THE
THREE
HEAVENS

THE THREE HEAVENS

ANGELS, DEMONS AND WHAT LIES AHEAD

JOHN HAGEE

WORTHY®
PUBLISHING

Published by Worthy Books, an imprint of Worthy Publishing Group, a division of Worthy Media, Inc., 134 Franklin Road, Suite 200, Brentwood, Tennessee 37027.

WORTHY is a registered trademark of Worthy Media, Inc.

HELPING PEOPLE EXPERIENCE THE HEART OF GOD

eBook available wherever digital books are sold.

Library of Congress Control Number: 2015931801

Any emphases in Scripture quotations are the author's.

Some names and identifying details have been changed within the stories in this book to protect the privacy of the individuals.

Published in association with Ted Squires Agency, Nashville, Tennessee

Cover design: Christopher Tobias, Tobias' Outwear for Books
Cover photo: ©Ig0rZh / istockphoto.com

ISBN: 978-1-61795-369-9
ISBN: 978-1-61795-599-0 (Ministry Edition)
ISBN: 978-1-61795-600-3 (Limited Edition)

Printed in the United States of America
15 16 17 18 19 LBM 8 7 6 5 4 3 2 1

This book is lovingly dedicated to Derek Prince, distinguished scholar and celebrated Bible teacher to the nations of the world. He was a man of God, a lover of Israel and orphans, and my dearest friend and beloved mentor.

CONTENTS

SECTION ONE

THE FIRST HEAVEN

CHAPTER 1

"MOMMY, GOD IS ALIVE!"

I t began as a normal day; I was at the office by 7 am, working on my next sermon series, when I received an unexpected call from Diana. She explained that our five-month-old grandson, Wyatt, had been admitted to the hospital with RSV (respiratory syncytial virus), a serious lung infection, and asked me to pray. We prayed for Wyatt's healing, and I made plans to meet her at the hospital.

However, before I could leave my office, Diana called again, informing me that Ellie, our eighteen-month-old granddaughter, was also being admitted to the same hospital with the same virus. My day was no longer normal. The Hagee family prayer chain was in full force, and we began to circle the wagons.

When I arrived at the hospital, I learned our two grandchildren were in adjoining rooms, which made it easier for "Nana" and "Papa" to divide our time between them. After a full day of assisting our daughters with our ailing grandchildren, Diana and I went home so I could prepare to leave town for a speaking engagement. I quickly packed, we drove to the airport, and Diana returned to the hospital.

As my wife walked back into Wyatt's room, she found him struggling for breath and his mother, our daughter Christina, frantically calling the nurse's station for help. A pediatric intensive care specialist raced into the room and instantly diagnosed Wyatt with a collapsed lung. He ordered our baby grandson into the pediatric intensive care unit and called for the respiratory therapist, who prepared to inflate Wyatt's tiny lung.

With the procedure successfully completed and Wyatt breathing without distress, Christina and Diana expressed their gratitude to the doctor for his swift and effective intervention. The specialist introduced himself by saying, "Mrs. Hagee, my name is Sam Zuckerman. I'm Jewish, and I have visited your church during the Night to Honor Israel. Because you are a woman of faith, I would like to tell you about an event that I believe will impact you as it has me." Diana was fully engaged and ready to hear what he had to say.

Once I reached my destination I immediately called home from the airport to get an update on our cherished grandchildren. As the Bible so rightly states, "Children's children are a crown to the aged" (Proverbs 17:6 NIV). I can say amen to that, for our thirteen grandchildren are our pride and joy!

Diana gave me her usual minute-by-minute update on Ellie and Wyatt and then said, "John, I have to tell you something remarkable that happened tonight!" And without taking a breath, she began to share the amazing account of a young patient Dr. Zuckerman had once treated.

The doctor said that three years earlier, a colleague and his wife had experienced a sudden tragedy in their family. The husband was the chief operating officer at the hospital where Dr. Zuckerman worked, and these friends had made the decision to add a pool to their backyard since their two children, Alexandria and Jackson, had learned to swim. The day the pool was completed, the family was informed by the installer that they could not use it for several days due to the high concentration of chemicals in the water.

David and Sherry took their two children into the house to prepare for dinner and celebrate the long-awaited addition to their home. Their youngest child, Jack, was an exuberant little boy of about four, so no one was alarmed that he did not come when first summoned for dinner. However, after his parents called for him several more times, there was still no sign of Jack, and it was unlike him to not respond at all.

The search was on, and suddenly David thought the worst: *Could Jack possibly be in the pool?* The father ran outside, and after searching the backyard, his fears were confirmed: his son was life-lessly floating in the pool, fully clothed and facedown.

David immediately pulled Jackson from the toxic waters as he frantically shouted for Sherry, who was frozen in shock, to call 911. The father attempted to revive his beloved son but instinctively knew the situation was grim.

The call to 911 was made; David continued CPR on Jackson for nearly ten minutes on the pool deck. The boy remained unresponsive, but his parents never gave up on saving him.

Finally, David and Sherry heard the piercing sound of sirens approaching their home. They were coming to *their* home . . . for *their* son. It was surreal.

Sherry kept their daughter inside the house as the ambulance and fire trucks arrived, explaining to Alex that Jack had fallen in the pool and that he would be taken to Daddy's hospital. Neighbors then took Alex to their home so she would not witness her brother being worked on.

The emergency responders quickly assessed Jack and began administering medications and inserting IVs. The EMS crew continued the father's valiant attempt to revive the lifeless boy but could not detect a heartbeat.

Once Jack had been transported to the hospital, the emergency room doctor, a respiratory therapist, and a talented team of nurses and other medical personnel fought for his life for over an hour. The physician administered a series of medications and treatments to the tiny patient, but to no avail . . . still no pulse. She decided to give Jack one last round of drugs before she would declare him dead.

The last treatment series produced a faint heartbeat. After stabilizing Jackson a bit more, the ER doctor informed the parents that their little boy only had a 40 percent chance of living through the first night.

The hours that followed were harrowing for all involved. That first night, as Sherry sat in the family room with their pastor, family, and friends, Dave stood in the corner of the room where Jackson was being treated and watched his son crash twice. Each time the heroic efforts of the expert medical team brought him back to life. The pediatric critical care physician knew the only way the patient could survive was to call for a helicopter transfer to Houston's Children's Hospital and place the boy on a heart-lung bypass.

Besides the fight for Jack's life, there was a fight against time. The chemicals in the pool had washed out all the pliability of the four-year-old's lungs; an artificial lubricant was essential to keep him alive. But the hospital had to wait for the vital drugs to be flown in.

When Jack's father asked why his son needed to be transferred to Houston, the physician responded, "Because we cannot sit here and watch him die."

Thankfully, the vials of surfactant (the lubricant) were delivered from Austin's Dell Children's Hospital before Jack could be transferred.

Later the ER doctor told Dr. Zuckerman that even though Jackson had regained his heartbeat, she was concerned he had gone so long without oxygen that he would be either brain dead or remain in a vegetative state.

In telling the story to Diana, Dr. Zuckerman said he and several other specialists gathered around the tiny patient and decided to place Jack in an induced coma to allow his fragile lungs to heal from the chemical burns. They sedated him with paralytic drugs to prevent the child from waking and pulling at the numerous tubes, IVs, and PICC (peripherally inserted central catheter) lines that covered his small body.

The temperature of the water in the pool had been 54 degrees; Jack's body temperature was 93 degrees when he came into the ER (normal is 98.6). His body had gone into hypothermia (when body temperature drops below 95 degrees). This slowed his vital functions down, allowing his brain and heart to receive the most oxygen possible. The medical team kept Jack in a state of induced hypothermia to help him heal from the trauma.

The four-year-old was on an oscillatory ventilator for nine days, followed by two additional days on a regular ventilator. Dr. Zuckerman explained that oscillatory ventilation forces as many as 540 tides (puffs) of oxygen into the lungs per minute. This special apparatus caused Jack's little chest to rapidly rise and fall, but it was the only way the doctors could prevent their patient's lungs from collapsing.

Jack's parents sat in vigil next to their motionless son's bed. Their baby boy had been so full of life a few hours ago; now he was desperately struggling to stay alive. They reeled from the tormenting questions flooding their minds.

This was not any patient . . . This was their Jackson. *How long was he in the pool? How much poison did he swallow before his lungs became filled with water? How long was he without oxygen? Will our son live or die? And if he lives, what effect will this trauma have on his brain? Will he ever be the same?*

ONLY GOD HAD THE ANSWERS

Minutes, hours, and days passed in drawn-out anguish as the family nervously anticipated the appointed time when the physicians would bring their beloved child out of his comatose state.

David, Sherry, and Alex were surrounded by loving family and steadfast friends during their ordeal. Their minister, Pastor Robinson, visited and prayed with them every day. All anyone could do now was wait.

Jackson's parents met with the dedicated team of specialists, who walked them through the next crucial steps of their son's life-and-death crisis. Once their son emerged from the medically induced coma, they would wait, hoping for his eyes to open and his lungs to breathe unassisted.

The next hurdle would be to confirm that Jackson's brain was functioning normally. The medical staff prepared David and Sherry that *if and when* Jackson woke up, he would most likely have significant neurological deficits.

The days were filled with fierce anxiety and raw emotions. Time dragged by as David and Sherry spent countless hours praying for an answer to Jack's dire situation. They knew they needed a miracle . . . and a miracle is what they received!

The evening before Good Friday, Sherry had a dream that her little boy would open his eyes. Early Friday Sherry held her son's hand and whispered, "Good morning," and true to her dream, Jackson opened his eyes for the first time since his accident. The doctors had to keep him sedated, but God had given Sherry the confirmation she needed: Jack was going to be okay.

The parents of this adorable boy watched in awe as he came back to life in the days that followed. As he was gradually weaned from the medications, Jack was able to breathe on his own, his motor skills were unimpaired, and amazingly, he managed a weak smile when he saw the faces of his ever-grateful parents.

At one point after the tubes were removed from his body and he was being held by his dad, Jack looked up into his father's eyes and said in a very weak whisper, "Daddy . . . I be okay . . . I be okay."

The night before Jack was released from the hospital, the pediatric neurologist came to the young patient's room and gave his parents a copy of his EEG, a test that diagnoses brain function. Their son's numbers were textbook perfect! "I have no medical justification for these results," admitted the neurologist. He had felt sure that Jack would suffer significant brain deficiency based on the length of time he had gone without oxygen.

His only explanation? "It was the grace of God."

Jackson had been given back to his family by an ever-merciful God. For that, David and Sherry would be eternally thankful. However, they quickly recognized their once high-spirited child was now uncharacteristically quiet and restrained. Upon Jack's discharge from the hospital, the doctor assigned to the case recommended that his parents not push to discuss the traumatic event right away, but wait instead for a time when Jack could better deal with its terrifying memory.

Because this little boy had lost nearly 20 percent of his body weight, the clinicians felt he would have to be sent to rehabilitation upon his discharge to regain his strength. Yet on day fourteen, the young patient ran out of the hospital!

The family was whole again, and soon their son's bubbling personality resurfaced. Following Jackson's cues, David and Sherry determined it was time to cross the bridge that would take them from the memories of that horrific day to a place where they could enjoy being together once again without worry. It was time to get Jackson back in the pool.

Four days after their son left the hospital, he went swimming in the same pool he had nearly drowned in. The family spent the afternoon together in the water, enjoying the Texas sunshine. It was almost as if their near-tragedy had all been a bad dream.

A doting Sherry was thankful her son was splashing water in her face, because it disguised the tears of gratitude that were welling up in her eyes. Eventually she took a deep breath and decided to ask Jack if he remembered what had happened weeks earlier. Jack immediately responded, "Yes, Mommy, I drowned."

"What happened, buddy? You are such a good swimmer!"

Sherry instantly wondered if she had overstepped her bounds by asking the question that had nagged her and her husband for weeks.

Things got quiet.

Jack didn't swim long; he had lost six pounds on an already small forty-two-pound frame, so he became cold quickly. Sherry took him from the pool, wrapped her little boy in a towel, and sat him on her lap in a nearby chair.

The grateful mother held her child closely as they enjoyed the sweet quietness around them. The sky was beautiful, with the sun just beginning to set. The rays reflecting against the clouds reminded Sherry of heaven.

Unexpectedly, Jack blurted out that he remembered how he fell in the pool that dreadful day. Sherry hugged him and said, "Mommy and Daddy are so sorry we weren't there to help you."

The boy then began to freely share the memory of that dark day. "I dropped a bucket in the pool by accident, so I went in to get it. My clothes got really heavy and I kept going down to the bottom, and then I couldn't hold my breath anymore."

"Buddy, were you afraid?" his mom asked.

Jack responded, "Yes. But then I saw the pool light and I swam to it."

Sherry was puzzled—the pool light had never been turned on. She thought for a moment, *Could Jack have seen the Light of God directing him to the other side?*

Then her son said, his voice still hoarse from being intubated, "Mommy, you know God is alive. I saw Him. He was as bright as the sun, and He told me to wake up. And I saw Nana and she told me to wake up. And then she shouted at me to wake up!"

Could this be? Sherry wondered. Nana was Jack's paternal grandmother who had died when their son was not yet two years old! *And God? What about God?*

Sherry looked at David, who was only a short distance away, in amazement. *Did our son just say that he saw God?*

Sherry held back a river of tears for fear she would startle her little boy. Wanting nothing to prevent Jack from telling his story, she sat quietly, nodding her head and silently thanking God for Jack's life and the wonderful miracle their family had experienced.

As her youngest child talked, what Sherry began to hear was the most beautiful story of heaven.

"Mommy, why did Jesus have to die?" Jack asked a few moments later.

"Well, He died so we could live," Sherry answered with a trembling voice.

Then their little boy made a statement that further astounded his parents: "I think that Holly is Jesus' dog now." Holly was the family dog that had died the previous year.

"Why do you think that, son?" his mother asked in disbelief.

"I saw her standing next to Jesus."

"What else do you remember seeing?" his mom asked softly.

"Oh, Mommy, I heard you telling me to open my eyes. I tried to open them, but I just couldn't."

Suddenly Sherry remembered that while Dave was performing CPR on their boy, she had repeatedly pleaded with Jack to open his eyes.

David was stunned, his heart pounding and his head reeling from the questions swirling in his mind. He tried not to show his astonishment as he joined in the conversation. "Wow, buddy, where were you?"

"I was in heaven, Daddy."

Heaven? Did Jack really die and go to heaven? This only happens in the movies . . . not to our boy!

Jackson then went on to describe gates, a throne with a rainbow behind it, faces with great color, and music that he could not easily explain.

"Son, what else did you see in heaven?"

"I saw Jesus, Daddy . . . I talked to Him."

David and Sherry could not believe what they were hearing. Jackson was so young; even though he attended church regularly, how could he possibly have seen Jesus?

The father continued, "What happened then?"

"Jesus held me and showed me heaven. I saw big houses and shiny yellow streets. I saw blue skies, and Nana and Holly were with me. Jesus looked at me and told me not to be afraid; I was going to see you and Mommy and Alex again."

"What did Jesus look like, son?" David asked in awe.

"His face had a big shiny light on it with lots of colors . . . I couldn't see it."

"How did you know it was Him?"

"He told me His name."

"And then what happened?" asked his father.

"He kissed me on the face and said it was time to come back."

In the following days, David and Sherry had several extraordinary conversations with Jack about his journey, and his descriptions of what he saw were always straightforward—not at all like a four-year-old's imaginings.

With this initial, mind-boggling chat over, Sherry felt compelled to go to her Bible, which they used for family study. She thought of Jack's descriptive phrases: "Big houses . . . shiny yellow streets . . . the light on God's face . . ." She remembered her Sunday school classes and went to the Gospels and the book of Revelation.

There it was: her four-year-old son was describing mansions, gates of pearl, the streets of gold . . . Jackson was speaking of the throne room of God!

In My Father's house are many mansions [big houses]; if it were not so, I would have told you. I go to prepare a place for you. (John 14:2)

And behold, a throne set in heaven, and One sat on the throne. And He who sat there was like a jasper and a sardius stone in appearance; and there was a rainbow around the throne, in appearance like an emerald. (Revelation 4:2–4)

The twelve gates were twelve pearls: each individual gate was of one pearl. And the street of the city was pure gold [shiny yellow], like transparent glass. (Revelation 21:21)

And He was transfigured before them. His face shone like the sun [big light], and His clothes became as white as the light. (Matthew 17:2)

Sherry closed her Bible. It was more than she could take in. This was the first of many conversations she and Jack would have about his time in heaven.

She remembered driving down the road with her son one day. Jack was looking out the car window and repeating, "No, that's not it . . . That's not it either!"

When she asked what he was talking about, Jack told her he

was looking for the color blue that he saw in heaven, but he "just couldn't find it."

According to Diana, "By the time Dr. Zuckerman was done sharing this extraordinary story, we were all in tears."

Dr. Zuckerman then asked her, "What do you think really took place, Mrs. Hagee?"

My wife answered without hesitation. "I believe Jackson saw heaven and spoke to Jesus."

And I agreed.

A LIFE-CHANGING MOMENT

When I began to outline this book, I knew that I wanted to include Jackson's miracle, which Diana and I have recounted to others many times over the years. Yet while my wife and I have always described the account as we remembered it, we felt we needed to verify the details for publication, so we began our search.

We learned that Dr. Zuckerman was no longer living in San Antonio, but through the help of another physician, we were able to locate him. Once Diana made contact, she asked if he remembered telling her about this miraculous event. He immediately responded, "Yes," and called it "a life-changing case" for him.

Dr. Zuckerman offered to help locate the parents of the child. Soon after, Diana received a call from Jack's father, David Kreye, who was more than willing to share their family's story in an effort to bring encouragement to others.

Mr. Kreye reported that Jack is now eleven years old and is a healthy, vibrant young man. He is also a straight-A student who also excels in martial arts; and yes, he still enjoys swimming!

Mrs. Kreye shared that she believes her son was witnessing to her of the peace and beauty he experienced in heaven. She also believes that God has a divine plan for Jack to let others know about heaven. "Maybe this was God's way of telling us to slow down and enjoy what we have in front of us," Sherry said. "Maybe it was His way of telling us that there is so much good we can do in this world."

In an effort to give back, Dave and Sherry became volunteers for an organization in Austin, Texas, called Colin's Hope. Colin was four when he drowned (exactly three months after Jack's accident).

For this book, David and Sherry verified their son's story[1] and sent a video that the hospital made of Jack's miraculous recovery. As Diana and I watched this four-year-old boy recount portions of his supernatural experience, we once again found ourselves rejoicing. Physicians, nurses, and respiratory therapists were interviewed, and they individually described Jack's condition as "severe," as one that statistically should have resulted in a "poor outcome." Over and over the hospital staff used the word *miracle*, but the best summary of all came from the president of the hospital, Jack Cleary:

> I don't know that everyone believes in miracles, but I still do, and I have the word *miracle* mentioned by a number of different people in regards to Jackson's experience . . . I think this whole building [hospital] was throbbing with prayer during the ten days or so that Jackson was a guest of ours on the Pediatric Intensive Care Unit . . . There is no understating the power of prayer and faith.[2]

And of course there is the statement from Dr. Zuckerman, who first told us the story: "I have often thought of Jackson. Perhaps he was brought back to awaken all of us to God's wonder and grace."[3]

WHAT LIES BEYOND

We are about to embark on a journey that will take us beyond the First Heaven—what we see with our natural eyes—into the realm of the Second Heaven where Satan and his fallen angels dwell, and ultimately into the Third Heaven where God rules and reigns over the universe, assisted by His innumerable angelic host.

King David and the apostle Paul referred to more than one heaven, and each of these heavens was created by God Himself.

I consider Your heavens [more than one], the work of Your fingers, the moon and the stars, which You have ordained. (Psalm 8:3)

Look! I see the heavens [more than one] opened and the Son of Man standing at the right hand of God! (Acts 7:56)

Nehemiah also declared that the majesty of God's creation includes the heavens.

You alone are the LORD; You have made heaven, the heaven of heavens [more than one], with all their host, the earth and everything on it, the seas and all that is in them, and You preserve them all. The host of heaven worships You. (Nehemiah 9:6)

The Bible teaches that each of us will spend eternity in one of two places: the "highest of heavens" with our Redeemer:

Thus says the High and Lofty One Who inhabits eternity, whose name is Holy: "I dwell in the high and holy place [Third Heaven] with him who has a contrite and humble spirit." (Isaiah 57:15)

or in hell with Satan, the Prince of Darkness:

The wicked shall be turned into hell. (Psalm 9:17)

Then I saw an angel coming down from heaven, having the key to the bottomless pit [hell] and a great chain in his hand. He laid hold of the dragon, that serpent of old, who is the Devil and Satan, and bound him for a thousand years; and he cast him into the bottomless pit, and shut him up, and set a seal on him. (Revelation 20:1–3)

THE HEAVENS

Where is the First Heaven? The First Heaven is located in the realm we see with our naked eye.

[God] brought [Abram] outside and said, "Look now toward heaven [the one we see], and count the stars if you are able to number them." (Genesis 15:5)

Take heed, lest you lift your eyes to heaven [the one we see], and when you see the sun, the moon, and the stars, all the host of heaven, you feel driven to worship them and serve them, which the LORD your God has given to all the peoples under the whole heaven as a heritage. (Deuteronomy 4:19)

The Second Heaven is where Satan has his throne and rules over the fallen angels that followed him in the rebellion against God in the genesis of time (Revelation 12:4).

The Third Heaven is where God has His throne and rules the universe.

Now this is the main point of the things we are saying: We have such a High Priest, who is seated at the right hand of the throne of the Majesty in the heavens. (Hebrews 8:1)

SO MUCH TO COME

Use the word *heaven* and it evokes images of a paradise, a place of eternal bliss and perfect happiness . . . but there is so much more!

Let us begin our supernatural journey through the Three Heavens by first exploring what the Word of God and science say about the First Heaven. Then we will expose Satan's diabolical tactics in the Second Heaven and how they impact each one of us. Finally, we will reveal the deep riches of the Third Heaven, which in the end will be the eternal home of those who choose Christ as Savior and Lord.

Most people believe there is only one heaven—the place where God lives with His holy angels. However, the truth is that our God has no limitation on earth or in heaven. He is omnipresent and omnipotent and has universal power and supremacy over all of His creation—which includes *all* three heavens!

> Will God indeed dwell on the earth? Behold, heaven [the First and Second Heavens] and the heaven of heavens [the Third Heaven] cannot contain You. How much less this temple which I have built. (1 Kings 8:27)

> Thus says the LORD: "Heaven [the Third Heaven] is My throne, and earth is My footstool." (Isaiah 66:1)

CHAPTER 2

THE HEAVEN WE SEE

The Bible begins its profound description of Creation with these words: "In the beginning God created the *heavens* and the earth" (Genesis 1:1).

The word *heavens* in the Hebrew (*shemayim*) is the plural form of the feminine noun, clearly indicating "more than one" heaven. Saint Paul reported, "[I] was caught up to the third heaven" (2 Corinthians 12:2). Logic dictates that if Paul was in the Third Heaven, there must be a First and a Second Heaven.

The First Heaven contains the sun, moon, and stars, yet it is a minuscule glimpse of God's creative majesty (Genesis 1). It was this majesty that inspired the songwriter to pen the words of one of the most celebrated songs in the history of Christendom, "How Great Thou Art":

O Lord my God, when I in awesome wonder,
Consider all the worlds Thy hands hath made . . .[1]

We begin our journey by looking heavenward.

THE WORK OF GOD'S HANDS

> You, Lord, in the beginning laid the foundation of the
> earth, and the heavens are the work of Your hands.
> (Hebrews 1:10)

Have you ever looked at the sky and seen a beautiful, blazing sunrise or a golden sunset unfolding? Have you witnessed the appearance of a Blood Moon in all its wonder? Did you ever, as a child, lie in the cool grass on a clear summer's night, gazing at a black sky lit with brilliant stars that appeared as a glowing canopy above the earth?

We have all observed the splendor of the First Heaven and probably wondered about its origin. Although there are many scientific theories regarding the formation of the sun, moon, and stars, we have only one eyewitness account—that Eyewitness is the Great I AM.

> Then God said, "Let there be lights in the firmament of the
> heavens to divide the day from the night . . . and let them
> be for lights in the firmament of the heavens to give light
> on the earth"; and it was so. Then God made two great
> lights: the greater light to rule the day [sun], and the lesser
> light to rule the night [moon]. He made the stars also. God
> set them in the firmament of the heavens to give light on
> the earth, and to rule over the day and over the night, and
> to divide the light from the darkness. (Genesis 1:14–18)

Man has tried to conquer the heavens for self-seeking purposes since Nimrod and the Tower of Babel: "Come, let us build ourselves a city, and a tower whose top is in the heavens; let us make a name for ourselves, lest we be scattered abroad over the face of the whole earth" (Genesis 11:4).

The tower was more than bricks and mortar and engineering genius. It was one of several *ziggurats*, which were rectangular temple-towers or tiered mounds. Erected in ancient Mesopotamia, the Tower of Babel was a religious structure where people worshiped the *created*, not the *Creator*. All ziggurats had runways leading to their apex where cult worshipers paid homage to the sun, moon, and stars.[2]

After touring the construction project for Himself, God responded definitively to man's idolatry and deliberate rebellion against His divine order. The Creator could not ignore man's insurgence against Him; He confused their tongues, causing them to speak different languages—"Therefore its name is called Babel" (Genesis 11:9)—and dispersed them to other places far and wide (Genesis 11:5–8).

Man's futile battle for supremacy ended for a time, but the war over man's soul continues.

God Almighty did not make the moon, sun, and stars for people to worship but to confirm His creative majesty, to sustain the earth, and to divide the seasons. The God of Abraham, Isaac, and Jacob even used the sun, moon, and skies to reaffirm His everlasting covenant with David and his descendants.

My covenant I will not break, nor alter the word that has gone out of My lips. Once I have sworn by My holiness; I will not lie to David: his seed shall endure forever, and his throne as the *sun* before Me; it shall be established forever like the *moon*, even like the faithful witness in the *sky*. (Psalm 89:34–37)

The earth and all that is in it belongs to the Lord and is under His control. David, the shepherd king, stood under the canopy of stars sprinkled like diamonds against the velvet of the night and said, "The heavens declare the glory of God; and the firmament shows His handiwork" (Psalm 19:1). Yes, the sun, the moon, and the stars are celestial evangelists that shout, "There is a God!"

Centuries after King David penned his declaration of the heavens, there were three men who followed the star (Matthew 2:2) that led them to God's greatest gift to mankind: a baby born to a virgin.

FROM THE THREE WISE MEN TO KEPLER

The magi from the East examined the prophecy of Numbers 24:17 found in ancient scrolls and searched the First Heaven for a star that would lead them to the King of the Jews.[3]

A Star shall come out of Jacob; a Scepter shall rise out of Israel. (Numbers 24:17)

The wise men found what they were looking for in Bethlehem.

But you, Bethlehem Ephrathah, though you are little among the thousands of Judah, yet out of you shall come forth to Me the One to be Ruler in Israel. (Micah 5:2)

Now after Jesus was born in Bethlehem of Judea in the days of Herod the king, behold, wise men from the East came to

Jerusalem, saying, "Where is He who has been born King of the Jews? For we have seen His star in the East and have come to worship Him." (Matthew 2:1–2)

The magi followed Scripture and a divinely appointed star to find their true future King. Man has continued to search the stars for what they can reveal about what lies beyond our realm.

THE STARS

Stars are composed of subatomic particles of gas and plasma and are cosmic energy "engines" that produce radiation in the forms of heat, light, and ultraviolet rays.

On a clear night, the earth's sky reveals only about three thousand stars to the naked eye. However, scientists cannot tell us how many stars exist because their number is beyond calculation. Our universe likely contains more than one hundred billion galaxies, and each of those galaxies may have more than one hundred billion stars. Acclaimed astrophysicist Carl Sagan could only account for the number of stars by saying, "There are billions and billions."

Look now toward heaven, and count the stars if you are able to number them. (Genesis 15:5)

Man has conceded that he cannot count the stars in the First Heaven, but King David declared that God can.

He counts the number of the stars; He calls them all by name. (Psalm 147:4)

Stars exist in various shapes, colors, and sizes. Some are classified as "dwarfs," while others are known as "super-giants" with a potential radius a thousand times larger than that of our own sun. The brightness of a star is determined by its luminosity (how much energy it puts out) in addition to its distance from Earth. Believers, however, know that there is only one Star that illuminates more than all the billions in the heavens, and that Star is Christ our Savior!

> I, Jesus, have sent My angel to testify to you these things in the churches. I am the Root and the Offspring of David, the Bright and Morning Star. (Revelation 22:16)

THE SUN

The best-known star in the First Heaven is the sun. The sun lies at the heart of our solar system. It composes more than 99 percent of the solar system's mass and is roughly 109 times the diameter of Earth—about one million Earths could fit inside the sun.[4]

The sun is orbited by eight planets, at least eight dwarf planets, tens of thousands of asteroids, and trillions of comets. The sun's core temperature is about 15,000,000 degrees Celsius (27,000,000 degrees Fahrenheit). Without its intense energy and heat, Earth could not sustain life.[8]

> He has set a tabernacle for the sun . . . Its rising is from one end of heaven, and its circuit to the other end; and there is nothing hidden from its heat. (Psalm 19:4, 6)

THE MOON

In 1609, Galileo was the first to point a telescope skyward, revealing discoveries in the First Heaven that the naked eye had never before seen. He observed mountains and craters on the moon and a subtle band of light arching across the sky that we now know as the Milky Way. Since then, science has confirmed that the moon is Earth's only natural satellite and is the most luminous object in the First Heaven after the sun. The moon is in synchronous rotation with the earth, and its gravitational influence produces the ocean tides and affects the length of each day.

He appointed the moon for seasons. (Psalm 104:19)

Because of its prominence in the sky and its cycle of phases, the moon has inspired language, calendars, art, and mythology since ancient times. What's more, the moon is the only celestial body other than Earth on which humans have to date set foot.

Science has shown that Earth orbits around the sun and the moon orbits around Earth. It is no accident that the Jewish calendar has always been rooted in this astronomical phenomenon: the rotation of Earth on its axis (a day); the revolution of the moon around Earth (a month); and the circling of Earth around the sun (a year). The sun, moon, and stars could only have been put into place by the hand of God, the Great Designer of our universe.

I have made the earth, and created man on it. I—My hands—stretched out the heavens, and all their host I have commanded. (Isaiah 45:12)

EXPLORING THE FIRST HEAVEN

The National Aeronautics and Space Administration (NASA) was created in 1958 for the purpose of space exploration and national security. The government agency didn't waste any time! Within twenty years of its inception, NASA conducted several major missions:

- Project Mercury, which determined whether a human could survive in space
- Project Gemini, which trained astronauts in space operations such as how to rendezvous and how to dock spacecraft.
- Project Apollo, which explored the moon
- Robotic missions programs such as the Moon Ranger, Surveyor, and Lunar Orbiter
- The Pioneer, Mariner, Viking, and Voyager explorations of Venus, Mars, and the outer planets
- Skylab, which is an orbital workshop for astronauts
- The Space Shuttle, a reusable spacecraft for traveling to and from Earth's orbit

Man's unquenchable desire to "go where no man has gone before" has led to enormous scientific advancements and discoveries.

For more than two decades, the Hubble Telescope has uncovered mysteries we never knew existed. It has probed into everything from black holes to planets around other stars and helped scientists discover as many as a million galaxies the size of ours yet to be explored.

NASA's Kepler Telescope, which is a space observatory dedicated to finding planets outside our solar system, has located hundreds of extra-solar planets. Most of them range between the size of Earth and Neptune, which is four times larger than our planet.

In February of 2014 Kepler scientists confirmed the discovery of 715 planets that are orbiting stars other than Earth's sun.[5] This means that more "super-Earths," or planets larger than Earth, have been found. More recently, millions witnessed two complete Blood Moon eclipses in 2014—both of which occurred during major Jewish Feasts (April 15, Passover; October 8, the Feast of Tabernacles)—and a total solar eclipse on March 20, 2015.

The Blood Moons were part of a Tetrad (four consecutive Blood Moons). This is a rare phenomenon in itself, but rarer still when an entire Tetrad falls on the Jewish Feasts.

The third Blood Moon appeared on April 4, 2015, at Passover. The fourth and final Blood Moon coinciding with a Jewish Feast in this century will occur on September 28, 2015, during the Feast of Tabernacles.

The significance of this Tetrad cannot be overemphasized; I have covered the subject exhaustively in my book *Four Blood Moons: Something Is About to Change.*

> It is very rare that Scripture, science, and historical events align with one another, yet the last three Four Blood Moon series or Tetrads have done exactly that [1492—the discovery of America; 1949—the rebirth of Israel; and 1967— the reunification of Jerusalem]. Several Tetrads have occurred in the past five hundred years but only three have corresponded to the Jewish Feasts as well as being linked to historical events significant to Israel. Seven more Tetrads will take place in the twenty-first century; however only

one of these seven, the Tetrads of 2014–2015, aligns . . .
with the Feast of the Lord![6]

Something big is about to happen!

The prophet Joel divinely prophesied that these wonders would occur, and the apostle Peter later quoted Joel's prophecy in Acts 2:20.

The sun shall be turned into darkness, and the moon into
blood, before the coming of the great and awesome day of
the LORD. (Joel 2:31)

Scientists the world over have dedicated their lives to learning how and why the sun, moon, and stars exist. Their efforts have only led them further and further into the unlimited dimensions of space. Even so, science's vast accumulation of data has barely penetrated the realities of the First Heaven.

God has clearly revealed through Scripture, science, and the events of history that He will use the First Heaven as His own high-definition billboard declaring the things to come.

Then God said, "Let there be lights in the firmament of
the heavens . . . ; and let them be for signs and seasons."
(Genesis 1:14)

The First Heaven is "as far as the eye can see," with or without the assistance of a telescope, a lunar orbiter, a space shuttle, or a sky lab. Whatever man discovers in the galaxies, by whatever apparatus he invents, it is part of the First Heaven. Saint Paul wrote in Romans, "Since the creation of the world His invisible attributes are clearly seen, being understood by the things that are made" (1:20).

What is this Scripture saying? Anyone who has the ability to look up and see the sun glistening in the day and the stars and moon shining at night should recognize that these celestial bodies were put there by a Power far greater than man. No military might on this earth is able to sweep the stars from the sky. No human influence can blot the sun from the heavens. No strength of man can command the moon to stop shining, the wind to stop gusting, or the waves to stop crashing onto the shore!

> Thus says the LORD, who gives the sun for a light by day,
> the ordinances of the moon and the stars for a light by
> night, who disturbs the sea, and its waves roar (The LORD
> of hosts is His name). (Jeremiah 31:35)

Mankind is not the product of NASA. We are not the product of the Kennedy Space Center. We are the *creation* of an almighty, all-knowing Force.

> When I consider Your heavens, the work of Your fingers,
> the moon and the stars, which You have ordained, what is
> man that You are mindful of him, and the son of man that
> You visit him? For You have made him a little lower than
> the angels, and You have crowned him with glory and honor. You have made him to have dominion over the works of
> Your hands; You have put all things under his feet. (Psalm
> 8:3–6)

This Force is not found in the Big Bang Theory. Our Force is supernatural! Our Force is the God of Abraham, Isaac, and Jacob! He is the Source of life, worthy of praise and glory! He is the Creator and Lord of all!

Our God is the Alpha and the Omega, the First and the Last, the Maker of heaven and earth! He is limitless and unconstrained! We give *Him* all our praise and glory!

No matter how much we try to make sense of all that we see and know, certain realities cannot be explained by human logic or science. There are experiences that can only be described as "supernatural."

We continue our exploration of the Three Heavens with testimonies of the life to come.

CHAPTER 3

JOURNEYS INTO
THE SUPERNATURAL

Throughout my fifty-seven years of ministry, I have stood by the bedsides of hundreds of people as they stepped from this life into the next. Comforting the families and friends left behind can be one of the most challenging roles in a pastor's life.

This responsibility is made easier when there is assurance that the person who has just passed from this world has stepped immediately into the arms of God. As my dear friend Derek Prince said, "The spirits of true believers through faith in Jesus, having been made righteous with His righteousness and redeemed with His blood, have immediate access into the heavenlies. The death and resurrection of Jesus robbed Death of its sting and Hades of its victory."[1]

I often share the following word pictures during memorial services. When the sun sets each day, we do not mourn its setting because we know it is rising on another horizon. When a ship sails out of our sight on the ocean, we do not grieve over our inability to see it any longer; it is only getting closer to its port of arrival. And so it is in life—our last breath here is our first breath there.

What is the way to the Third Heaven where Jesus resides? The directions are simple: we are to turn to the *right* and then walk *straight* ahead.

You will show me the path of life; in Your presence is fullness of joy; at Your right hand are pleasures forevermore. (Psalm 16:11)

Walk in the way of goodness, and keep to the paths of righteousness. (Proverbs 2:20)

Since time immemorial, man has searched for the answers to what exists beyond this life. Movies set in the world beyond are highly successful, and books on the subject of heaven and hell remain on bestseller lists for months because they attempt to deal with the difficult questions we all ask.

Is there really a literal heaven and hell? Is there such a thing as an afterlife, and if so, who will be there? What lies beyond man's final breath? Will we see bright lights and hear angels sing, or will we step into an abyss of eternal darkness?

The following are five testimonies of individuals who journeyed into that supernatural realm. The first two are personal accounts from my own relatives. One was on the brink of prematurely moving into eternity, and one saw the other side and was more than ready to cross the Jordan River into heaven.

"IT WAS NOT MY TIME"

This is the story of my father's younger brother, Reverend Joel Lavonne Hagee, who was the fourth of ten sons and one daughter born to my grandparents, John Christopher and Laverta Hagee.

My grandfather had nicknames for all his children, and he called Joel "Tink" because he was always *tinkering* with one gadget or another, trying to discover how it worked or how he could improve on it.

Uncle Tink was a bright and genuinely happy man who never met a stranger, so he quite naturally became a pastor and dedicated himself to the purposes of the gospel until the day he died. His incredible journey into the supernatural changed not only his life but the lives of thousands of people around the world.

While in his mid-forties, Uncle Tink suffered a severe heart attack. His wife, Vivian, raced him to the hospital where, by the grace of God, he received treatment and made a full recovery. Like most people who have survived similar experiences, he was greatly impacted by the fact that he almost died in the prime of his life.

Always the Bible scholar and pastor, Uncle Tink began to study God's scriptural promises concerning healing for all believers. He then personally recorded those collective passages and gave a copy of the audiotape to his wife and emphatically instructed, "Vivian, if I ever have another heart attack, put headphones on my ears and start playing the healing scriptures that I have recorded." Aunt Vivian, who was totally committed to Tink's well-being, solemnly promised to do exactly that.

Several years later Uncle Tink had a second major heart attack. EMS was called, and the medical technicians worked for some time to revive him, but only a faint pulse could be detected—no other signs of life remained.

Immediately Aunt Vivian did what she had promised to do: she placed the earphones over Uncle Tink's ears as he was being moved from the living room floor into the ambulance. The lead paramedic informed my aunt that the recordings would be of no benefit because the patient was unresponsive. She firmly instructed the emergency responder to leave the headphones on her husband's ears. Recognizing there was no room for debate, the paramedic agreed.

At the hospital, the emergency room physician was brought up-to-date on my uncle's condition. He and his team also heroically attempted to bring Tink out of his comatose state—but to no avail.

The ER doctor sought out Aunt Vivian, who was gathered with family in the waiting room, and informed her that her beloved husband had experienced a massive heart attack that left him clinically brain dead. Our much-adored Tink—whose mind was filled with brilliant ideas, who was always inventing and creating, who was at all times kind and loving—was now being sustained by machines.

Vivian looked directly into the eyes of the doctor, and with fearless conviction she firmly stated, "Then it won't hurt for him to hear these Bible verses about God's healing power, will it?"

Everyone in the room thought that once the shock of her husband's irreversible diagnosis wore off, Aunt Vivian would allow the doctors to remove Uncle Tink from life support. But she was not about to break the promise she had made to him.

Some people might wonder why she didn't just let him go. I firmly believe that God Almighty, in all His infinite wisdom, has an appointed time for our life on earth to end—and Aunt Vivian was absolutely sure it was not Uncle Tink's time. She was confident the

Word of God would not return void but would bring healing and life to his mind and body, and she remained faithful to keep the recorded healing scriptures in his ears.

Dr. Rob, my cousin by marriage, was the chief of staff at the hospital where Uncle Tink was being treated. He reviewed the charts and personally consulted with the cardiac specialist before visiting Uncle Tink. When Rob walked in and saw the earphones on our uncle's ears, he gave Aunt Vivian a puzzled glance. Uncle Tink lay motionless other than the forced rhythmic movement of his chest created by the respirator. His monitors showed only a faint heartbeat and no significant brain activity.

In Rob's characteristic, matter-of-fact manner, he said, "Aunt Vivian, it's over for Uncle Tink. Why do you insist that he continue to listen to what he can't hear?"

"You don't really know if he can hear it or not," she countered. "Hagee told me to put these healing scriptures in his ears if he ever had another heart attack, and that's *exactly* what is happening."

Rob too recognized that this was not a battle he was ready to fight, so he instructed the medical staff to move the patient into the cardiac intensive care unit until his wife could come to grips with the fact that her husband was gone.

Twenty-four hours passed, and Aunt Vivian kept a faithful vigil at Uncle Tink's bedside. Though his prognosis remained grim, she made sure that no one removed the headphones from his ears.

While the healing scriptures played continually, a miracle of miracles began to unfold: his electrocardiogram picked up a stronger heartbeat with a consistent rhythm. The charge nurse, who was charting Uncle Tink's vital signs, called in the CICU doctor to personally examine the patient. There was not only a stronger heartbeat and better respiration but, most importantly, Uncle Tink was showing increased signs of brain activity.

The doctor confirmed the good news, and with Aunt Vivian's permission, the team began to wean Uncle Tink off the ventilator and the other devices that had sustained him. The healing scriptures, however, played on.

By the next day Uncle Tink was conscious and on his way to recovery. When he heard the doctor's review of all that had transpired since his massive heart attack, Uncle Tink quickly responded, "I know exactly what happened!"

The doctor looked at him with a confused expression. "How could you know what occurred? You were unconscious!"

"I was standing in the corner of the room watching every one of you work on my body," my uncle replied.

The doctor was extremely skeptical until his patient began to describe what he'd seen. Uncle Tink recounted in exact detail how many doctors and nurses were in the room, where they were standing, and what each of them was doing. He went on to describe what they were wearing and what they had said to each other about his condition. The attending physician was stunned at the absolute accuracy of my uncle's account.

So what happened to Uncle Tink?

Simply stated, his spirit left his earthly body, yet was still very much present in this world. It was not Uncle Tink's appointed time to cross over into heaven. Instead, God and His ever-powerful Word, along with the advances of modern medicine, sustained his frail heart. He and Aunt Vivian had faith that God's miraculous Word would not fail him—and it didn't!

Soon after my uncle was released from the hospital, the

paramedic who had gallantly attempted to revive him moments after his heart attack showed up on my aunt and uncle's front porch. When Uncle Tink answered the door, the young man could not hide the shock on his face. "I am sorry to bother you, Reverend Hagee, but I had to see it with my own eyes. When the medical staff informed me that you actually walked out of the hospital, I just couldn't believe it. You do realize that you were beyond resuscitation?"

My uncle smiled and invited him in for a cold glass of tea.

Uncle Tink visited with the young man and shared his miraculous story. The paramedic walked out of my uncle's home shaking his head in amazement at what God, through the power of His faithful Word, had done.

Uncle Tink gave me a copy of the healing scriptures that brought him back from the edge of eternity. I rerecorded those passages and have sent them to the ends of the earth by the tens of thousands to those who have contacted our ministry and asked to receive the encouragement and miracle-working power that the Word of God offers our spirit, mind, and body.

The last time Uncle Tink and I discussed the details of his journey into the supernatural, he made a statement that I have never forgotten: "John, I was not afraid to die. What I experienced proved that the easiest thing you will ever do is die. I was not afraid, but I knew it was not my time; God had more for me to do, and I was going to do it!"

Uncle Tink lived well into his eighties and remained faithful to the call of preaching the gospel of Jesus Christ to America and the nations of the world. He and all of his ten siblings have since made the journey to heaven. They are safe in the arms of God, and one day very soon, Jesus, our Savior and Lord, will appear in the clouds of the First Heaven to take us all home. I can assure you, there will be a Hagee reunion like no other just inside the Gates of Pearl!

It would be impossible for this book to contain all the testimonies of the people who have listened to God's healing scriptures and miraculously recovered from their physical, spiritual, or mental afflictions. Know this truth: Jesus Christ has conquered disease and death through the power of His Word, His blood, and His holy Name.

"I SEE HEAVEN"

Martha Swick was my maternal grandmother. She lived in Goose Creek, Texas, with her husband, Charles Albert, and their six children. My name, John Charles, pays tribute to both of my grandfathers, even though I only remember being with my paternal grandfather, John Christopher Hagee, a few times and never met Charles Albert Swick.

Martha Swick lived a hard life filled with painful trials and tribulation. My grandmother was thirty-three years old and expecting her seventh child when my grandfather suddenly died. He had developed a small hernia while working for the local oil refinery. The company required that it be surgically repaired before he could continue on the job. With the responsibility of a large family to support, my grandfather knew he had no choice, so he scheduled what should have been minor surgery. While in the hospital, though, he contracted a severe infection that took his life within ten days.

Grandmother Martha buried her cherished husband in a pauper's grave in Goose Creek and went home with six small children and a seventh on the way. The family's world was completely shattered!

Martha had been trained as a nurse in Goose Creek, a very small town with no hospital. When someone was critically ill, the town's two doctors—Dr. Duke and Dr. Lilly—sent Grandmother to the ailing person's home, and she stayed until the patient recovered or passed on. It was an early form of hospice, deep in the heart of Texas. Years later, Doctors Duke and Lilly built a hospital in Goose Creek, and I was one of the first to be born there in April of 1940.

My mother, Vada, was nine years old when her father died. She was the second oldest of the children and the only girl living at home. Her older sister, Alta, was married and had moved away; and her baby sister, Esther Gladys, who was born after Grandfather's death, stayed with an aunt and uncle through the week.

It was a very difficult life for the Swick family. Grandmother's work sadly kept her away from her children from early Monday until late Friday almost every week, so my mother accepted the enormous responsibility of caring for her four siblings. She did all the housework and the cooking for her rambunctious brothers Burl, Glen, Woodrow, and Paul.

Adding to Grandmother Martha's sorrow was Esther Gladys's tragic death at the age of ten. She, along with the aunt and uncle who had cared for her, drowned when their car was bumped off a ferry into Cedar Bayou as they were traveling to a revival in a neighboring town. Esther's passing was almost more than my grandmother could bear.

Martha Swick continued to work as a nurse until she retired in the mid-1940s. Grandmother was a brilliant woman, tenacious and as tough as nails; she said what she meant and she meant what she said, without apology. Once she made up her mind about any issue, she pursued her goal with relentless persistence. Life left her no other choice.

My grandmother was eighty-eight years of age when she lay in a deep coma after a lengthy illness. My mother stayed by her side day and night, praying for her mother to recover. Grandmother Martha had fought a good fight; she had successfully carried her cross the last mile of the way and endured unspeakable heartache during her life.

As the end drew near, my mother reached over to pray for my grandmother one more time. Suddenly my very plain-spoken grandmother, who could make General Patton snap to attention, came out of her comatose state, looked my shocked mother straight in the eye, and declared with a strong voice and a clear mind, "Vada, stop praying for me! I see heaven, and every time I get close to the other side, your prayers bring me back! I don't want to come back. It's so beautiful there. Charles and Esther Gladys are waving at me from the other side. Good-bye, Vada; I'm crossing over!"

My very astonished mother sat back, caught her breath, and stopped praying as ordered. Within minutes Grandmother's face broke into a radiant smile, and she stepped across the finish line of this life.

Martha Swick was escorted by angels to the other side, where her loving husband and beautiful daughter were waiting in glistening white robes for their reunion just inside heaven's pearly gates.

People on earth speak of my grandmother as dead, but she has never been more alive than she is right now. She is sheltered in the arms of God. She is home! She is in the paradise God created for those who love Him.

She served her generation by the will of God before entering her eternal rest. She exchanged her cross for a crown; she turned in her worn-out body for a glorious and beautiful supernatural one that will never grow old or weary.

My mother asked me to preach the funeral of my grandmother. It was a difficult task for me. Here was the woman who had rocked me to sleep as a child, who had read Bible stories to me when I spent the night with her. She taught her children and grandchildren how to work from dawn to dusk, but most importantly, to honor and obey the Word of God above all else.

As I write this book this very day, her youngest child, Paul Swick, has passed to his eternal reward at age ninety-two. Today, Grandmother Swick is reunited with all of her seven children and her treasured husband, Charles Albert. They are together in the Third Heaven, celebrating the joy and peace that only the righteous in Christ will ever know.

When my mother first told me of my grandmother's passing, I reminded her of a tune we sang around the piano as a family when we were children. Before everyone arrived at the memorial service, I stood beside Grandmother's open casket and sang her favorite song, which she taught me:

> How beautiful heaven must be,
> Sweet home of the happy and free;
> Fair haven of rest for the weary,
> How beautiful heaven must be.[2]

ANGELS, HEAVEN, AND A MOTHER'S LOVE

Some of you may think that my grandmother, who lived a long life, was of course ready to see heaven. But what about a child?

I ask that you read the account of a pediatric intensive care specialist, who shares the story of a young patient under his care.

Several years ago I treated a little boy who had been diagnosed with acute lymphocytic leukemia. He was receiving chemotherapy and was responding well before being discharged to his home in a neighboring city.

Soon after his release from the hospital, he contracted chicken pox, which can be devastating to someone with immune problems. Due to the leukemia and chemotherapy, he had profound immune deficiency and consequently developed a severe case of chicken pox-related pneumonia, which required readmission.

His condition quickly worsened, and he was transferred to the pediatric intensive care unit. Shortly after, he suffered respiratory failure. We inserted a breathing tube into his throat and placed him on a breathing machine. He began to fail conventional mechanical ventilation, and next required the aid of a high-frequency oscillatory ventilator. This device helps patients by rapidly vibrating oxygen into their lungs.

The young boy remained critically ill, needing continued assistance to his heart and lungs. He was heavily sedated and required paralyzing medications in order for us to properly care for him. He was on high doses of antibiotics,

IV nutrition, and various blood products, including IVIG, which is a plasma derivative rich in antibodies.

In my estimation, the boy's chances of pulling through this assault on his body were less than 20 percent. Yet miraculously, after about three weeks of intense treatment, he survived his ordeal and was able to be successfully taken off respiratory support.

The child slowly improved and began to speak to his mother, who had lovingly and prayerfully remained by his side. None of the PICU (pediatric intensive care unit) staff really knew what the boy's developmental and personality baselines were. But according to his mother, he seemed to be moping after reemerging from his comatose state.

As the youngster talked to his mother in Spanish (their native tongue), a PICU nurse and I had the privilege of witnessing their fascinating conversation.

The little boy kept repeating: "Mommy, I am very mad at you! Mommy, I am very mad at you!"

"Why are you mad at me, son?" his mother asked with obvious concern.

"You kept calling me to come back to you, but the angels were calling me to play. I felt so good there, Mommy, and I wanted to stay; but I could hear you calling me back."

The mother was visibly moved to hear her son's clear description of the joy he felt while he was "away from her."

"What else do you remember, my son?" she asked with tears running down her face.

"The angels told me to come back to you, but I was so happy there. I felt so good. Mommy, why did you call me to come home?"

His mother told me she had spoken to her son about angels in the past—that they were sent by the God of heaven to look after us—but nothing more. Because I understand Spanish, it was very touching to hear this young boy speak so clearly of his experience with the angels in heaven.[3]

Personally, this story reaffirms for me the existence of angels and of heaven, and it is also a testimony of the power of a mother's love.

"LISTEN TO THE ANGELS"

The great country music legend Johnny Cash shared a supernatural experience surrounding the death of his brother, Jack. Jack was two years older than Johnny and had always been his hero and role model. On a Saturday in 1944, Jack went to work at a woodshop cutting fence posts. Johnny had tried to talk Jack into going to a movie with him that day, but funds were low and the family needed the money, so Jack dutifully decided to go to work instead.

While at the shop, Jack fell across a table saw and was severely injured. He was rushed to the hospital for treatment, but the doctors informed the family they didn't expect him to live through the day.

Jack lingered for a week, in and out of consciousness—sometimes hallucinating, then relapsing into a coma. His condition continued to worsen as his body swelled from the trauma of his injury.

Jack's family, recognizing that his death was imminent, gathered in the hospital room to say their good-byes. Johnny Cash recounted the rest of the story:

> I remember standing in line to tell him good-bye. He was still unconscious. I bent over his bed and put my cheek against his and said, "Good-bye, Jack." That's all I could get out.
>
> My mother and daddy were on their knees. At 6:30 a.m. he woke up. He opened his eyes and looked around and said, "Why is everybody crying over me? Mama, don't cry over me. Did you see the river?"
>
> And she said, "No, I didn't, son."
>
> "Well, I thought I was going toward a fire, but I'm headed in the other direction now, Mama. I was going down a river, and I saw a fire on one side and heaven on the other. I was crying, 'God, I'm supposed to go to heaven. Don't You remember?' All of a sudden I turned, and now, I'm going toward heaven. Mama, can you hear the angels singing?"
>
> She said, "No, son, I can't hear them."
>
> And he squeezed her hand and shook her arm, saying, "But Mama, you've got to hear it."
>
> Tears started rolling off his cheeks and he said, "Mama, listen to the angels. I'm going there, Mama."
>
> We listened with astonishment.
>
> "What a beautiful city," he said. "And the angels singing. Oh Mama, I wish you could hear the angels singing."
>
> Those were his last words. And he died.

The memory of Jack's death, his vision of heaven, the effect his life had on the lives of others and the image of Christ he projected has been more of an inspiration to me, I suppose, than anything else that has ever come to me through any man.[4]

AN IRRESISTIBLE PARADISE

Dr. Mary Neal's riveting personal testimony[5] gives us another glimpse of the life to come for those who believe.

In her book *To Heaven and Back,* she writes about caring for a patient who had suffered complete liver failure at the age of fourteen. This girl told Dr. Neal that she was not afraid of dying because God had told her He was with her and that He loved her. Furthermore, she had heard God tell her to "come home." Right before surgery the young patient told Dr. Neal that she wouldn't be coming back and thanked her for all she and the other medical professionals had done.

Dr. Neal writes in her book, "I listened and accepted the truth of her words. Still, my tears flowed freely later in the day when her heart stopped beating." She had a hard time accepting the loss of this beautiful girl, and she didn't fully comprehend her patient's claim that angels were with her and that no one should be sad because it was time for her to go. Then one day Dr. Neal died herself, and that is when she saw the light and understood what her patient had told her.

Mary and her husband are athletic and avid outdoors people. One of their greatest passions is kayaking, and they have done so on rivers throughout the United States as well as internationally. So one year they decided to head to Chile, where they would experience a river well known for it's treacherous white waters and challenging ten- to twenty-foot falls.

With some of their fellow travelers being less experienced in waters so difficult to navigate, their guide decided to take a more narrow, less-challenging channel. However, one kayaker with very limited skills hit the path with too much angle and got stuck between two boulders at the entrance of the drop. Attempting to avoid the novice kayaker, Dr. Neal went over the main drop, plunging more than fifteen feet down the waterfall. The sudden dive tore the paddle out of her grip as she became caught up in the wild gush of water that ended below the falls under violent, churning waves. There was no escape. She recounts this harrowing experience in an interview with *Christianity Today*:

> When I hit the bottom of the waterfall, the front of my boat became pinned in the rocks underwater. I and my boat were completely submerged in the water.

She desperately tried to get out of her kayak by using every escape procedure in which she was expertly trained. Dr. Neal pushed her foot against the braces and she wiggled the boat with all of her body strength . . . nothing! She tried reaching her "grab loop" that would free her spray skirt from the boat so she could swim to safety, but she couldn't reach it due to the pressing weight of the waterfall crashing down on top of her. Tragically, the apparatus meant to keep water out of her kayak was now trapping her inside of it.

It was no use. I was stuck. My kayak, my coffin. "You're not in control," I told myself. "Just let go!"

Nothing she attempted would free her and allow her to reach the fresh air just a couple of feet above her. But instead of panic, a great calm came over Mary as she acknowledged God's love for her. She prayed, "Your will be done," and all of a sudden, she became aware that Jesus was there with her, holding her and comforting her. At that very moment she knew that everything would be all right. She was profoundly reassured that her husband and children would be fine, even if she died. She surrendered and thought, *Okay God, hurry up.* Her panic left and she no longer felt herself struggling to hold her breath; she instinctually knew she had been underwater too long to still be alive. Yet, strangely, she felt more alive than ever before.

She could still feel the weight of the water as it pounded against her, then suddenly, the raging current separated her body from the boat. Facing downstream, with her legs straight in front of her, the orthopedic doctor felt the breaking of her bones and the tearing of the ligaments in her knees. In her book, she wrote,

> While my body was being slowly sucked out of the boat, I felt as though my soul was slowly peeling itself away from my body . . . It felt as if I had finally shaken off my heavy outer layer, freeing my soul. I rose up and out of the river, and when my soul broke through the surface of the water,

I encountered a group of fifteen to twenty souls . . . who greeted me with the most overwhelming joy I have ever experienced.

She started traveling down a path with these spiritual beings, all the while still being able to witness what was happening below on the bank of the river—her body being pulled ashore, someone administering CPR to her lifeless body, and prayers being lifted up on her behalf.

All the while the path she was on with her "human spirits" led toward a great hall, which she described in a *Guideposts* article as "larger and more beautiful than anything I could conceive of, with an immense dome and a central arch built with shimmering gold blocks . . . Heaven . . . irresistible paradise . . . eternal home."

But before she crossed the threshold, the spiritual beings turned to her and said that it was not her time, that she must return to her body, to the earth, to her family, in order to finish the work God still had for her. At that moment she was filled with a sadness equal to the joy she had felt when she was about to come into the presence of God. It was time to go back to her loved ones, but she knew now what that precious young patient of hers had meant. Someday she would once again walk into that "ever-present radiance," but not now.

She summarizes her experience this way in her book:

God and His angelic messengers are present and active in our world today and this involvement and intervention is both ordinary in its frequency and extraordinary in its occurrence. Despite leading what I would consider a very ordinary life, I have had the privilege of being touched by God in visible and very tangible ways.

Everyone will leave this world someday and enter into an eternal home. When we depart this life, we will walk into the next one, for every exit from one place is also an entrance into another. The question we must ask ourselves is, "What world am I entering into?"

The Scriptures speak of heaven and hell, of the angels of God and the fallen angels of Satan, and of the war between these two powerful celestial forces. We live in a world of good and evil, a world of light and darkness, a world of angels and demons. There is no doubt that we are surrounded by supernatural beings infinite in number and great in power. Their ongoing battles over the human soul take place in the Second Heaven.

SECTION TWO

THE SECOND HEAVEN

CHAPTER 4

THE MIDST OF HEAVEN

I know a man in Christ [Paul speaking of himself] who
fourteen years ago—whether in the body I do not know . . .
God knows—such a one was caught up to the third heaven.
And I know such a man . . . how he was caught up into
Paradise and heard inexpressible words, which it is not
lawful for a man to utter.

2 Corinthians 12:2–4

Saint Paul's statement clearly describes a specific place called
Paradise. Paul also said he was caught up into the Third
Heaven. As I have stated before, logic would dictate that if there is
a Third Heaven, then there must be a First and a Second Heaven.
Paul's personal experience also verifies that people who are very
much alive can be "caught up," or supernaturally transported,
through the First and Second Heavens and into the Third Heaven,
which is the believer's eternal home. Elijah and Enoch have been
there thousands of years and have yet to die!

John the Revelator spoke of a region described as "the midst of heaven," or "mid-heaven," which is the Greek word *mesouranema*.

> And I looked, and I heard an angel flying through the midst of heaven [mid-heaven], saying with a loud voice, "Woe, woe, woe to the inhabitants of the earth, because of the remaining blasts of the trumpet of the three angels who are about to sound!" (Revelation 8:13)

The battle of Daniel 10:12–13 is an example of an ongoing conflict between the forces of good (God's elect angels) and the forces of evil (Satan's fallen angels). These battles could very well take place in the mid-heaven.

The references above scripturally validate the existence of a Second Heaven. But who dwells there, and what takes place in the Second Heaven?

Before we answer these questions, we must define who Lucifer *was* and who Satan *is*.

LUCIFER

The traditional depiction of the devil as a horned, sharp-toothed, cloven-hoofed, insidious creature is taken from pagan mythology, not Scripture. God created an inexpressibly beautiful angel named Lucifer. He was a cherub and the overseer of the Garden of God. He was also wise, the most glorious of all the angels, and the worship leader in Paradise.

Lucifer displayed such splendor and radiance that he was called "son of the morning" (Isaiah 14:12). The Hebrew translation of the name Lucifer is *helel,* which means "to shine" or "to bear light." He reflected the magnificent majesty of God's radiance.

Ezekiel vividly depicted Lucifer:

> Thus says the Lord GOD: "You were the seal of perfection, full of wisdom and perfect in beauty. You were in Eden, the garden of God; every precious stone was your covering . . . The workmanship of your timbrels and pipes was prepared for you on the day you were created.
>
> "You were the anointed cherub who covers; I established you; you were on the holy mountain of God; you walked back and forth in the midst of fiery stones." (28:12–14)

Lucifer's wings "covered" the place where God's glory was manifested in His heavenly temple, just as the cherubim in the tabernacle of Moses covered the mercy seat and the place where the visible glory of God appeared (Exodus 37:9). So what went wrong?

How did God's creation—the "seal of perfection, full of wisdom and perfect in beauty"—become God's bitter adversary?

BIRTH OF A REBEL

The Word of God says this about Lucifer's fall from the Third Heaven:

> How you are fallen from heaven [the Third Heaven], O Lucifer, son of the morning! How you are cut down to the ground, you who weakened the nations! (Isaiah 14:12)

God created a cherub who had free will to make decisions; He did not create the monster that Lucifer became. The angel Lucifer willfully chose to attempt to overthrow God and His Kingdom.

Why did God cast him out of Paradise? Lucifer's declaration of defiance is recorded in Isaiah:

> You have said in your heart: "I will ascend into heaven, I will exalt my throne above the stars of God; I will also sit on the mount of the congregation . . . I will ascend above the heights of the clouds, I will be like the Most High." (14:13–14)

Five times Lucifer said, "I will." He lusted for the throne of God, and in his self-centeredness he became dissatisfied with his position, exalted though it was. Lucifer was consumed by his desire to be worshiped, an ambition that will be vicariously experienced through the Son of Perdition—the Antichrist (Revelation 13:4).

What motivated Lucifer to make such vainglorious pronouncements? Pride! Because of pride, Lucifer challenged God's ultimate authority by seeking to claim a place of equality with his almighty Creator.

Derek Prince concisely explained Lucifer's prideful rebellion:

> Lucifer's heart was lifted up in pride because of his beauty and this was the reason . . . he was cast out of the Mountain of God [the Third Heaven] . . . It is vitally important for all of us to realize that the first sin in the universe was not

murder, nor adultery, but . . . pride. It was pride that produced rebellion. It was God who gave Lucifer his power, his authority, his beauty, his wisdom; all those were gifts from God. Yet Lucifer's wrong attitude turned them into instruments of his own destruction.[1]

C. S. Lewis wrote this about the sin of pride:

The essential vice, the utmost evil is pride. Unchastity, anger, greed, drunkenness, and all of that are mere fleabites in comparison: it was through Pride that the devil became the devil. Pride leads to every other vice. It is the complete anti-God state of mind.[2]

And Scripture warns, "Pride goes before destruction, and a haughty spirit before a fall" (Proverbs 16:18).

Remember this truth: "Pride cannot live beneath the cross."[3] Pride is sin, and God cannot coexist with sin.

As a consequence to Lucifer's rebellion, God banished him from Paradise. In that instant the chief cherub was no longer "the bearer of light"; he would forever be called Satan. The beautiful Lucifer was no more.

SATAN'S NATURE AND INTENT

Since the fall of Lucifer, Satan is known by many names that not only epitomize his evil nature but also define his brutal and vicious mission to destroy God's purposes.

Scripture references Satan as our adversary the Devil, a roaring lion (1 Peter 5:8), the Strong Man (Mark 3:27), a murderer, and the Father of Lies.

> He was *a murderer* from the beginning, and does not stand in the truth because there is no truth in him. Whenever he speaks a lie, he speaks from his own nature, for he is a liar and *the father of lies.* (John 8:44 NASB)

He is also known as the Great Dragon, the Ancient Serpent, and the Deceiver (Revelation 12:9) who has the power of death (Hebrews 2:14). Satan is the Evil One (1 John 5:19 NASB)!

Satan is the Tempter (Matthew 4:3), Beelzebub, the Ruler of Demons (Matthew 12:24), the Prince of this World (John 14:30), the Prince of the Air (Ephesians 2:2), and the Angel of the Bottomless Pit.

> They had as king over them the angel of the bottomless pit, whose name in Hebrew is *Abaddon*, but in Greek he has the name *Apollyon*. (Revelation 9:11)

Think of it . . . Lucifer was lovingly and perfectly created by the Great I AM. Almighty God had a divine assignment for this anointed cherub, but instead, Lucifer chose a path that would lead him to be branded as an agent of death and destruction. He is now known as Satan.

Since the time of his fall until now, the Adversary has attempted to foil God's plan of redemption by destroying His chosen line from which our Messiah comes. There was Cain, who "was of the wicked one" (1 John 3:12), and there was the evolution of universal disobedience that caused God to redeem mankind through Noah (1 Peter 3:19–20), whose lineage included Abraham, Isaac, and Jacob—the fathers of God's chosen people.

When God establishes, Satan opposes. Therefore, it is within Satan's evil nature to direct his hostility toward God's faithful remnant. This blatant resistance was personified in Ishmael's opposition to Isaac, Esau's desire to kill Jacob, and Pharaoh's oppression of the Israelites.[4] Then there was Haman's gallows, Herod's killing of the innocent, and the temptation of Christ in the wilderness.

The Serpent's goal was to thwart the Father's plan of redemption, but he failed! This ages-long conflict will reach its climax when an angel from heaven seals Satan in the Abyss for one thousand years (Revelation 20:1–3).

Once banished from Paradise (the Third Heaven), the Rebel of all rebels established his throne in the Second Heaven, or "midheaven," where he and his fallen angels rule over all the kingdoms of the world.

The whole world lies in the power of the evil one. (1 John 5:19 NASB)

Jesus knows where Satan's throne is.

Says He who has the sharp two-edged sword: "I know your works, and where you dwell, where Satan's throne is." (Revelation 2:12–13)

If there is a throne, there is also a kingdom.

THE KINGDOM OF SATAN

Christ plainly stated during His ministry that Satan has a kingdom (Matthew 12:26). While delivering a demon-possessed man, the Pharisees tried to discredit Jesus' miracle by saying that He had cast out the demons by the power of Beelzebub, the Ruler of the Demons. Christ answered their accusation by saying that a kingdom or city divided against itself cannot stand, and if He were casting out demons by Satan's authority, Satan was defeating himself. He closed His argument by asking, "How then shall his kingdom stand?" (Matthew 12:24–26).

Take note: Satan's Kingdom was recognized by no less an authority than Jesus Christ.

Satan's reign and influence encompass the First and Second Heavens, but he roams freely about the earth. He has even visited the Third Heaven since his fall, disguising himself as an angel (2 Corinthians 11:14) and presenting himself before God in the Third Heaven along with the righteous angels. It was only God who recognized him.

> Now there was a day when the sons of God [angels] came to present themselves before the LORD, and Satan also came among them. The LORD said to Satan [disguised as an angel of light], "From where do you come?" Then Satan answered the LORD and said, "From roaming about on the earth and walking around on it." (Job 1:6–7 NASB)

Be warned that Satan does not confine his influence to the wicked and the corrupt; he attends religious gatherings, as reflected by his presence at the angelic convocation (Job 1). His agents posture as "ministers of righteousness" (2 Corinthians 11:15), and references such as "doctrines of demons" (1 Timothy 4:1) point to Satan's evil intent to destroy God's Church.

Both Satan and his Kingdom have distinct traits.

Both thrive in darkness: "He has delivered us from the power of darkness and conveyed us into the kingdom of the Son of His love" (Colossians 1:13). Most importantly, Satan and his Kingdom are temporary.

The Scriptures confirm that his authority will be taken from him by the angel of God.

> Then I saw an angel coming down from heaven [the Third Heaven], having the key to the bottomless pit and a great chain in his hand. He laid hold of the dragon, that serpent of old, who is the Devil and Satan, and bound him for a thousand years; and he cast him into the bottomless pit, and shut him up, and set a seal on him, so that he should deceive the nations no more till the thousand years were finished. (Revelation 20:1–3)

Until Satan's Kingdom is no more, he and his evil minions maintain dominion over the First and Second Heaven as permitted by God Almighty. However, remember this: Satan's authority is always limited by God's sovereignty.

Once Lucifer devised his rebellious plot against God, he recruited the angelic beings under his authority to follow after him. He eventually organized one-third of the angels (Revelation 12:4) to join his revolt against the God who created the heavens and earth.

The same spirit of rebellion that Lucifer employed to recruit one-third of the angels in the Third Heaven is the same spirit he used against Adam and Eve in the Garden, and it is the unchanged tactic he uses to lure every one of us from God's Kingdom today. We, like the angels and Adam and Eve before us, have been given the free will to choose between good and evil—between becoming servants of Christ or slaves to sin and Satan.

Once *Lucifer* and his followers were cast from heaven, *Satan* established his opposing Kingdom as a counterfeit reflection of God's governmental structure, which is chronicled in Colossians 1:16.

The apostle Paul spoke of Satan's illegitimate government within this false kingdom.

> We do not wrestle against flesh and blood, but against *principalities*, against *powers*, against the *rulers of the darkness* of this age, against *spiritual hosts of wickedness* in the heavenly places. (Ephesians 6:12)

The Kingdom of Satan is comprised of four evil divisions. The first is the fallen angels, or *principalities*, which serve as Satan's highest-ranking rulers. The second division is the *powers*, who are given authority to execute the will of the chief rulers. The third is the *world rulers* of the darkness of this age, and finally, the earthbound demons, who are the *spiritual hosts of wickedness*; they are Satan's servants and do his bidding on the earth.

There is only one reason for Satan to organize his legions into ranks, and that reason is spiritual warfare! His obsession is *still* fueled by pride, which produces an insatiable craving for absolute power.

Satan's foremost goal is for the world to bow before him and worship him as God. Yet there is a greater Kingdom than Satan's, led by Jesus Christ Himself, who will rule the earth for a thousand years of perfect peace.

> The wolf also shall dwell with the lamb, the leopard shall lie down with the young goat, the calf and the young lion and the fatling together; and a little child shall lead them. (Isaiah 11:6)

> He shall judge between the nations, and rebuke many people; they shall beat their swords into plowshares, and their spears into pruning hooks; nation shall not lift up sword against nation, neither shall they learn war anymore. (Isaiah 2:4)

Until that millennial Kingdom comes, however, the fight is on!

CHAPTER 5

THE CLASH OF TWO KINGDOMS

There is at this moment a war going on in the spiritual realm that affects every person on the face of the earth. It is the clash of two Kingdoms. One Kingdom is under the command of Almighty God, the Prince of Peace (Psalm 103:19; Isaiah 9:6); the other Kingdom is under the command of Satan, the Prince of the Power of Darkness (Matthew 12:26; Colossians 1:13).

THE KINGDOM OF GOD

We have discussed the Kingdom of Satan in the previous chapter. Allow me to introduce you to the Kingdom of God. A noted Bible scholar defined the Kingdom of God thusly:

> The Kingdom of God means the sovereignty of God over the universe and includes and embraces the Kingdom of Heaven and all other realms in the whole universe. It is moral and universal and has existed from the beginning and will know no end. The Kingdom of God existed even

before the creation of the Earth. The angels and other spirit beings were in this kingdom when the Earth was created (Job 38:4–7). The Kingdom of Heaven could not have existed then, for there was no Earth for the kingdom from the heavens to rule.[1]

Of this Kingdom, Scripture says:

[The Lord to Job:] "Where were you when I laid the foundations of the earth? Tell Me, if you have understanding. Who determined its measurements? Surely you know! Or who stretched the line upon it? To what were its foundations fastened? Or who laid its cornerstone, when the morning stars sang together and all the sons of God shouted for joy? (Job 38:4–7)

The LORD has established His throne in heaven, and His kingdom rules over all. (Psalm 103:19)

How great are His signs, and how mighty His wonders! His kingdom is an everlasting kingdom, and His dominion is from generation to generation. (Daniel 4:3)

God established a blueprint for governmental structure within His heavenly Kingdom as recorded by Saint Paul in Colossians 1:16:

By Him all things were created that are in heaven and that are on earth, visible and invisible, whether thrones or dominions or principalities or powers. All things were created through Him and for Him.

Here Paul listed four levels of authority within God's Kingdom in descending order: thrones, dominions, principalities, and powers. Paul also referred to *Satan's* hierarchy in Ephesians 6:12: principalities, powers, rulers of darkness, and spiritual hosts. Note that Satan's command is void of "thrones" and "dominions." This exclusion suggests that the angels at these levels chose not to join Lucifer's rebellion when the third of the angels followed him.

WAR IN THE HEAVENLIES

Surrounding us is a spirit world, far more populous, powerful, and resourceful than our own visible world of human beings. Spirits, good and evil, wend their way in our midst. With lightning speed and noiseless movement they pass from place to place. They inhabit the spaces of the air about us. Some we know to be concerned for our welfare, others are set on our harm. The inspired writers draw aside the curtain and give us a glimpse of this invisible world, in order that we may be both encouraged and warned.[2] (Myer Pearlman)

Picture in the theater of your mind two Kingdoms: one belonging to God, and the other to His great adversary, Satan. One stands for good and the other for evil. One stands for light and the other for darkness. One stands for blessings and the other for curses.

One stands for life and the other for death. These two opposing Kingdoms cannot coexist; they are at war!

When did this spiritual war begin? What were its causes? Where did the initial battle take place? How long will the battle last, and who will be the victor?

The "war of all wars" began sometime before Genesis 1:1, in an era that biblical scholars refer to as "the dateless past."[3] At that time there was only one Kingdom under the command of the triune Godhead (God the Father, God the Son, and God the Holy Spirit).

What started this war? We know that Satan was cast from the Third Heaven as a result of his rebellious pride. Once he entered the Second Heaven, Satan established his Kingdom for the sole purpose of coming against the Kingdom of God.

The driving force of this epic clash is the same as in any war: It is a struggle for power. A struggle to attain what rightfully belongs to someone else. And the only way to achieve this objective is to take that power by force.

> War broke out in heaven: Michael and his angels fought with the dragon [Satan]; and the dragon and his angels fought, but they did not prevail, nor was a place found for them in heaven [the Third Heaven] any longer. So the great dragon was cast out, that serpent of old, called the Devil and Satan, who deceives the whole world; he was cast to the earth, and his angels were cast out with him. (Revelation 12:7–9)

Once they were expelled from the Third Heaven, Satan and his followers pledged themselves to each other and formed the Rebel

Kingdom that exists to this day and will exist until it is terminated by God's ultimate power.

> The devil, who deceived them, was cast into the lake of fire and brimstone where the beast and the false prophet are. And they will be tormented day and night forever and ever. (Revelation 20:10)

INVASION OF THE GARDEN

Satan's initial attack on God's authority on earth occurred in the Garden of Eden. The Godhead had created man and had given him a "place, a purpose and a partner"[4]; Adam and Eve were instructed to "be fruitful, and multiply, and replenish the earth, and subdue it: and have dominion over the fish of the sea, and over the fowl of the air, and over every living thing that moveth upon the earth" (Genesis 1:28 KJV).

Satan considered the earth *his* domain (Matthew 4:8) and saw Adam and Eve as God's invaders in his territory. If God created mankind to dwell upon the earth to establish *His* Kingdom, then Satan needed a plan of counterattack. He must destroy the destiny of man, but how?

That old serpent, the Devil, made his way to Eve and employed three strategic tactics against her. The first one was doubt: "Has God indeed said . . . ?" (Genesis 3:1). You can almost hear the Father of Lies as he interacts with Eve: "Are you *sure*? Is that what He told you? Doesn't sound like the God I know!"

Then the Deceiver used his second tactic—that of supposition—causing Eve to question whether the consequences of her disobedience would *truly* lead to her death as God had stated:

"You will *not* surely die" (Genesis 3:4). Satan continued his diabolical dialogue with Eve: "How could a loving God destroy *you* over one small act? He loves you unconditionally; He wouldn't hurt you!"

The third and final approach he used against Eve was temptation: "God knows that in the day you eat of it [the tree of the knowledge of good and evil] your eyes will be opened, and you will be like God, knowing good and evil" (Genesis 3:5). Eve looked at the tree . . . and it was beautiful! How could eating from it harm her? It would produce wisdom equal to God's; what is wrong with *that*?[5]

Ultimately, the Tempter succeeded. Reaching for immortality that was already hers, Eve succumbed to the serpent's subtle enticements, and in the type of rebellion established in the Third Heaven by Lucifer, she influenced another to follow her in sin. Adam, of his own free will, chose to follow Eve out of the state of innocence into a world of suffering, sickness, tears, and death. The threefold presentation of sin was established: sin is first a fascination, then it takes a form, and finally it becomes a fact.

God is omnipresent and omniscient, which means that He is *in* all things and *knows all* things. When Adam and Eve fell, God questioned them and their actions, and in doing so He gave them the opportunity to repent. They chose instead to rationalize their sin and cast blame—Adam blamed Eve, and Eve blamed the serpent. To this day, rationalizing sin is Satan's substitute for confession and repentance. The Accuser had left his mark!

I can only imagine how brokenhearted God must have felt as He banished Adam and Eve from the Garden. Before doing so, though, He covered their nakedness with animal skins. With this one act, the biblical pattern that the innocent must die for the guilty was set in place. It was a foreshadowing of the spotless Lamb of God slain on the Cross for the sins of the world.

Almost all things are by the law purged with blood; and without shedding of blood is no remission. (Hebrews 9:22 KJV)

God already knew the Adversary's plan; God knew how Adam and Eve would respond. And in the moment that Adam and Eve rebelled, the sovereign God set into motion His miraculous plan of redemption.

The reasons for Satan's attack were twofold: First, he wanted to initiate a subtle assault on God's creation, causing humanity to be separated from God. Second, once he had successfully estranged the created from the Creator, Satan put in place his most calculated onslaught: he seduced man and woman into forming an allegiance with him so that he might become the god of this world.

Satan's subversive counterattack overpowered the humans completely. But God established a beachhead in the Garden of Eden, promising that the seed of the woman would bruise the head of the serpent. In this way, He demonstrated His complete mastery of Satan by reversing the tables on the Tempter before driving Adam and Eve out of the Garden (Genesis 3:15).

God Almighty issued His victorious declaration over the war of life and death there in the Garden of Eden, and it was confirmed on the Cross of Calvary when Jesus said, "It is finished!" (John 19:30).

Eternal redemption for humankind was foreshadowed in these two verses. And though the warfare would continue, the Cross of

Christ was to become the final battleground where Satan's fate—and that of his Kingdom of fallen angels—was sealed for all eternity.

There was no room for diplomatic negotiations; sin must forever be punished. God drove Adam and Eve from the Garden, knowing that the violent and vicious war that the Evil One had initiated would leave a path of destruction, with all of humanity wounded and many forever destroyed. And the first human casualty of this war was about to be claimed as the clash of the two Kingdoms continued.

MURDER IN THE FIRST DEGREE

God's divine plan of redemption was in place, but it was not acceptable to Satan. In response, he devised a plan to annihilate the seed that would birth the Savior of the world.

Adam and Eve had two sons, Cain and Abel. Satan was convinced that if he destroyed the first family's offspring, he would thwart God's efforts to establish His Kingdom on earth through mankind.

In order to carry out his destructive plot, the Prince of Death introduced the spirit of murder on the earth.

Genesis records that "Abel was a keeper of sheep, but Cain was a tiller of the ground" (4:2). At the set time, the brothers brought two separate offerings to the Lord. Cain's was "of the fruit of the ground" (4:3) while Abel sacrificially presented the firstborn of his flock (4:4). These diverse gifts characterize two prototypes of religion found throughout man's history.

Cain offered the fruit of the ground, which was under God's curse (Genesis 3:17). Cain's offering was the product of self-will and unbelief; in other words, it involved no divine revelation, no acknowledgment of sin and its consequent curse, no recognition of the need for a sacrifice to make amends for sin. The product of the curse could not remove the presence of the curse.[6]

Abel, on the other hand, sacrificed from the firstborn of his flock. Through this act he acknowledged the presence of sin and the necessity for restitution through the shedding of blood. This understanding came to him, not through his own reason, but by divine revelation. Abel's religion was founded on his faith in God and not by his own works.

> By faith Abel offered to God a more excellent sacrifice than Cain, through which he obtained witness that he was righteous, God testifying of his gifts; and through it he being dead still speaks. (Hebrews 11:4)

God respected Abel's righteous sacrifice but rejected Cain's corrupt offering because Cain's reflected the humanistic pride of his flesh (Genesis 4:4–5).

Cain responded violently to God's rejection, murdering Abel in a fit of rage fueled by jealousy for his brother and rebellion against God. The accomplice to that murder was Satan; he, through wickedness, was the motivating force that provoked Cain to slaughter his brother.

It is significant to realize that the first murder was over religion—one founded on humanism and the other on faith in God. Sadly, religion has continued to be the cause of many wars and much bloodshed.

Scripture points a condemning finger squarely at Satan for Abel's murder by declaring:

> In this the children of God and the children of the devil are manifest: Whoever does not practice righteousness is not of God, nor is he who does not love his brother. For this is the message that you heard from the beginning, that we should love one another, not as Cain who was of the wicked one and murdered his brother. And why did he murder him? Because his works were evil and his brother's righteous. (1 John 3:10–12)

Satan's assault on Abel through Cain was tragically successful: he orchestrated the end of one life and the banishment of another, as Cain was exiled for shedding his brother's innocent blood. However, Eve bore another son, Seth, through whom God's eternal purposes would be accomplished as the clash of the two Kingdoms continued.

INVASION OF THE NEPHILIM

Satan's obsession with total power prompted him, as the self-appointed Commander of the Kingdom of Darkness, to call upon his evil legions to infiltrate mankind with the intent to pollute the Adamic line leading to the Messiah.

> Now it came to pass, when men began to multiply on the face of the earth, and daughters were born to them; that the sons of God saw the daughters of men, that they were

beautiful; and they took wives for themselves of all whom they chose. (Genesis 6:1–2)

Who were the "sons of God"? Chapters 1, 2, and 38 of the book of Job define them as "angels." We have established that two-thirds of the angels remained with God in the Third Heaven (elect angels) while one-third were banished (Satan's fallen angels).

Please note: Genesis 6 refers to a time when "men *began* to multiply." Seth did not have a son until 235 years after Creation, and his son did not have a son until 90 years later (Genesis 5:3–9). These unsanctioned marriages occurred before Seth's sons were of age. The sons of God of Genesis 6 were fallen angels referred to in the sixth verse of Jude.[7]

The [fallen] angels who did not keep their proper domain, but left their own abode, He has reserved in everlasting chains under darkness for the judgment of the great day.

God's Kingdom was flourishing in number and in strength; feeling threatened, the Prince of Darkness called upon his evil legions to infiltrate mankind. These fallen angels came to earth and produced a race of Nephilim, or giants. The meaning of the word *Nephilim* in the Hebrew is "fallen." This satanic invasion of Genesis 6 corrupted the whole world.

Then the LORD saw that the wickedness of man was great in the earth, and that every *intent* of the thoughts of his heart was only evil continually. (Genesis 6:5)

Consequently, God sent His judgment to crush Satan's wicked invasion of earth. Watchman Nee described this evil evolution:

> For Adam it is a sinful act, for Cain it has become a lust, and by the time of the flood, sin has developed so quickly that man has become flesh (carnal); that is, sinning has now become a habit.[8]

For this great apostasy there was no remedy but the absolute judgment of God. And that absolute judgment was the Flood, exterminating the human race save for those on the ark.

Great sin demands great judgment. With the exception of Noah and the inhabitants of the ark, every living creature on earth was destroyed in the Flood. Satan had attacked; man had surrendered. It seemed that the Evil One had won the battle, yet God had a greater plan and used the ark to save the Adamic line that would one day lead to Christ's redemption of man at the Cross. This is why we say, "Jesus is the ark of our salvation!"

The clash of the two Kingdoms continues once more.

KNOW THE ENEMY

If you know the enemy and know yourself, you need not fear the result of a hundred battles. If you know yourself but not the enemy, for every victory gained, you will also suffer a defeat. If you know neither the enemy nor yourself, you will succumb in every battle. (Sun Tzu, Ancient Chinese Philosopher)

In World War II General George Patton studied the life and military philosophies of the German general Erwin Rommel, also known as the "Desert Fox." Rommel was recognized as one of the greatest minds in military history, "brilliantly successful in attack and remarkably resourceful in defense."[9] Patton, however, realized a truth that many Christians choose to disregard: to know your enemy is to possess the power to defeat him.

Underestimating the enemy is suicide; it is akin to becoming an ally with the opposition for your own defeat. This is why every strategic military invasion is preceded by extensive reconnaissance and an intensive study of the enemy. Every battlefield position is charted. Every landmark is identified. The personalities of opposing generals are psychoanalyzed to determine how they might react under the pressure of war.

No area of scrutiny is exempt. The war will be won or lost on the knowledge of the enemy.[10]

The apostle Paul, through divine revelation, provided us with a clear picture of Satan's chain of command in Ephesians 6. Paul warned us to be mindful of our primary target so that we are empowered to "stand against the wiles of the devil" (v. 11) and not turn against one another! He underscored that our enemy is not "flesh and blood" (v. 12) but the henchmen of the Evil One.

The Devil is a roaring lion who seeks to devour his prey (1 Peter 5:8). And his demons have been given direct orders to seek out and destroy those who will not submit to him and imprison those who will (John 10:10).

Under Satan's command, demons work together to inflict every conceivable form of harm, deception, and torment on humanity.

In order to be triumphant in spiritual warfare, God's children must accept the fact that the enemy walks among us, deploying every sinister scheme for the sole purposes of domination and destruction.

INVASION OF DEMONS

We discussed in chapter 4 that the Enemy has structured his Kingdom by levels of authority. The fourth and lowest position in Satan's realm is held by the "hosts of wickedness" (Ephesians 6:12), most commonly known as demons. They are the foot soldiers of his evil army and are dominated and directed by the higher-ranking rulers, powers, and principalities.

The terms *Devil*, *devils*, and *demons* are often confused. There is only one Prince of Devils, and that is Satan, but there are many demons. The word *demon* is derived from the Greek word *daimon*, meaning evil spirit or devil (*demons* is the plural form).

Satan (*the* Devil) has an angelic body and cannot physically enter into anyone, but he can be in union with man for evil purposes (Luke 22:3). Demons, on the other hand, are evil spirits that operate in the world by possessing the bodies of humans (Luke 8:30) or beasts (Luke 8:33).[11]

I have stated that Satan mimics God through counterfeit means, and demonic invasion is no exception. Those who are submitted to the Lord have a divine personality dwelling in them in the form of the Holy Spirit (John 14:23). Those who are ruled in some area of their life by demons are influenced by Satan's evil spirit (Acts 19:16).

Jesus Christ came to earth to deliver the oppressed from the power of demons (Acts 10:38). Once liberated, believers are transformed by the power of God's Spirit—a supernatural transformation that Satan cannot imitate!

WHAT CHARACTERIZES DEMONS?

Like their leader, demons have personalities and purposes that define their objective.

Demons are distinct creatures:

Now when He [Jesus] rose early on the first day of the week, He appeared first to Mary Magdalene, out of whom He had cast *seven* demons. (Mark 16:9)

Demons have a will:

When an unclean spirit goes out of a man, he goes through dry places, seeking rest, and finds none. Then he says, "*I will* return to my house from which I came." And when he comes, he finds it empty, swept, and put in order. Then he goes and takes with him seven other spirits more wicked than himself, and they enter and dwell there; and the last state of that man is worse than the first. (Matthew 12:43–45)

Demons have the ability to speak.

The Gospels of Matthew (8:29), Mark (1:24), and Luke (8:30) repeatedly present illustrations of this, as does the book of Acts (19:15).

Demons have understanding:

> [The demon said,] "Let us alone! What have we to do with You, Jesus of Nazareth? Did You come to destroy us? I know who You are—the Holy One of God!" (Mark 1:24)

Demons have self-awareness:

> Then He [Jesus] asked him [the demon], "What is your name?" And he answered, saying, "My name is Legion; for we are many." (Mark 5:9)

Demons have faith:

> You believe that there is one God. You do well. Even the demons believe—and tremble! (James 2:19)

Demons have emotions:

> And he [the demon] cried out with a loud voice and said, "What have I to do with You, Jesus, Son of the Most High God? I implore You by God that You do not torment me." (Mark 5:7)

Demons have fellowship:

> I do not want you to have fellowship with demons. You cannot drink the cup of the Lord and the cup of demons;

you cannot partake of the Lord's Table and of the table of demons. (1 Corinthians 10:20–21)

Demons have doctrines:

Now the Spirit expressly says that in latter times some will depart from the faith, giving heed to deceiving spirits and doctrines of demons. (1 Timothy 4:1)

Demons have desires:

So the demons begged Him [Jesus], saying, "If You cast us out, permit us to go away into the herd of swine." (Matthew 8:31)

Demons have controlling power over those they occupy:

Then the man in whom the evil spirit was leaped on them, overpowered them, and prevailed against them, so that they fled out of that house naked and wounded. (Acts 19:16)

Demons have miraculous powers:

For they are the spirits of devils, working miracles, which go forth unto the kings of the earth and of the whole world. (Revelation 16:14 KJV)

In His model prayer, Jesus instructed His followers to pray for deliverance from the Evil One on a daily basis (Luke 11:4). Christ is the example for the New Testament Church. He spent much of His time delivering people from the bondage of evil spirits. He cast demons from possessed individuals often, publicly, and successfully, yet the demons did not relinquish their hold on humanity even after Jesus was crucified! They will continue to torment and possess till Christ comes again to redeem His Church. Until then, we remain at war!

The clash of the two Kingdoms continues.

CHAPTER 6

INVASION OF DEMONS IN SOCIETY

Man is drawn to the supernatural like a moth to a flame. A divine spark in each of us senses something more beyond our world. The question is, what? My book *Invasion of Demons*, released in 1973, attempted to answer at least part of that question.

Presently Cornerstone Church has an extensive Pastoral Care Department; we visit the sick, minister to the needy, and provide counseling for our membership. But in the early 1970s, it was just me—I was the pastor, the choir director, the adult Sunday school teacher, the janitor, the yard man, and the *only* counselor.

It was a typical Tylenol Tuesday—a day when I would hear people's problems (most of them self-inflicted) from early morning until late evening. But this day would be different; it was a day that would inspire my first book.

My first counseling appointment that morning walked into my office and sat across the desk from me. After we exchanged pleasantries I asked my standard opening question, "How can I help you today?"

My counselee seemed normal enough; she was well mannered, attractively dressed, and gave the impression that she was reasonably educated.

She took a deep breath, and then it happened . . .

"I am here to tell you that I worship Satan! He's the god of this world and my life. He is more powerful than Jesus Christ. My prayers to him are answered with absolute miracles. I can control people with dolls and pins through which I impart misery and sickness at will."

As a minister of a prospering suburban church, I tried valiantly to exercise a very fundamental counseling skill: express no visible shock.

I'm afraid I failed miserably.

I could not believe the words that were coming from this woman's mouth. I tried to analyze the situation. She was not there entirely by choice. She had come to my office at the recommendation of her family—church members who were very concerned with her unusual behavior and the unexplained powers she seemed to possess.

Something was very wrong with this picture. We were not talking about a primitive tribe in some remote jungle of the world. I was the pastor of an evangelical church located in the Bible Belt of America and was listening to a seemingly civilized individual.

I was bewildered. She was bewitched! Here was a woman glorifying the Devil with passionate fervor, right in the pastor's study!

The impact of her words might have been comical had my office not been filled with an onerous evil spirit that made my skin crawl.

As my visitor continued to spew her vitriol, her eyes were

literally aglow with a phosphorous coloring, and at times her eye-balls seemed to protrude on invisible stems as she fervently professed her allegiance to Satan. Every inch of my frame cringed as I listened to her satanic testimony.

When she paused for breath, I instinctively interrupted her monologue with a scriptural counterattack. Her reaction to the Word of God was instantaneous and venomous. Every time I mentioned Jesus and the authority of His Name, she totally denounced it.

Utter condescension and mocking contempt flowed from her lips as would sulfurous water gushing from a poisonous spring. I felt like a fighter on the ropes in my own study, and I knew without a doubt that I was in a spiritual battle with an enemy unlike any I had ever encountered or believed existed!

At the earliest possible opportunity I suggested that we terminate the session. The woman was frazzled from our verbal exchange, and I was both physically and spiritually exhausted. We had been locked in a literal war of spirits that could be likened to a hostile wrestling match. The woman left, and I was delighted to see her go.

Following this demonic encounter, I sat at my desk in a very contemplative mood, pondering every detail of my maiden voyage into the world of demons. I rescheduled the remainder of my counseling appointments and called my ministerial colleagues to ask if they had ever had a similar experience. I took great care to describe the dreadful episode just as it happened, yet not one of the pastors I contacted had ever encountered this type of situation.

Overall, they reacted as if I had told them about an earthly invasion of extraterrestrials.

After several conversations I began to realize that what had happened in my office was certainly real but completely new territory—to me and to the ministers in my area.

It is my conviction that everything that happens in this universe is under the control of a sovereign, almighty God. The question that plagued me at that moment was, "What was the 'thing' that accompanied the woman into my office, and why did it come?"

Recognizing that my peers didn't have the answer, I called upon my constant Companion and the Source of infinite knowledge, Jesus Christ and the Word of God.

Let me affirm that I'm not what some would consider "hyperspiritual"; I do not seek the signs and wonders, but I do pursue their Source. I believe every word of God's sacred Scripture, so I began to pray to the Lord for direction. I asked for wisdom (James 1:5) and discernment (Proverbs 3:1–3) and ventured the question, "Lord, why did You allow this to happen?"

The next morning during my devotions I read of Christ's ministry to the demoniac of Gadara. I felt the profound movement of the Holy Spirit as God's presence began to surround me like a majestic cloud hovers over a mountain peak. I immediately connected the previous day's experience in my office with Luke 8:26–33.

Compelled by an instinctive motivation, I started an in-depth study of God's Word relating to the works of Satan and his legions of demons. I searched the Scriptures; I fasted and prayed. In addition, I read everything I could regarding the occult, witchcraft, and other spiritist movements that were sweeping America.

One of the pastors with whom I shared my experience referred me to a British Bible scholar named Derek Prince, who was an expert in demonology. I made contact with this brilliant man of God and was drawn to his profound insights based on Scripture and his personal experience with demonized people. It would begin a cherished thirty-two year friendship filled with love, admiration, and mutual respect.

What I learned from Derek Prince and his Bible teachings opened a new dimension of ministry for me. He was a mentor; a fearless spiritual leader who loved the Word of God, who loved Israel, and who fought the Prince of Darkness with a passion.

It's been forty-four years since my first eye-opening experience with demonic forces. The more I researched these oppressive spirits, the more I recognized that their presence invades our daily lives and has a far more destructive effect on every aspect of our society than we can imagine.

INVASION OF THE HOME

Train up a child in the way he should go, and when he is old he will not depart from it. (Proverbs 22:6)

Most of us are familiar with this biblical adage and its exhortation to instruct our children in the ways of the Lord. Sadly, Bible truths are not what our society is planting in the fertile minds of our children. Yet in faithful accordance with the promise of the ancient proverb, our children *will not* depart from what their young minds are taught, whether good or evil.

The Hagee grandchildren love to sleep over at Nana and Papa's house. We are thrilled to hear the sounds of laughter on a Saturday morning as they awake, ready for a Mexican breakfast and playtime.

While Diana prepares their tacos, I try to find entertaining and wholesome cartoons for them to watch. That task has become nearly impossible in this day and age.

SATAN'S DAYCARE

I remember Bugs Bunny, Winnie the Pooh, and Yogi Bear. I remember cartoons filled with moral messages. I remember being able to discuss with my children the life lessons learned from some of these programs: from "Be kind to others" to Smokey the Bear's slogan of "Only YOU can prevent forest fires!"

Those days are virtually gone.

Now I am appalled at what I see as I surf through the Saturday-morning cartoon channels. Many animated children's programs feature witches, warlocks, violence, and utter pandemonium.

A highly respected study sponsored by the American Academy of Pediatrics recommended no television for children under the age of three. The study suggested that when compared to more gently paced animated features, "fast-paced" cartoons negatively and immediately affect a child's ability to think creatively and regulate his or her behavior. Researchers have further discovered that a four-year-old is negatively affected after viewing just nine minutes of overstimulating animated content. Yet the average cartoon is eleven minutes long.

This study analyzed not only the pace of the programs but the themes of the storylines. The researchers concluded that fast-paced cartoons that were also "fantastical" in nature (meaning, with little relation to reality) further deteriorated a child's cognitive resources. The study additionally found that slower-paced cartoons depicting familiar themes and routines of childhood did not have the same negative impact on young viewers.

Furthermore, the research advanced the theory that when children are faced with interpreting an animated tale that has absolutely nothing to do with real life, they are more likely to have a hard time refocusing on reality afterward.[1]

The developing minds of our children and grandchildren are not capable of transitioning from "fantastical" to "reality" in the blink of an eye. These same children are 100 percent of our future. The avalanche of imaginary media activity is engraving itself in their vulnerable young minds.

I can assure you that our children, for the most part, will become what they behold. And what they have the opportunity to behold in today's media is alarming.

For as he [a person] thinks within himself, so he is. (Proverbs 23:7 NASB)

Satan, the Prince of the Air, knows that the most effective way to desensitize society to the occult is to start with the young; the younger the better. The impressionable minds of our children are blank canvases primed for the influence of vivid animation and beguiling music.

Satan planned to subtly capture the mind, heart, and soul of our youth from the beginning, just as he planned the demise of Adam and Eve. Consequently, the occult was slowly introduced into children's cartoons, toys, games, and books in the modern era under the guise of good overcoming evil.

Next, good witches and well-meaning sorcerers were programmed into fledgling imaginations. Fortune-telling was presented as a noble means of saving the distressed and death a temporary consequence, as if one were being placed in "time-out." Primetime television shows such as *Bewitched, Sabrina the Teenage Witch,* and *Charmed* opened the way. Then our children were introduced to charming vampires via *Buffy the Vampire Slayer.*

Young girls three and older are the target market for the "Secret Spells Barbie" and her "Charm Girls," Barbie's Wiccan friends Christie and Kayla. These dolls are not decked out in long black robes and pointed hats; they are adorned in their trademark elaborate, brightly colored gowns. What then makes them different from their predecessors?

As their marketing ad boasts, "By day they are just fashionable school girls, but by night they turn into magical enchantresses." Each doll is accessorized with the standard wardrobe change plus a spell book, potions, a cauldron, and other paraphernalia needed to cast her spells. The little girls who enjoy this newfangled version of Barbie and her "white magic" learn about incantations and horoscopes while they play.[2]

Books are no different; our youngsters have been familiarized with handsome vampires in *Twilight*; survivalist, defeatist themes in *The Hunger Games*; and good warlocks in *Harry Potter.* Probably many of you have read at least one of the four hundred million copies of the Harry Potter series that have sold to date. This mind-boggling number does not include sales of Harry Potter–themed movies, games, and toys.

Diana and I shopped at a local wholesale warehouse on a busy Saturday morning several years ago (what were we thinking?). As we waited in the long line to check out, we noticed a girl of about ten deeply engrossed in a book she was tightly cradling in her hands.

"What are you reading?" I asked. The young reader did not lift her head; she was riveted.

Her mother smiled and said, "It's Harry Potter's latest novel. She has been pestering me every day for weeks to call the store and ask when it would be available for purchase." The mother added, "I'm so thankful for Harry Potter; it's the only book that has motivated her to read."

I ask you: What made this book so mesmerizing that this young child could not wait to get her hands on it? Yes, it's probably well written, but there are many well-written books available about topics that don't pertain to witches, warlocks, casting spells, or incantations.

The popularity of these subjects is part of a bigger picture: our children are being indoctrinated to believe that the occult is acceptable within our society.

The *Twilight* series is a line of vampire-themed, fantasy-romance fiction that chronicles the life of a teenage girl who falls in love with a 104-year-old vampire. These blockbuster novels have sold well over 120 million copies and won multiple awards, including the 2008 Children's Book of the Year.[3] The books have gained immense popularity and commercial success around the world, especially with young adults, charting on the *New York Times* bestseller lists for more than 235 weeks.[4]

Then there is the extremely popular dark tale of *The Hunger Games*. Its universe is set in a postapocalyptic society consisting of the wealthy Capitol and twelve districts in varying states of poverty. Every year twenty-four children between the ages of twelve and eighteen are chosen to compete in a compulsory and vicious televised "death match" called the Hunger Games. Bottom line: The chosen teenagers fight other teenagers to the death for the entertainment of the masses.[5]

If our children don't read the books, they can watch them on the big screen, rent them On Demand, or simply view them on the Internet via YouTube clips. Or they can play with the toys, board games, or video games. Some of the merchandise associated with these books is even geared to preschool children!

These products are not entertainment; they are a proselytizing technique orchestrated by Satan himself to cultivate his evil seed in the fertile minds of our children! There is a calculated plan, and that plan is to awaken them to the power of the occult. And true to that wicked plan, these vulnerable young boys and girls will be shaped by their exposure to the domain of the Kingdom of Darkness.

SATAN'S SIMULATORS

Popular board games like Dungeons and Dragons opened the door to more overtly violent and occultic video and Xbox games with top-selling titles such as *Diablo III: Reaper of Souls*, a role-play featuring a defeated lead character, Nephalem, who is trying to retrieve the Black Soulstone that contains all seven great evils; and *The Assassin's Creed*, which originates from historical fiction and features "good assassins" who predate humanity versus the evil Knights Templar.

The Walking Dead, based on a graphic comic novel that takes place after the zombie apocalypse, is branded as a "character development game" which, depending on the choices of the player, can determine the demise of a character or an adverse change in the character's disposition. In the past three years *The Walking Dead* has sold more than twenty-eight million units and was voted the 2014 Game of the Year.[6]

Is this how you want your child's *character* to be cultivated? The millions who participate in this video "game" will be at risk to become what they behold.

We are being manipulated and dominated by destructive terrorization.

Can you visualize a video game in which the player decapitates police officers, kills them with a sniper rifle, massacres them with a chainsaw, and sets them on fire? Now think about the 185 million who purchased units[7] of *Grand Theft Auto*, which fantasizes such grotesque acts of violence and murder. The player is a street hoodlum trying to take over a city. In one scenario, he or she can enter a police precinct, steal a uniform, free a convict from jail, escape by shooting the police, and flee in a squad car.

In a segment for *60 Minutes*, CBS News correspondent Ed Bradley reported, "*Grand Theft Auto* is a world governed by the laws of depravity. See a car you like? Steal it. Someone you don't like? Stomp her. A cop in your way? Blow him away. There are police at every turn, and endless opportunities to take them down. It is 360 degrees of murder and mayhem: slickly produced, technologically brilliant, and exceedingly violent."[8]

According to the *60 Minutes* report, the game has been blamed for triggering several acts of violence: the robbery and killing of six people in Oakland, California; a shooting death in Newport, Tennessee; and a triple murder in Fayette, Alabama, in 2003.

In Fayette, eighteen-year-old Devin Moore, who had played the controversial video game day and night for months, was accused of gunning down the victims—a 911 dispatcher and two police officers—in the local police station after being arrested for suspected auto theft. "[In] *less than a minute*," summarized Bradley, ". . . three men were dead."[9] And after Moore was recaptured, the teen reportedly remarked to police, "Life is like a video game. Everybody's got to die sometime."[10]

The murders in Fayette put *Grand Theft Auto* at the center of a civil lawsuit filed by families of two of the victims. Their attorney stated, "Devin Moore was, in effect, . . . given a murder simulator . . . The video game industry gave him a cranial menu . . . And that menu offered him the split-second decision" to do "just as the game itself trained [him] to do."[11]

Moore was found guilty of first-degree murder and sentenced to death by lethal injection. His sentence was upheld in a court decision in 2012.[12] And the lawsuit? After years of debate, it was dismissed.[13]

The fact remains that despite its violence—or because of it—millions of people continue to amuse themselves with *Grand Theft Auto*.

Many lives were tragically affected on that dismal day in Alabama. Three men were viciously murdered, and their grieving families will forever mourn their absence. And Devin will be executed for his actions—actions that were orchestrated by the ultimate Murderer, who took this young man's mind and programmed him to become exactly what he beheld!

Some of you are breathing a sigh of relief. Your school-aged children are not allowed to play occult games or violent videos, and they've grown past the cartoon stage. But what about music, television, and films?

SATAN'S SYMPHONY

God sings to His creation:

The Mighty One, will save; He will rejoice over you with gladness, He will quiet you with His love, He will rejoice over you with singing. (Zephaniah 3:17)

And God's creation sings praises to His Name for His glorious works:

Hear, O kings! Give ear, O princes! I, even I, will sing to the LORD; I will sing praise to the LORD God of Israel. (Judges 5:3)

The book of Revelation records the angels singing the song of the Lamb to celebrate God's judgment, power, and sovereignty:

They sing the song of Moses, the servant of God, and the song of the Lamb, saying: "Great and marvelous are Your works, Lord God Almighty! Just and true are Your ways, O King of the saints!" (Revelation 15:3)

Music has been with us from the beginning and will be with the redeemed throughout eternity. The art of music has evolved through various eras. There is the medieval era (476–1475); the Renaissance (1600s) and baroque ages (1700s); the classical era (1750–1800s) and the romantic age (1900s); up to the modern and postmodern eras (late 1900s to present) that we know today.

For discussion, let's contrast the classical period—represented by the works of Bach, Mozart, and Beethoven—with today's music. These three classic composers filled concert halls with heavenly sounds through their symphonies, concertos, opuses, and operas. Within their sacred masterpieces are timeless works such as Mozart's *Requiem Mass*, Beethoven's *Moonlight Sonata*, and Handel's unforgettable *Messiah*.

Several of these compositions were commissioned by the Church as works of praise unto the Lord. For everything that God created for good, however, Satan has devised a counterfeit for evil. Many of today's musical expressions include messages of sodomy, blasphemy, drugs, adultery, illicit sex, female degradation, suicide, and murder.

Have you noticed the number of young people walking around with earbuds seemingly attached to their brains? They probably aren't listening to a concerto by Mozart or Josh Groban's "Ave Maria." They are most likely listening to songs that are currently in the Top 40 on the *Billboard* charts. These songs can be instantly downloaded on an MP3 player or through their iTunes accounts, and listened to over and over and over again.

I ask you: What kind of music is your child listening to? Are they songs with harmless messages or songs with blatantly subversive lyrics accompanied by alluring rhythms? The latter are composed by the Master Architect of Evil for the purpose of destroying our future generation.

Parents need to awaken to the fact that some of today's trendy tunes on the pop charts include lyrics that glamourize illicit drug usage, encourage demoralizing sexual activity, and blaspheme God. It was difficult enough for me to read the lyrics to some of these songs in my research for this book, much less think about what they represent and how they mock godly principles.

"Just harmless music," you say; "another form of artful expression." After all, "no one bothers listening to the words anyway; they're just interested in the beat . . . right?"

Think on this disturbing story:

A twenty-nine-year-old man confessed to police that he sang songs while fatally stabbing his wife and daughter. His four-year-old son survived the attack despite being stabbed eleven times. According to police, the husband and father said he was possessed and believed that his wife was a demon. (Note: It is not possible for a human being to become a demon, but one can be controlled by demonic forces.)

The man reportedly told the police that just before stabbing his wife, he started screaming lyrics from a popular rap song, saying, "Here comes Satan. I'm the anti-Christ; I'm going to kill you."

Police said this father admitted that when the kids awoke to their mother's screams, he stabbed them too. He said he stabbed his son the most because he loved him the most. Then he rolled a cigarette, said another prayer, and called 911.[14]

Then there was the infamous 1992 heavy-metal song about the killing of police officers. The artwork inside the CD cover depicts a man with a gun pointed at the viewer's face. The songwriter commented, "To us that was the devil [****] what's more scary than [****] some gangster with a gun pointed at you?"[15]

A critic evaluated the music style of this particular album as "a kinship between gangster rap and post-punk, hard-core rock, both of which break taboos to titillate fans. But where rap's core audience is presumably in the inner city, hard-core appeals mostly to suburbanites seeking more gritty thrills than they can get from Nintendo or the local mall."[16]

The use of profanities and the phrase "cop killer" are repeated a combined total of twenty-two times in this song. Experts on memory retention recommend repetition as the cornerstone of recall. It helps the brain form a strong link to a specific piece of information. It also aids in storing that piece of data into long-term memory.[17]

So much for harmless lyrics and music.

Satan has successfully planned and is currently executing a full-frontal assault to capture the minds and souls of our children and our children's children. Meanwhile, our generation is apathetic or is blinded to the reality of Satan's demonic plot.

One old saying goes, "If the camel once gets his nose in the tent, his body will soon follow." Satan is in the tent, and he is in control!

TOXIC TELEVISION

You would never allow a known murderer to walk through the front door of your home without putting a gun in his face to protect your family. However, too few parents hesitate to click a remote, and so they invite him in to their family's mind and soul through their television set.

American families currently own more than 116 million TV sets[18] with thousands of channels to choose from. In a year, the average youth attends school 900 hours yet watches television 1,200 hours. By age eighteen, our children have viewed an estimated 150,000 acts of violence through their TV sets.[19] What type of entertainment are families choosing?

He's smart, he's good looking, and he's got a great sense of humor. He's Dexter Morgan, everyone's favorite serial killer. As a Miami forensics expert, he spends his days solving crimes, and nights committing them. But Dexter lives by a strict code of honor that is both his saving grace and lifelong burden. Torn between his deadly compulsion and his desire for true happiness, Dexter is a man in profound conflict with the world and himself.[20]

The preceding is a description of a primetime, award-winning television program that aired from 2006 to 2013 and is currently in syndication. The series enjoyed wide critical acclaim and popularity, including four straight Primetime Emmy nominations for Outstanding Drama series and two Golden Globes.[21] A record-breaking audience of 2.8 million tuned in for its series finale, making *Dexter* one of the most-watched original series episodes ever.[22]

I'm sure that the two million–plus viewers sat on the edge of their sofas in their comfortable family rooms, glued to their sixty-inch flat-screen televisions, all the while eating snacks and enjoying HD-quality entertainment. But is this type of "entertainment" simply for our amusement and viewing pleasure?

Have we as a society become radically desensitized to the violence and depravity that is flooding from movie and television studios? It is not that we have become more broad-minded and intellectual; it is that we have adapted to the demonic and have become comfortable in the presence of evil.

Consider Steven, a sixteen-year-old teenager obsessed with TV serial killer Dexter, who was jailed for the murder of his seventeen-year-old girlfriend, "who he ferociously stabbed before dismembering her body in a 'blood-curdling' killing."[23]

Steven was convicted of premeditated murder. At the sentencing, the court heard that the young political science student "had a fascination with horror movies and the macabre."[24] They also heard that Steven wanted to do as Dexter, the television character, had done.

At the start of the hearing, the judge warned the court that the case involved details that "are extremely unpleasant and may cause considerable distress to anyone listening," and advised anyone of a nervous disposition to leave.[25]

This compels me to ask: Why was it "extremely unpleasant" to view the actual end result of this horrific murder, but it wasn't "unpleasant" to watch the dramatization of death on television?

Steven's defense attorney "described the murder as a 'chilling, blood-curdling and sustained' killing . . . The evidence points to the defendant trying to emulate the actions of the character Dexter, who he idolised."[26]

An evil seed was planted in fertile ground, and it produced evil fruit.

Either make the tree good and its fruit good, or else make the tree bad and its fruit bad; for a tree is known by its fruit. (Matthew 12:33)

SATAN'S CINEMA

What about the motion picture industry?

To quote famed movie critic Roger Ebert, "Catholic priests in the movies were once played by Bing Crosby and Spencer Tracy and went about dispensing folksy wisdom, halftime pep talks and pats on the back. Times have so changed, alas, that these days movie priests are almost inevitably engaged in titanic confrontations with the forces of darkness . . . What Jesus was to the 1950s movie epic, the devil is to the 1970s."[27]

Rosemary's Baby, The Exorcist, and *The Omen* were three in a cycle of pioneering "demonic child" films produced from the late 1960s to the mid-1970s, and they began a trend that has escalated into all types of occultic films in recent years.

The lead character in *Rosemary's Baby* is a pregnant woman who suspects that her husband has made a demonic pact with their peculiar neighbors. The woman believes that in exchange for success in his acting career, her husband promised the wicked couple her baby as a human sacrifice in their satanic rituals. The tragic tagline for the film was "Pray for Rosemary's Baby."

When the movie *The Exorcist* debuted, it took the world by storm. This supernatural horror film deals with the demonic possession of a twelve-year-old girl and her mother's desperate attempts to win her back through an exorcism conducted by two priests.

Several religious leaders spoke out against the film, suggesting that it was aligned with the forces of darkness. How right they were. No matter the protests, the movie earned ten Academy Award nominations and was the first horror film to be nominated for Best Picture of the Year. *The Exorcist* became one of the highest-grossing films of all time, earning over $440 million worldwide.

The Omen is about a priest who wickedly substitutes the spawn of Satan for a newborn baby. The Devil's evil offspring is raised by an American ambassador to Great Britain (implying, of course, the demonic infiltration of government). Roger Ebert stated, "There is the usual technical stuff like Biblical prophecies, formulas for warding off evil spirits and great use of the cabalistic sign 666. As long as movies like *The Omen* are merely scaring us, they're fun in a portentous sort of way. But when they get thoughtful . . . well . . ."[28]

It's important to know that there were four sequels to *The Omen*. But let's go back to *The Exorcist* for a moment.

When the movie premiered, some viewer reactions were less than promising. Theaters reportedly offered vomit bags to audiences, some locations kept a supply of smelling salts on hand for those who fainted, and there were even some injuries. Yet all of this ironically fueled the success of the film.

I will speak further about this movie and its effect on a young girl in my church later in the book. But for now, let me ask: When is the last time someone fainted or became ill in the theater due to the contents of a demonic horror flick? It was most likely in the 1970s.

Is this because the special-effects industry has plateaued in its creativity, or because of weak storylines or bad actors? *Not hardly!* Could it be that we have become so accustomed to dark messages that we are insensitive to what this genre of movies represents? *Most definitely!*

I repeat, these are *not* examples of harmless entertainment in search of accolades and good ratings. The forces of evil are on a rampage in our society and have taken captive the minds, hearts, and souls of many in this generation who are addicted to the ever-evolving enticements of the supernatural and the demonic.

We must recognize that Satan craves control of the world. The battle rages for the minds of our future generations. There will be a winner and a loser in this war, and to the winner goes our children! Satan hates God and the image of God in us. He despises Jesus

Christ and the redemption He has afforded us. He covets the eternal joy to which we are destined. He envies our relationship with God the Father, His Son, and His Holy Spirit because he forfeited his. Therefore, Satan is totally determined to do everything within his power to destroy God's creation!

This destructive path includes the Church of Jesus Christ. Satan seeks to destroy it from within through false teachings, and from without through persecution, as the clash of two Kingdoms continues.

CHAPTER 7

INVASION OF DEMONS
IN THE CHURCH

*Now the Spirit expressly says that in latter times
some will depart from the faith, giving heed to
deceiving spirits and doctrines of demons.*

1 Timothy 4:1

I often tell my congregation and our national television audience that church membership will not save you, denominations will not save you, ritual will not save you, and singing "Amazing Grace" at the top of your lungs will not save you. And by all means, sitting in church will not guarantee immunity from satanic attack. Salvation only comes through faith in Christ. When you confess and forsake your sins, you are cleansed by the shed blood of Jesus.

When the Japanese Imperial Navy attacked Pearl Harbor on December 7, 1941, the Second World War began for America.

News of the attack was carried to citizens of every society and culture. In a matter of hours, the world recognized that mankind was involved in a life-and-death struggle between democracy and dictatorships.

Pictures of our ships sinking into watery graves after being ripped apart by Japanese bombs covered the front pages of the world's newspapers. The bodies of thousands of sailors floating facedown in the waters of Pearl Harbor were forever burned into the memory of Americans. A war had begun in which there was no compromise. Leaders of western civilizations demanded the absolute surrender of the enemy.

England's Prime Minister Winston Churchill told the world, "You ask what is our aim? I can answer in one word: Victory. Victory at all costs. Victory in spite of all terror. Victory, however long and hard the road may be. For without victory there is no survival."[1]

The Kingdom of God has been at war with the Kingdom of Darkness under the leadership of Satan since the fall of Lucifer, yet astoundingly, very few Christians are aware of this ongoing battle. Most live their lives believing that an armistice was signed with the Devil at the Cross.

In truth, we are all participants—and many are casualties or prisoners of war. The victims of the spiritual warfare between the Kingdom of Light and the Kingdom of Darkness are the twisted and tortured targets of Satan's legions.

Let the Church understand this truth: we are at war with Satan and his Kingdom, and we *will* be until he is cast into the Lake of Fire by the Conqueror of Calvary, Jesus Christ our Lord!

The fight is on and the victory is ours through Christ the King!

THE DEVIL AND MRS. SMITH

Soon after my initial encounter with the occult, when the woman visited my office to declare that she had committed her soul to Satan, I received a phone call from a Mrs. Smith.[2] She opened the conversation with these words: "Pastor Hagee, could you come pray for me? I think I have a demon!"

Dumbfounded, I replied, "Are you a member of my church?" I felt a measure of relief when she answered no. She said that she and her family attended a well-established denominational church, but she felt sure that her pastor would not understand her situation.

"Why did you call me?" I asked, looking for an out. She responded, "I drove past your church and remembered that a friend told me you are a sound Bible teacher, and I was hoping you could help me."

There was no escape! This was the second time in as many weeks that someone connected to the occult had crossed my path. I took her name and address and committed to be at her home within the hour. As I drove through one of the most upscale neighborhoods in town, I thought, *God, I know You are trying to get my attention, but why?*

I parked in front of a very beautiful mansion and sat in my car for a moment to collect my thoughts. I told myself to have an open mind and to stay focused on the Word during this most unusual house call.

I rang the doorbell, and Mrs. Smith graciously received me into her home. She was an attractive, middle-aged woman dressed in crisp white slacks and a tailored blouse. Every detail of her appearance and domestic décor testified of a well-ordered life.

She escorted me into her den, which was quite spacious and beautifully appointed. I sat down in a posh chair, and after we'd exchanged some polite conversation, I began to question her in-depth as to why she felt I could help.

As she answered my questions, I hurriedly reviewed my mental file on abnormal psychology. I had just completed graduate school at the University of North Texas; there was nothing about Mrs. Smith that fit the "abnormal" criteria.

I learned that my hostess was college-educated, and her husband was a very successful executive who worked for a national firm on the East Coast, Monday through Friday. She was a stay-at-home mom, and from all appearances, they were a model upper-class American family.

Eventually Mrs. Smith admitted to playing with a Ouija board and Tarot cards while her husband was out of town to combat boredom.

There it was—the connection to the occult!

For those of you who aren't familiar with either one of these "games," the Ouija board was invented in 1890 by Elijah Bond. (Its name is said to derive from the French word *oui* and the German *ja*, both meaning "yes.") The Ouija board is also known as a spirit board, talking board, or witch-board. A heart-shaped or triangular piece of wood serves as a movable indicator, spelling out words on the board to convey the spirit's message to players during a séance.

Bond was granted a trademark on his originally named "Nirvana [spiritual enlightenment] Talking Board" in 1907. The game's manufacturer, the Swastika Novelty Company, adorned many of Bond's boards with its broken-cross symbol.

Since the late eighteenth century, mystics, fortune-tellers, and occultists have been using Tarot cards in the practice of divination in an attempt to predict the future. If the Lord Himself were the Author of this book, what warning would He give to those who participate in these so-called games?

You have trusted in your wickedness; you have said, "No one sees me"; your wisdom and your knowledge have warped you; and you have said in your heart, "I am, and there is no one else besides me."

Therefore evil shall come upon you; you shall not know from where it arises. And trouble shall fall upon you; you will not be able to put it off. And desolation shall come upon you suddenly, which you shall not know.

Stand now with your enchantments and the multitude of your sorceries, in which you have labored from your youth—perhaps you will be able to profit, perhaps you will prevail.

You are wearied in the multitude of your counsels; let now the astrologers, the stargazers [followers of horoscopes], and the monthly prognosticators stand up and save you from what shall come upon you.

Behold, they shall be as stubble, the fire shall burn them; they shall not deliver themselves from the power of the flame; it shall not be a coal to be warmed by, nor a fire to sit before!

Thus shall they be to you with whom you have labored, your merchants from your youth; they shall wander each one to his quarter. *No one* shall save you. (Isaiah 47:10–15)

And the story continues . . .

"Mrs. Smith, you stated you felt your body had been invaded by a demon spirit. Could you explain what you mean by that?"

I had been in the church since I was born and never personally known of anyone who was involved with these kinds of "games."

She was quick to answer, "As I was playing Tarot cards last week, I heard the front door of my home open unexplainably. I could hear footsteps walking down the hall and into this room; then suddenly I felt *that something . . . that presence* . . . enter me."

As I heard her tell this mind-boggling story, the hair on the back of my neck stood straight up. I was pondering where she might like a new door measuring about five feet eight inches tall by four feet wide, because I was ready to run right through the wall of her house.

I asked for clarification. "You felt this *thing* enter you?" She answered forcefully and without hesitation, "Yes! It entered me, and it's still there NOW!"

"What evidence do you have to make you believe a demon spirit is in you right now?" I asked incredulously.

She began to weep and said, "From the moment this presence entered me, I have been obsessed with the most vulgar and deviant sexual thoughts. I have never cursed in my life, and I find myself using the filthiest language you can imagine. I have never been a violent person either, but I feel I am capable of committing murder without remorse. Pastor, I know something is very wrong, and I have no control over it."

Her stare was piercing; she had my complete attention. My theology had just collided with reality, and I had no solution for her spiritual condition other than the Word of God. I reached for my Bible and said, "I am going to read you a story."

As I took the Word of God in my hands, Mrs. Smith instantly slapped at it like a frightened cat. I had never seen such a vehement reaction to the presence of a Bible. In desperation, I started reading the story . . .

Then they sailed to the country of the Gadarenes, which is opposite Galilee. And when He [Jesus] stepped out on the land, there met Him a certain man from the city who had demons for a long time. And he wore no clothes, nor did he live in a house but in the tombs. When he saw Jesus, he cried out, fell down before Him, and with a loud voice said, "What have I to do with You, Jesus, Son of the Most High God? I beg You, do not torment me!" For He had commanded the unclean spirit to come out of the man. For it had often seized him, and he was kept under guard, bound with chains and shackles; and he broke the bonds and was driven by the demon into the wilderness.

Jesus asked him, saying, "What is your name?"

And he said, "Legion," because many demons had entered him. And they begged Him that He would not command them to go out into the abyss.

Now a herd of many swine was feeding there on the mountain. (Luke 8:26–32a)

I glanced up from reading the passage and witnessed a demonic manifestation with my own two eyes: Mrs. Smith began to physically contort! While sitting on the sofa, she grabbed her ankles and yanked them into the air, tucking her head between her legs, all the while still looking at me! Her face was the image of a vicious, feline-like creature! An overpowering dark presence filled the room; it was very real and very terrifying!

Absolutely nothing in my ministerial training provided a rational resolution for this paranormal situation! I did the only thing I instinctively knew to do . . . I kept reading the Bible!

I remembered the Word of God declaring that the New Testament Church had overcome Satan "by the blood of the Lamb and by the word of their testimony" (Revelation 12:11). So I continued reading . . .

> So they [demons] begged Him [Jesus] that He would permit them to enter them [swine]. And He permitted them. Then the demons went out of the man and entered the swine, and the herd ran violently down the steep place into the lake and drowned. (Luke 8:32b–33)

What I heard next was blood curdling. A deep, guttural, masculine voice came out of Mrs. Smith's mouth: "I hate you, John Hagee!"

It was the threatening pronouncement of a demon sent by the Prince of Darkness.

I held the Bible in both hands and began to call on the name of Jesus to deliver this tormented woman. Initially she let out an ear-piercing shriek, but each time I mentioned the name of Jesus and the blood of the Cross, the screeches became less and less intense.

After several minutes, her ferocious growling turned into soft whimpers. Suddenly Mrs. Smith fell to the floor as though she'd been shot. She lay motionless before me.

I thought, *Here I am, alone in a home with a dead woman. My ministerial career is over!* I sat in my chair, nervously waiting for some sign of life.

I was comforted to see her eyes slowly begin to blink. Then she looked up at me with a radiant but puzzled expression and asked, "What am I doing on the floor?"

I explained, "I believe you have just been delivered from the demonic force that you invited into your life when you began to play these occultic games."

She got up, sat on her couch, and we silently stared at each other for a few moments. Finally, Mrs. Smith cleared her throat and said emphatically, "I believe it's gone! I don't feel its presence! It's gone! Thank you! Thank you! Thank you!"

"Don't thank me," I said, "thank God. Only He delivers from the power of evil."

I invited her and her husband to come to church the next Sunday, and in time the entire family received Christ as Savior and Lord. They were faithful and active members of our church until they moved out of the city.

The Lord was showing me that an invasion of demonic spirits can happen anywhere, not only in the far reaches of the world, as I had previously been taught. I discovered through this extraordinary episode with Mrs. Smith that these forces must be confronted and can only be defeated through spiritual warfare and the ultimate power of God's Word.

Therefore submit to God. Resist the devil and he will flee from you. (James 4:7)

The Devil *in* Mrs. Smith was *no more*!

THE SHOOTER

With all I was learning about satanic activity after these two overt, eye-opening experiences, I felt it was time for my congregation to be educated on the subject of demonic invasion.

For months our church had enjoyed a spiritual revival with a large number of salvations, healing miracles, and manifestations of the Holy Spirit. Our congregation was prospering on every front as God's blessing poured from heaven beyond our capacity to contain it. It was like a fresh, sweet-smelling rain falling on lush green fields.

I announced to my church that I would be teaching on the topic of the invasion of demons. Some of our members received the announcement with nervous smiles and guarded doubt. Why would I choose to teach on such an unpleasant subject when things were going so well? Still, I persevered.

I was determined to remove any false perceptions of demonic activity and to teach my sheep regarding this spiritual warfare, which was just as real as World War II, the Korean Conflict, or the Vietnam War of that time.

The first three Wednesday evenings were very well attended, and the dedicated Bible students in the congregation were surprised at how little they knew of this spiritual invasion. However, as I began to detail the attack of demonic forces in our society, I started receiving serious backlash from some of our membership.

Some said, "Pastor, demons operate among the ignorant and

superstitious in faraway countries, not in America." Still others said, "I've never seen the Devil at church. I don't bother the Devil, and he doesn't bother me!" (Little did we know that within a matter of days, this latter statement would be retracted.)

In spite of these comments, I firmly but kindly held my ground, knowing that this invisible warfare was simply beyond the scriptural knowledge and spiritual experience of the protesters.

The fourth session was approaching, and I was confident that God would validate the teaching. However, none of us could have possibly been prepared for the demonic demonstration that was about to occur in our midst.

As the congregation gathered for the final teaching, it became obvious that we were going to have the lowest attendance of any of the sessions. My first thought was, *My people have boycotted my teaching because they're uncomfortable with this controversial subject.*

On the previous three Wednesday nights the church had been comfortably full, but not so this night. Disappointment would be the first impulse for most preachers in this circumstance. Yet I felt greatly encouraged to go forward; a deep river of peace was flowing within me for a reason I would soon understand.

I promptly began the service by leading the congregational singing, which I seemed to be enjoying more than anyone else. I scanned my flock to see if those who had expressed doubt about my subject were present. They weren't.

It didn't matter; I felt the powerful presence of God and began teaching on the final theme, "Seven Steps to Deliverance." I had been speaking for about twelve minutes when, like a thunderbolt of lightning, our church was challenged by the power of Satan.

A crazed man burst through the front doors of the sanctuary

with a drawn and cocked .22-caliber pistol. The man, in his mid-thirties, walked up the aisle behind one of our congregants, grabbed him by the nape of the neck, and roared like a wild beast. The enraged intruder yelled obscenities at our entire church and demanded that his victim leave the pew.

"We are in the presence of a demonized man!" I shouted into the microphone, loud enough to be heard above the frightened screams of the congregation. "Be calm and pray for deliverance in the name of Jesus and the blood of His Cross!"

Some of the church attendees immediately knelt between the pews and fervently prayed; others crawled out of the sanctuary in terror, desperately seeking safety. Many of those who were there later admitted they thought they were witnessing a staged, illustrated sermon, since several of the principles I'd taught for the past three weeks occurred in rapid succession.

As the assailant approached the platform of the church, he commanded his hostage to stand beside me. The church member instantly obeyed. There we stood, shoulder-to-shoulder behind the pulpit, staring into the barrel of a loaded gun with a demonically controlled man on the other end.

My terrified congregation grew remarkably calm as the intruder held us at gunpoint. It was increasingly obvious to all that this was the clash of two Kingdoms, and unless God's miracle-working power prevailed, no less than two people would be murdered in front of eighty-plus eyewitnesses.

For nearly two very long minutes I tried to reason with the man, but without any success. As he stood there staring at us, eyes raging with fury and his face twisted by inner torment, I knew by the threats that poured from his mouth that he would attempt to shoot us.

He shouted, "I have come to kill you to demonstrate that Satan's power is greater than that of Jesus Christ! Get on your knees and beg for your life!"

I held up my Bible as a shield and stated, "No weapon formed against me shall prosper!"

He screamed, "I have a gun!"

I responded, "I have a Bible!"

Even though I believed he had a sinister intent, I felt absolutely no fear. God was present, and Satan's Kingdom would be defeated.

The demonized agent from hell pointed his weapon at our heads and swore that he was going to murder us at the count of three. Instantly the following passage flashed through my mind: "For He shall give His angels charge over you, to keep you in all your ways" (Psalm 91:11).

I knew at that moment I was staking my life on God's Word!

The man's spiteful voice resonated throughout the church as he counted, "*One . . . two . . .*" and then began shooting at us from point-blank range, no more than eight feet away.

Miraculously, every shot missed!

The first bullet zipped between our heads and struck the wall behind us. He shot five more times—and each bullet was deflected by the angels of God, who were sent to defend us.

This miracle was the power of Almighty God in action! And I thank God for His supernatural protection every day!

The tortured man tried to escape after his failed murderous attempt, but another member of the church apprehended him with a flying tackle in the rear of the sanctuary. The police were summoned, and the attacker was taken to police headquarters and charged with attempted murder. When the interrogator asked about his motive, he replied that he believed a voodoo hex had been placed on him, adding that he strongly believed in witchcraft and had been actively practicing it for years.[3]

He had consulted a witch, who informed him that the only way to remove the curse was to kill the person whom he felt had spoken it over him. Ironically, his chosen target was one of the skeptical church members who did not believe demons existed!

This demented man, under the guidance of the Prince of Darkness, tried to challenge the Kingdom of Light. But he was publicly defeated by the angels of the living God. Satan did, however, demonstrate to every skeptic in my church that he is very real, he is very alive in our society, and he can control any life that gives him the slightest opportunity to invade.

The evening news carried the story of "bullets flying in church as sermon on demons is interrupted." As for the demonized man who entered our building that fateful night, he underwent psychiatric evaluation and, upon being diagnosed as mentally unstable, was committed to an asylum for treatment. The shooter was a model patient, and within ninety days of his hospitalization, the attending doctors declared him well enough to reenter society.

Once released, the attacker left the hospital and drove directly to his home, climbed a tree in his backyard, and hung himself. Satan took the life of his prey, for he comes to steal, kill, and destroy (John 10:10).

The Bible pronounces that "the angel of the LORD encamps around those that fear Him" (Psalm 34:7). Except for a few holes in the church walls and furniture, the pastor and all members were unharmed. Satan's deadly plan was defeated and God was glorified!

After this incident, I resolved that if what I was teaching made the Enemy angry enough to try to kill me in cold blood, in my own pulpit, in front of my congregation, then I had no choice but to continue to educate the body of Christ about demonic warfare.

My message is simple: Satan and his demonic Kingdom truly exist, his power is real, and his objective is to destroy God's people.

Some of you may still doubt, but many in bondage have been and will continue to be delivered from the subtle and subversive assaults of Satan through the liberating power found in God's Word, and I will never stop exposing the truth about the Adversary.[4]

THE EXORCIST COMES TO CHURCH

Shortly after *The Exorcist* was released, I was in my pulpit on Sunday morning preaching a sermon series on the Cross. As I spoke, I heard sobbing coming from the congregation.

I scanned the room for the source of the disruptive and ever-increasing cry, and found its origin: a strikingly beautiful girl in her teens. Her weeping progressed to loud moaning, and I motioned to one of our elders to help. As the elder compassionately escorted the young lady from the service, the two of them passed in front of Diana, who was very pregnant at the time.

The girl, obviously distressed, was cupping her face in her hands. Diana thought she might need a woman's comfort, so she followed the young lady and the elder down the hall toward my office.

When they got there, the teen turned to the wall and continued to sob uncontrollably. Diana placed her hands on the girl's shoulders to calm her, and then it happened: this gorgeous young woman suddenly transformed into an ambassador of evil as she spun around.

Her eyes were like deep pits of black pitch. She looked directly at Diana with a piercing stare that cut my wife to the core. Diana felt her belly tighten, as if our innocent baby was drawing back from this satanic confrontation.

As the elder attempted to extend a helping hand, the teenager yelled out a blood-curdling scream that could be heard throughout the building. "Get your hands off me! I hate you! I hate all of you!"

The elder withdrew his hand in shock. Meanwhile, the mother of the distraught teenager came looking for her daughter after she heard her screams. The elder escorted both women into my office and asked them to wait until I could visit with them following the service.

When the service ended, Diana and the elder gave me their chilling report. I walked into my office to find the girl cradled in her mother's arms; both were embarrassed over the incident.

I asked the mother about their family. Her husband was a prominent doctor, and she stated that they were Christians.

The mother told me that her daughter had gone to see *The Exorcist* the week before. She then reported, "When my daughter returned home she told me, 'Something changed in me while I watched that movie. I feel different inside; I don't want to be near my friends anymore.'"

The concerned mother continued, "I have seen her become very withdrawn in the last few days, which is not like her. She is normally happy, kind, and loving. I knew something was wrong, and a friend suggested we visit your church."

"I believe that a demonic spirit entered your daughter while she watched the movie," I responded. "I further believe that the demon inhabiting your daughter protested the message I was preaching. This evil spirit was angry, for it knew it would be exposed." I then advised the mother to immediately seek deliverance for her daughter.

She agreed and said she would inform her husband of my recommendation. After we prayed, the mother promised to call me with a follow-up.

The next morning she contacted me and said that her husband was adamantly against any spiritual intervention. As a medical professional, he believed he was better trained to diagnose and treat his daughter. They had agreed to admit her to a local hospital for evaluation.

I thanked her for the call and said good-bye. I grieved for the young woman, for I knew only God and His redeeming power could deliver her from the true source of her torment. The father admitted his daughter into treatment the next day, and we never heard from the family again.

It is a fact that when you open your mind to a demonic force, you are in very real danger of being invaded by that spirit emotionally, physically, and spiritually. Be careful what you allow your children to watch—they will become what they behold, and not every movie has a happy ending!

WITCHCRAFT IN COSTA RICA

I was invited to speak in Costa Rica several years ago by a godly pastor who hosted an annual evangelical convocation. As the attendees gathered from Central and South America, I was deeply moved by their desire to hear the Word of God. I will never forget the sight of the faithful who packed the large tin building, its back and side walls raised like massive garage doors. Other precious saints stood for hours outside in the pouring rain as they listened to the preaching.

After one of the evening services, our host took Diana and me to a popular restaurant located above the city. As we exited the van, we heard sounds much like howling wolves and noticed what looked like campfires on the mountainside.

We asked the pastor about the unusual noises and flickering lights, and he responded very matter-of-factly, "Those fires are lit by witch covens; they are preparing for their worldwide convention that will soon take place in our city."

Diana and I couldn't believe our ears . . . A sanctioned, worldwide convention of witches being held in this beautiful place? But indeed it was! We later learned from the pastor that belief in witchcraft is very common.

For example, the town of Escazú is a colonial metropolis spread out over a hillside overlooking San Jose. Escazú is one of the most affluent cities of the nation and is known as "La Cuidad de las Brujas," or "The City of the Witches." It is renowned for witches who specialize in casting spells.

After speaking to overflow crowds at the convocation a second time, the host pastor and I decided it was time to take the meeting to a larger venue. A year later, after months of planning, we held a three-day healing service at the local arena.

The building was filled with expectation as I presented the Bible truth about God's healing power. I vividly remember calling the people forward for prayer on the first night so I could personally anoint each one of them. What happened next was truly frightening! Hundreds stampeded toward us, dangerously pressing against those who were standing directly in front of the platform. I instantly shouted repeatedly to the throng, "Stop right where you are!"

The rushing multitude heeded as my voice thundered through the speakers. I informed them that I was postponing the healing portion of my teaching until the following evening, when we could conduct our event in an orderly manner in accordance with Scripture. I thank God that no one was injured.

Early the next morning I visited the arena and marked four horizontal lanes with tape across the front of the platform to designate where people could wait for personal prayer. That evening after the sermon, I gave the congregation direction as to how the healing service would be conducted. The presence of the Holy Spirit saturated the building as the crowd approached with the full expectation of receiving a miracle from God.

While hundreds came to receive healing, Diana translated for them in Spanish and I anointed each individual—men, women, and children—with oil and prayed over them. It would prove to be a powerful night of restoration.

One of those who came forward was a woman dressed in a tailored suit. Diana asked her to state her need. She responded, "I want the pastor to pray for my mind."

I felt in my spirit that there was more to her request, so I urged Diana to ask again and have the woman be more specific.

"I think I am losing my mind," the woman detailed. "I will be in conversation with someone and suddenly I feel as though I have blacked out. When my mind 'returns,' whoever I've been in conversation with tells me I sounded different, and yet I have no recollection of the incident. It seems to be happening more often over the past several years. I have no control over my mind, and I am extremely frightened."

I knew then that this seemingly sophisticated woman needed deliverance from a demonic influence. I informed her of what I believed and asked her if she desired to be free from the spirit that held her mind captive. "Yes!" she emphatically replied.

The moment I anointed her head with oil and demanded that the tormenting demon leave, she fell to the floor like she had been shot and began to writhe like a snake. Next, she forcefully exhaled for an inhuman amount of time until her face turned a dark purple. Her eyes bulged from her head and her hair was dripping with sweat. This previously attractive woman was now almost too hideous to look upon. The people surrounding her stood back in terror.

I continued to pray and then I commanded the demon to identify itself. Out of the woman's mouth came the shocking words, "*Soy el espíritu de brujería*" ("I am the spirit of witchcraft"). I pled the blood of Jesus Christ and demanded the demon to release its hold on her. After several minutes the demon was gone and the woman was left physically spent on the floor.

As the assisting ministerial staff lifted her to her feet, I asked if they knew who she was. Their answer stunned me: "Yes, Pastor Hagee, she is the wife of one of our local pastors."

How could this be?

I asked the staff to locate her husband. Once they did, I asked him harshly, "How did you allow this to happen? Your wife has been demonized for years while living in your home and you are the pastor of a church?"

Embarrassed, he replied, "Witchcraft rules our city. These spirits are strong and ruthless. Pastor, I am ashamed to say that I was afraid to admit or confront the fact that there were demonic forces in my home."

I heard it with my ears, but I still could not comprehend that the leader of a large congregation would allow demons to invade his wife, his home, and his church. I instructed the pastor on the absolute necessity to expel the wicked influences once and for all. The Devil will not leave unless he is resisted!

We prayed until after midnight for the hundreds who came forward for healing. It was a night that is etched in my memory forever. I had encountered a minister's wife who was living in spiritual slavery in a church that was simply failing to teach the words and actions of Jesus Christ in dealing with evil spirits.

THE KACHINA DOLL

Kachina is a Hopi Indian term meaning "spirit father" or "spirit being." It is also a term used by the Pueblos, who believe Kachinas are the spirits of the ancestral dead, which are their intermediaries to the gods.

There are more than four hundred different Kachinas in the Hopi and Pueblo Indian cultures, with the local pantheon of Kachinas varying from the dead, to the sun, the stars, thunderstorms, wind, corn, or even insects.

Each Kachina is viewed as a powerful being that, when given adoration and respect, can use his or her particular ability for human good such as bringing rainfall, healing, fertility, or protection. "Evil" Kachinas, on the other hand, are believed to have the power to attack and kill.[5]

One observer noted, "The central theme of the Kachina [religion] is the presence of life in all objects that fill the universe. Everything has an essence or a life force, and humans must interact with these or fail to survive."[6]

Kachina dolls are highly sought after by collectors who are captivated by the unique American-Indian art form found in parts of the southwestern United States. A collector can pay anywhere from a few hundred dollars to as much as $250,000 for older, well-crafted, handmade dolls.[7] However, what unsuspecting buyers may not know is, they are also investing in an ancient spiritual realm that is part of the idolatrous Kingdom of Darkness.

Let all be put to shame who serve carved images, who boast of idols. (Psalm 97:7)

Their land is also full of idols; they worship the work of their own hands, that which their own fingers have made. (Isaiah 2:8)

Such was the case with some very good friends of ours who love and serve the Lord. They were unaware of the spiritual power these dolls possess.

Several years ago we invited these friends to attend a special teaching seminar at Cornerstone Church conducted by Derek Prince on the subject of exposing and expelling demons.

For two nights Brother Derek methodically laid the scriptural foundations found in the Word of God regarding this subject matter. Then, on the third and final night of the seminar, he conducted a deliverance service. It was during this service that Brother Prince called out idols and idol worship. Among the idols he listed were Kachina dolls.

After the service, our friends asked Brother Derek and me for a private meeting. They explained that within their extensive art collection were several highly valued Kachina dolls. The couple informed us they had no previous knowledge of the dolls' occultic ties but were concerned once they heard the teaching. What should they do?

Brother Derek listened intently and immediately responded, "You must rid yourselves of these items as quickly as possible."

Our friends said they would find buyers for the dolls when they returned home. But Brother Derek was adamant: "No, you can't sell them; the money that you receive from their sale would be cursed. They must be destroyed. I recommend burning them."

The couple was stunned since these dolls represented a sizable investment, but they dutifully agreed.

Several days later I received a call from them. "Pastor Hagee, we burned our entire Kachina collection as Brother Derek instructed, and we want to share the bizarre things that happened!

"As we tossed all the dolls into the bonfire, a wailing noise came from the blaze. We stood in shock because the sound was almost human-like. It seemed to take forever to get these old wooden dolls to burn,[8] but finally after several hours, we felt satisfied that they were totally incinerated." I listened closely as they continued their story.

"We then walked back into our home to dust off the shelves where we had displayed the dolls and were shocked to find a snake coiled in the middle of the room. Pastor Hagee, we have never found a snake anywhere in our home before!

"The snake was unlike any that are common to our area," the wife said. "We managed to drag it outside of our home, only to find it nearly impossible to kill. After attempting to destroy the large snake several times, my husband had to finally chop it into pieces before it stopped moving. He then threw the fragments into the fire, and we walked back into the house thoroughly exhausted, both physically and emotionally.

She added, "We were more determined than ever to rid our home of any trace of the Kachinas. As we reorganized the room, I came across the ledger that contained the appraised value and pictures of each of the dolls. As I leafed through the book, I stopped and stared in shock at what I saw! One of the most prized of our now-cremated Kachina collection was holding a perfect replica of the live snake that invaded our home! What could this mean, Pastor?"

I gave them my answer: "The spirit world has supernatural power. The demon that was in this doll was trying to survive, and to do so, it manifested in the snake."

I commended the couple for their obedience to Derek Prince's scriptural direction (Leviticus 26:1) and prayed that God's peace would saturate their lives and home.[9]

This Christian family unknowingly opened the door to evil when they purchased these "dolls" to adorn their dwelling. Remember this truth: Satan is the great Deceiver; he will tempt you with items that look, feel, or sound appealing. He knows that, if and when you allow these objects entrance into your home, the wickedness they represent will infect your entire family.

What do you have in your possession that may be influenced

by the occult? Are you aware of the history behind the objects you collect or decorate with?

Search your home with a new set of eyes!

Are you reading occultic books or listening to music with demonic themes? Do you play with Tarot cards or collect statues and artwork of dubious origins? If so, I strongly suggest that you purge yourself of them as soon as possible. It is up to you to resist the devil and his tactics in the protection of your household. You are the gatekeeper of your heart, mind, and soul!

I have shared these true stories to make you aware of the very real and threatening presence of evil in our society and within our churches. No one is immune from Satan's attacks, but we can be victorious over them.

Let us walk on the path to deliverance clearly marked by the words and works of Jesus Christ: "If the Son makes you free, you shall be free indeed" (John 8:36).

CHAPTER 8

THE EVOLUTION OF EVIL

One would think that the products I cited in the previous chapters—toys, video games, books, music, and movies—were destructive and heinous enough. However, the evolution of evil in our society through these various gateways has reached horrific levels.

DEVIL'S GATE

When I wrote the book *Invasion of Demons* in 1973, occult movies such as *The Exorcist* were especially popular. Consequently, occult games like Ouija board sales surged. In fact, just five years prior to the release of *The Exorcist*, when Parker Brothers purchased the rights to manufacture Ouijas, it sold two million boards, surpassing Monopoly sales![1]

To date, up to an estimated twenty-five million boards have sold worldwide since the Ouija's creation. This does not include the immeasurable number of players on the Internet who have free access to a virtual Ouija board and other occult games such as

"Tarot Card Readings," "Ask the Crystal Ball," "Numerology," and "Asylum," among many more.

If the actual or virtual Ouija game was not enough to entice our society, we now have a movie by the same name, released in the fall of 2014. *Ouija* was an instant box-office success, grossing $35 million domestically in the first two weeks of its release.[2]

The *Ouija* movie plot revolves around a girl who is mysteriously killed after recording herself using an ancient Ouija board. Friends of the young victim investigate the mysterious power of the board, only to find that there are some things not meant to be played with, especially on the "other side."[3]

Ouija boards are not harmless!

Involving yourself with them is like leaving the gate to your home wide open in the middle of the night in a neighborhood with a sexual assault and murder rate that is the highest in the nation, hoping no evil monster will enter your home to murder or rape you.

Your open gate is the Devil's invitation to enter.

Three young Americans were recently taken to the hospital after allegedly becoming overpowered by evil spirits while using a Ouija board. The gate was opened as Alexandra, age twenty-two, played the game with her twenty-three-year-old brother and her eighteen-year-old cousin while visiting family in southwestern Mexico. Minutes into their "fun," Alexandra began "growling and thrashing around" in a "trance-like state." Her brother and cousin also started showing signs of "demonic manifestations."

Paramedics were called to the house and restrained Alexandra first, to prevent self-inflicted injuries, and then treated all three of the young people with painkillers, stress medication, and eye drops.[4]

The paramedics applied *conventional* medicines to treat an *unconventional* condition!

A spokesperson later commented, "The medical rescue of these three young people was very complicated. It was difficult to restrain and transfer them to the hospital because of their erratic and involuntary movements . . . [The three Ouija participants complained of] numbness, double vision, blindness, deafness, hallucinations, muscle spasms, and difficulty swallowing."[5]

There is no update on their condition.

Another personal account of the evil fruit of the Ouija was shared by a woman from the Northeast. She and her sisters bought a Ouija board while in their teens. As they led séances with their friends, they were often visited by various spirits, and one unfriendly spirit in particular that identified himself as "Zozo" (the open gate).

The girls later heeded their priest's warnings to stop using the board. But then a classmate lost her own sister in a tragic accident and asked them to bring out their Ouija board again so she could speak to her deceased sister (the open gate).

What happened next? Their grieving friend "bawled and told her sister how much she loved her and missed her. She didn't want to live anymore without her and wished she could be with her."[6]

Only a few weeks later, the woman reported, this teenaged girl also died in a car accident, "exactly the way . . . her sister had died. My sister took the Ouija Board and put it out with the trash, and none of us has touched one since."[7]

This is not a new phenomenon. King Saul had a similar experience in 1 Samuel 28.

The prophet Samuel was dead, and the Philistines were

gathering their armies to fight with Israel. King Saul became afraid and inquired of the Lord, but the Lord did not answer the king's petitions (v. 6). God had previously departed from Saul because of his sin of disobedience and rebellion, which the Lord equates to witchcraft (1 Samuel 15:22–26).

In God's silence, Saul chose to seek out Samuel through the witch of Endor (1 Samuel 28:7). The Bible plainly teaches that communication with the dead is actually contact with demon spirits that are imitating the departed (Deuteronomy 18:10–12; 1 Chronicles 10:13). If God refused to answer Saul, He certainly would not have answered through a demon spirit imitating Samuel.

The deceptive appearance of Samuel to the witch was actually a *familiar spirit* impersonating the dead prophet. This demon knew both Samuel and Saul and their past relationship, and was in fact speaking through the witch (1 Samuel 28:15).

The demon spirit revealed his identity when he predicted that Saul and his sons would be with him tomorrow. Just as Lazarus dwelt safe in the bosom of Abraham, so did the prophet Samuel; and just as the "rich man" was in hell (Luke 16:22–23), so was the demon.

Saul inquired of a demon and was answered by one.[8]

THE PROGRESSION OF EVIL

During my study for this book, I was astonished to observe the progression of evil within various areas of the entertainment industry in the past four decades. The following are a few examples of the meteoric advance of the Kingdom of Darkness in our society through these recreational outlets.

In 1973, the top ten television shows were: *All in the Family*, *Sanford and Son*, *Hawaii 5-0*, *Maude*, *Bridgette Loves Bernie*, *Sunday Mystery Movie*, *The Mary Tyler Moore Show*, *Gunsmoke*, *Wide World of Disney*, and *Ironside*.

Compare that programming with the top ten television shows of 2014: *Breaking Bad* (contains extensive drug use, violence, and sex); *Game of Thrones* (a fantasy series filled with sex and violence); *The Returned* (a supernatural crime series); *Mad Men* (a drama featuring sex and nudity with a recommended viewing audience of fourteen and older); *Girls* (follows college-age women who engage in multiple sexual encounters ranging from mild to graphic); *Orange Is the New Black* (a true prison "dramedy" filled with sex and obscenities); *The Walking Dead* (a drama filled with murderous zombies, sex, and nudity that has consistently outrated *Sunday Night Football* among viewers aged eighteen through forty-nine); *Nashville* (featuring a teen character who sleeps with multiple partners); *Masters of Sex* (chronicles the sex lives of Masters and Johnson); and *The Americans* (features sex, violence, and gore).[9]

The evolution of evil continues.

Among the top pop music titles in 1973 were "Tie a Yellow Ribbon 'Round the Ole Oak Tree," "My Love," "You're So Vain," "Keep on Truckin'," "Top of the World," "Midnight Train to Georgia," "Time in a Bottle," and "Will It Go Round in Circles."[10]

Then, in less than two decades, our society's youth were introduced to the blasts of Marilyn Manson. His stage name was formed by combining two American cultural icons: actress Marilyn Monroe and the infamous, demon-influenced mass murderer Charles Manson.

When asked about his pseudonym, Marilyn Manson commented, "It kind of defined my style . . . philosophies that God is a man . . . It almost sounds like 'abracadabra.' It has a real power to it."[11]

In 1996, Marilyn Manson released his self-proclaimed autobiographical album *Antichrist Superstar*, inspired by books such as *Antichrist* by Nietzsche. Manson described his work: "Just by the title, people might perceive it as a satanic album. And it is. But people's perception of Satanism is a little different from mine. I consider it to be a record about individuality and personal strength; putting yourself through a lot of temptations and torments, seeing your own death, and growing from it. In the end it has an almost positive, even Christian element to it."[12]

When Manson was asked if *Antichrist Superstar* was an "apocalyptic record," he responded, "I'd say so, in many ways, whether it's the Armageddon of the self-conscious or the destruction of the physical world. The mythology of the Antichrist could be as simple as someone disbelieving in God . . . I look at myself as the person to awaken individuals. The record is a different interpretation of the classic story of the fallen angel."[13]

In the United States alone, three of Marilyn Manson's albums have gone platinum and three more gold.

And the evolution continues.

The progression of satanic influence within certain music genres has also resulted in offensive spectacles at one of the most coveted music awards ceremonies in the world, the Grammys.

In the past forty years, these same Grammys featured such artists as Bette Midler, Marvin Hamlisch, Natalie Cole, Christopher Cross, Mariah Carey, LeAnn Rimes, Norah Jones, and Carrie

Underwood, to name a few. However, the performances and antics of some of the most popular artists of recent years have glorified Satan and his Kingdom.

At the 2012 Grammy Awards, Nicki Minaj walked the red carpet in a nun-like hooded red satin robe. She was channeling "Roman Zolanski," her self-proclaimed demonic alter ego, while being escorted by a man dressed as the pope.

Nicki debuted her *Roman Reloaded* album by performing an onstage self-exorcism complete with a mock confessional and stained glass.

The longer the performance, the more it mocked the Catholic faith. A white-hooded choir sang as Minaj strapped herself to a leather table with flames burning beneath her. The presentation culminated with Minaj levitating to the choir's rendition of "O Come All Ye Faithful" as a man posing as a bishop walked on stage.[14]

Do you think that Minaj only appeals to extremists in limited numbers? I don't think so! The *New York Times* called her "the most influential female rapper of all time." In April 2013, Minaj became the most-charted female rapper in the history of the *Billboard Hot 100*.[15]

And the gate continues to open wide.

At the 2014 Grammy ceremonies, another award-winning artist, Katy Perry, performed her song "Dark Horse." Perry said she wanted this piece to have a "witchy, spell-y kind of black magic-y idea," so she wrote it from a witch's perspective. The song was originally inspired by the 1996 movie *The Craft*, an American horror film that centers on a group of four teenage girls who pursue witchcraft and use sorcery for their own gain.[16]

In her performance, Perry dressed in a witch's costume bearing an illuminated Knights Templar cross. As she danced around an upside-down broomstick, she was encircled by fire and "burned at the stake," all the while surrounded by dancing demons. Even *E! Online* tweeted in amazement that Perry's performance resembled "actual witchcraft"![17]

To demonstrate the alluring popularity of this type of music, I will share some of the song's impressive statistics. From its debut, "Dark Horse" has been a commercial success, charting at number one in Canada, the Netherlands, and the United States. It reached the top ten in nearly twenty countries, including New Zealand, the United Kingdom, Sweden, and Venezuela, as well as *Billboard* magazine's Digital Songs chart.[18] To date, the song has sold over eight million copies worldwide, becoming one of the best-selling singles of all time.

Remember, these are only a few examples of the thousands of songs through which Satan subtly seduces our innocent. Today's music abounds with lyrics and images that exalt the occult, promiscuous and abusive sex, violence, murder, drugs, and suicide . . . *all* in the name of "free expression" and "art."

The evolution continues . . .

In 1973, the box-office hits included such films as *The Sting*, *American Graffiti*, *Papillon*, *The Way We Were*, *Magnum Force*, *Live and Let Die*, *Robin Hood* (Disney animated), and *Paper Moon*.[19] However, a dark and evil trend developed in the movie industry as well; films no longer portrayed art imitating life, but rather, life emulating death.

The 1994 film *Natural-Born Killers* inspired the greatest wave of copycat killings to date. The movie depicts homicidal lovers who embark on a rash of senseless murders that ultimately catapult the killers into fame. Not only has this notorious movie been linked with the highest number of separate murder sprees in history, but it is one film where the killers readily admit it motivated their actions.

One such crime was the 1994 decapitation of a thirteen-year-old girl by a fourteen-year-old boy. The boy said he wanted "to be famous like the Natural-Born Killers."[20]

In the same year, a seventeen-year-old who admitted to watching *Natural-Born Killers* more than ten times murdered his stepmother and half-sister while they were sleeping. The youth said he shaved his head and donned sunglasses to mimic Mickey, the film's male lead, before committing the murders.[21]

After being tossed out of a bar in Chicago in 2001 for harassing female customers, an enraged Luther Casteel went straight home and shaved his hair into a mohawk. He then changed into military fatigues and armed himself with two handguns, two shotguns, and two hundred rounds of live ammunition. Casteel returned to the bar and began shooting while he laughed and screamed, "I'm the king . . . How do you like me now?" Acquaintances said Casteel was obsessed with guns and the movie *Natural-Born Killers*.

Casteel fatally shot two people and wounded sixteen others, some of whom remain permanently disabled.[22]

The infamous black trench coat and mass school killings were introduced to the big screen the following year in *The Basketball Diaries*. The movie depicts a heroin-addicted high school basketball player who, in a dream sequence, enters his classroom clad in a long black coat and proceeds to massacre his classmates with a shotgun.

In 1996, a shooting at Frontier Middle School in Washington State involved a fourteen-year-old gunman who killed his algebra teacher and two students. The student admitted that he tried to model his life after Charlie Decker, the protagonist in Stephen King's novel *Rage*, who kills two teachers and takes his algebra class hostage. Prosecutors stated that Barry Loukaitis was influenced by King's novel as well as the films *Natural-Born Killers* and *The Basketball Diaries*.[23]

In Paducah, Kentucky, in 1997, fourteen-year-old Michael Carneal opened fire on a group of praying students, killing three and injuring five more. Carneal had wrapped a shotgun and a rifle in a blanket at home, placed a loaded Ruger MK II .22-caliber pistol in his backpack, and calmly gone to school. After methodically inserting earplugs, he took the pistol out of his backpack and fired eight rounds in rapid succession into the prayer gathering.

A friend of Carneal's who disarmed him after the shootings testified that Carneal looked into his eyes and said, "Kill me, please. I can't believe I did that."[24]

After this school shooting, a lawsuit was filed against the distributors of *The Basketball Diaries* and other media companies, claiming that the movie's storyline, along with Internet pornography sites and several computer games, inspired the young killer.[25]

Natural-Born Killers also had a decisive influence on Eric Harris and Dylan Klebold, the perpetrators of the April 1999 Columbine High School massacre in Colorado. The assassins wrote the phrase "going NBK" (Natural-Born Killers) in their journals, signaling the start of their demonic rampage.[26] They also wore black trench coats in their planned killing spree, murdering thirteen innocent students and a teacher before taking their own lives.

The obsessive compulsion with occultic products is like any addiction that eventually overtakes the user.

Author John Grisham made a statement after two senseless

shootings in Mississippi. Benjamin Darrias, eighteen, and Sarah Edmondson, nineteen, murdered Bill Savage, a "soft-spoken solid citizen, who was a devout Christian" and maimed Patsy Byers, a thirty-five-year-old mother of three. The teenagers admitted to their deeds after watching *Natural-Born Killers*.

The following is what Grisham wrote about the attacks:

> We are expected to believe that Mickey and Mallory [the main characters of the movie] are tormented by demons, and that they are forced to commit many of their heinous murders, not because they are brainless young idiots, but because evil forces propel them. They both suffered through horrible, dysfunctional childhoods, their parents were abusive, etc.
>
> Demons have them in their clutches, and haunt them, and stalk them, and make them slaughter fifty-two people. This demonic theme, so as not to be missed by even the simplest viewer, recurs, it seems, every five minutes in the movie.
>
> Guess what Sarah Edmondson saw when she approached the checkout stand and looked at Patsy Byers? She didn't see a thirty-five-year-old woman next to the cash register. No.
>
> She saw a "demon." And so she shot it.[27]

The Matrix, released in 1999, has reportedly played a pivotal role in several murder cases as well. Aside from the main character's trench coat, the movie subtly presents this philosophical principle: our reality is not real; rather, it is a virtual program that yields to self-gratification. Several killers have embraced this make-believe concept as "actual truth"; by their logic, any person killed was not a real person.

After dismembering his landlady, a Swedish exchange student told police he'd "been sucked into the Matrix." Tonda Lynn Ansley also killed her landlady, but believing herself to be in the Matrix, she likened the killing to a dream.[28]

Perhaps the most well-known murderer influenced by *The Matrix* is Lee Boyd Malvo. Malvo, a teenager at the time, assisted John Allen Muhammad in the 2002 Washington, DC-area sniper attacks in which ten people were killed, three others critically injured, and thousands of citizens terrorized.

Malvo told psychiatrist Dewey Cornell that he had watched *The Matrix* "more than 100 times." The young man's attorneys cited this and Muhammad's indoctrination as grounds for insanity. Their defense was unsuccessful; Malvo was sentenced to life without parole.[29]

You would think that after suffering such horrific movie-linked murders, society would be crying out for sanity. However, we have become so desensitized to the reality of violence that when the news reports the latest killings, we somehow think we are simply watching another movie that will soon be over.

But it doesn't end.

The evolution of evil continues.

DARKNESS RISES

The rash of violence in connection with films has continued into this decade. In 2012, America was confronted with the horrific news of yet another mass murder. This bloodbath, however, did not take place on a school campus or in a rural town but in a movie theater in the peaceful suburbs of picturesque Aurora, Colorado.

Imagine the setting. Friends, couples, and families are sitting with their soda and popcorn to watch the much-anticipated premier of a sequel in the Batman series, *The Dark Knight Rises.* Then suddenly, life decides to emulate death once again.

James E. Holmes, a top neuroscience graduate enrolled as a PhD student at the University of Colorado, entered the theater in Aurora through an exit door near the movie screen, outfitted in what filmgoers described as a bulletproof vest and gas mask. Witnesses told what happened next:

> He throws something into the theater which begins hissing and emitting smoke. The man then shoots into the ceiling and . . . starts firing into the crowd.
>
> Pandemonium breaks out as people desperately scramble to hide . . . and escape the vicious attack . . .
>
> Aurora police report that hundreds of calls start flooding 911. The dispatcher calls to units: "They're saying someone is shooting in the auditorium" . . .
>
> Inside the theater . . . the gunman continues to calmly fire into the crowd with some of the shots penetrating the wall of a neighboring theater. Victims were seen slumped on the floor; others are running out of the theater wounded.[30]

This tragic shooting was said to bear eerie similarities to a scene in the 1986 comic book *Batman: The Dark Knight Returns.* There, a crazed, gun-toting loner walks into a movie theater and begins shooting, killing three in the process.

The 1986 comic, written and illustrated by Frank Miller, was indeed a key inspiration for Christopher Nolan, the director of the Batman films. This comic helped to "reimagine the character away from his Saturday morning cartoon image and into a dark, grim avenger."[31]

Was the shooter imitating this caricature?

James Holmes's obsession with the Batman character may have developed long before he was accused of opening fire inside a Colorado movie theater. MTV's *Pimp My Ride* host, "Diggity" Dave Aragon, recalled a phone conversation several weeks before the Colorado shootings with someone identifying himself as James Holmes. Holmes said he had watched *The Suffocator of Sins*, a violent movie trailer for a spoof on Batman that Diggity Dave wrote, directed, and starred in.[32] According to Aragon, Holmes claimed to have seen the trailer dozens of times. He also had very specific questions, such as the number of Batman's victims and how he chose his victims.

Clinical psychologist Dr. Michael Mantell called Holmes's obsessive interest "frightening and alarming" and assessed: "That aggressiveness or assertiveness, that extra bit of interest [in] 'how many people were killed? Was it a mass murder?' . . . says . . . he had been thinking a great deal about this . . . This was part of his plan." Mantell concluded that he believes something is very wrong with society. "In this country, we tend to tear down what's good and in a freakish way, celebrate what is evil."[33]

Even this secular psychologist, who isn't trained to give credibility to spiritual matters, understands far too well the evil that is being celebrated in our culture.

RIGHTEOUSNESS *VERSUS* LAWLESSNESS

The wave of suffering from that fatal event reached my office in San Antonio, Texas, when I received the brokenhearted parents of one of the victims.

There they stood, tears streaming down their faces, shaking their heads in stunned disbelief. I hugged the mother tightly, hoping I could relieve some of her sorrow. We sat in my office, and I listened as these grieving parents recounted their daughter's story.

Their precious twenty-four-year-old Jessica—a beautiful, fledgling journalist who friends described as "spunky and quick-witted"—was dead. Only a month earlier she had moved to Colorado, and now she had been murdered by a man who, in his "freakish way," chose to unemotionally, calmly, and methodically gun down innocent moviegoers.

Her family wanted people to know everything about Jessica. They wanted the world to remember her kind and giving spirit, her warm, outgoing personality—not that she was another victim of a madman.

"She would walk into a room and the place would light up. She was a jolt of lightning," her mother tearfully recounted. "She just had a spirit that was larger than life."[34]

Know this truth: There exists good and evil, light and darkness, truth and deception. The movie *The Dark Knight Rises* was driven by the spirit of darkness.

The killer immersed himself in a world of murderous fantasy and chose to emulate a psychopath. According to police reports, Holmes identified himself as "The Joker," even dyeing his hair red in order to look like his idol.

Movie director Nolan highlighted the Joker's character as an example of "diabolical, chaotic anarchy" who has "a devilish sense of humor."[35] And he was right!

In Scripture, Satan as the Prince of Darkness has dominion over the power of darkness (Colossians 1:13). Saint Paul asked the question, "What fellowship has righteousness with lawlessness? And what communion has light with darkness?" (2 Corinthians 6:14). None! There can be no fellowship between the spirit of light and the spirit of darkness.

Jesus told His Church, "You are the light of the world" (Matthew 5:14). Logic requires that if you are not a part of the Kingdom of Light, then you are a slave to the Kingdom of Darkness.

What you see, you think on! Your thoughts will become your speech, and your speech eventually will become your actions. What you behold, you become! The evil you allow into your mind can overpower you and ultimately destroy you and others.

The apostle Paul warned New Testament believers about controlling their thought life:

> For the weapons of our warfare are not carnal but mighty in God for pulling down strongholds, casting down arguments and every high thing that exalts itself against the knowledge of God, bringing every thought into captivity to the obedience of Christ. (2 Corinthians 10:4–5)

We have invited demonic forces into our society through a series of wide-open gates, and evil has gladly walked in. Satan has raped the minds, hearts, and souls of our young and indoctrinated them through *his* form of entertainment, and we have allowed it through occultic toys, books, games, music, and movies.

Some young people proudly display the number *666* on their tattooed arms, their schoolbooks, and their T-shirts. They are not looking for the coming of Jesus Christ; they are waiting for Satan's messiah, the Antichrist!

The end result is the rejection of God Almighty and the acceptance of the devil, witchcraft, and all the evils of the occult. This highly calculated, well-executed, and very seductive campaign will pay off for the Evil One when those he has evangelized into the Kingdom of Darkness bow their knee and worship his son, the son of perdition known as the Antichrist.

CHAPTER 9

THE SPIRIT OF
THE ANTICHRIST

*A*nti means to oppose or to be antagonistic to a particular person, practice, party, policy, or action. Logically speaking, if one opposes Jesus Christ and His Kingdom, the same is influenced by the "spirit of the Antichrist." This spirit personifies lawlessness and rebellion against delegated authority and defies all that Christ is: His Word, His virgin birth, and His death and resurrection.

> Many deceivers have gone out into the world who do not confess Jesus Christ as coming in the flesh. This is a deceiver and an antichrist. (2 John 1:7)

There is a distinct difference between the "spirit of the Antichrist" and the man referred to as "*the* Antichrist," who has yet to be revealed: "As you have heard that the Antichrist is coming, even now many antichrists have come, by which we know that it is the last hour" (1 John 2:18).

Scripture states that in the last days, the Antichrist will arise and assume great religious, political, and economic power (Revelation

17:1–15). He will blaspheme God, persecute believers, and abolish the observance of the Lord's feasts.

> And he shall speak words against the Most High [God] and shall wear out the saints of the Most High and think to change the time [of sacred feasts and holy days] and the law; and the saints shall be given into his hand for a time, two times, and half a time [three and one-half years]. (Daniel 7:25 AMP)

Knowing that mankind must have a religious belief, he will create a one-world religion based on the divinity of man and the supremacy of the State. As the personification of the State, he will demand adoration and appoint his priesthood (false prophet) to enforce this worship (Revelation 13:12–15).

This diabolical transference of faith in God to belief in the State embraces the doctrine that government is the ultimate power to which man and his moral conscience must submit. The Antichrist's ultimate goals are to abolish God and to coronate his State, the Kingdom of Darkness.[1]

Believers will be taken up in the Rapture of the Church (1 Corinthians 15:51–52; 1 Thessalonians 4:16-17) before the Antichrist appears, but until that time, they will battle with the spirit of the Antichrist.

> Every spirit that does not confess that Jesus Christ has come in the flesh is not of God. And this is the spirit of the Antichrist, which you have heard was coming, and is now already in the world. (1 John 4:3)

When the Antichrist's spirit is manifested, it blatantly attempts to counter all that the God of Abraham, Isaac, and Jacob embodies. One such opposition is the Church of Satan, which was founded for the purpose of defying God.

THE CHURCH OF SATAN

The Church of Satan is the antithesis of the Church of Jesus Christ. Founder Anton LaVey, born Howard Stanton LaVey in 1930, introduced his religion to American society in 1966, and immediately satanic worship began to multiply like an aggressive cancer.

LaVey accused churchgoers of employing double standards and cited in his *Satanic Bible* that this hypocritical lifestyle was his motivation for defying the Christian religion.[2]

He attained notoriety through his paranormal research and live performances as an organist at various bars in San Francisco, and eventually formed a group called the Order of the Trapezoid, which he dedicated to the Prince of Darkness.[3]

LaVey established his evil religion on *Walpurgisnacht* (the night of the witches)—April 30, 1966. He ritualistically shaved his head, allegedly "in the tradition of ancient executioners," put on a Roman collar and a black full-length robe, and declared the founding of the Church of Satan. LaVey also declared 1966 as "*Anno Satanas*," Year One of the Age of Satan.[4]

The *Los Angeles Times* and *San Francisco Chronicle* dubbed him "The Black Pope" after he performed satanic masses, weddings, and funerals. And in the first satanic baptism in history, LaVey dedicated his three-year-old daughter to the Devil.[5]

LaVey quickly reached celebrity status and is credited for the mainstreaming of Satanism and witchcraft in America. Believing "there is a demon inside man . . . It must be exercised, not exorcised—channeled into ritualized hatred," he expanded his Black House in San Francisco through subsidiary branches of the Church of Satan, or "grottoes," in America and throughout the world. The church's membership was dedicated to the practice of "black magic, curses, and indulgence, not abstinence."[6]

The broad expansion of the Church of Satan remains frightening, but it is only one tentacle of a mighty, evil octopus that has wrapped itself around our society, threatening our physical and spiritual survival.

MARKETING THE PRINCE OF DARKNESS

In the 1980s, the media reported concerns of criminal activity involving the Church of Satan. Dubbed as the "Satanic Panic," Satanism was blamed for satanic ritual abuse (SRA). This panic caused the Church of Satan to go underground for a period of time, but not for long.

After LaVey's death in 1997, the role of High Priest remained empty until 2001, when longtime Satanic Church members assumed the offices of High Priest and Priestess. The Church of Satan is still alive and well, persisting in attempts to make itself a socially accepted religion through various public displays and ritual practices.

The year 2014 marked the fourth anniversary of satanic rituals performed at the Civic Center Music Hall in Oklahoma City. Satanist Adam Daniels said of the Black Mass:

> We're calling Jesus a mute God . . . a fugitive God. That he's done nothing, he's a chamberlain of nothing . . . The whole

basis of the mass is that we take the consecrated host and give it a blessing or offering to Satan . . . We're re-consecrating it [the host body of Christ], or the Devil does.[7]

Archbishop Coakley of the Archdiocese of Oklahoma City agreed that this ritual is "evil in its purest form" and went on to say: "The Satanic ritual . . . is to invoke those dark powers, which I believe are very real, and call them into our city, into our community."[8]

The Church of Satan's efforts to expand the occult into mainstream society is reflected in additional news reports.

The Satanic Temple in New York City rolled out a campaign to adopt a highway in 2013 to further increase public understanding and acceptance of Satanism.

"We truly look forward to this opportunity to serv[e] our community and raise public awareness of socially responsible Satanism," stated Satanic Temple spokesperson Lucien Greaves, "and this is only a small beginning. You can expect more public community involvement from us in the future."[9]

During the 2014 Christmas holiday, the Detroit chapter of the Satanic Temple set up its "Snaketivity Scene" on the lawn of the State Capitol in Lansing, Michigan. The display featured a snake wrapped around a satanic cross offering a book titled *Revolt of the Angels*.

The Temple's spokesperson, who wore an upside-down Christian cross necklace, said the group wanted to promote "views outside Christian and conservative beliefs." They felt the government's endorsement of only one method of celebrating the season (the birth of Christ) was "problematic."[10]

The Satanic Temple of Florida was also permitted to place its exhibit in Tallahassee. The display showed an angel falling into flames with the message, "Happy Holidays from the Satanic Temple."[11]

Satanists have hijacked our nation's sacred freedoms and used them to promote themselves, their beliefs, and their leader, the Prince of Darkness. Standing on the First Amendment of our Constitution, which prohibits discrimination based on a person's faith, the Church of Satan and Wicca are now on the list of religions authorized to practice on American military bases.

The Church of Satan's incessant efforts to legitimize itself as an accepted part of American society will continue until the Antichrist himself makes his appearance as the global dictator of Planet Earth. Let us not be deceived but be courageous in our constant battle for truth and righteousness as defined in the Word of God.

SATANIC RITUALS

The Church of Satan and its anti-God, anti-Christ philosophy has made a gruesome impact on our society, harvesting evil results.

In 1995, fifteen-year-old Elyse Pahler was "sacrificed to Satan" by three San Luis Obispo teenagers in what was one of California's most grisly murders on record. The suspects took the girl to a hidden area near her home, drugged and raped her, and tied a belt around her neck "to make it easier to stab her." The killers then offered up their victim as the "ultimate sin against God," stabbing her to death at an alleged "Satanic altar." The boys "selected and stalked" Elyse, believing that a virgin sacrifice would earn them a "ticket to Hell."[12]

In early 2014, Houston, Texas, prosecutors confirmed that the murder of fifteen-year-old Corriann Cervantes was part of a satanic ritual. Authorities alleged that seventeen-year-old Jose Reyes and a sixteen-year-old accomplice lured Cervantes to a vacant apartment near her home, sexually assaulted her, and beat her to death.

The alleged killers carved an inverted cross on her stomach, an act that Reyes admitted was part of a satanic ceremony. The Harris County District Attorney reported, "Mr. Reyes says he had sold his soul to the devil. And if they ended up killing this teenager, it would allow the 16-year-old accomplice to also sell his soul to the devil."[13]

In the fall of 2014, two skeletons were found in shallow graves in Clemmons, North Carolina. Pazuzu Illah Algarad—formally known as John Alexander Lawson, a self-described Satanist—his wife, and an accomplice were charged with the murders of Joshua Fredrick Wetzler, thirty-seven, and Tommy Dean Welch, thirty-six.

According to *Camel City Dispatch*, Lawson adopted "the name of Pazuzu, the demon at the center of *The Exorcist* movie, and cultivated a personality that was a combination of Charles Manson, Anton LaVey and Alistair Crowley." His erratic behavior included befriending Middle East jihadists on Facebook and filing his teeth into points with a Dremel tool.[14]

Lawson boasted to friends that he ate parts of human bodies, burning the remains in a fire pit before burying them in his backyard. His neighbors referred to Lawson as "the local boogeyman."

His house featured a painted black door decked with upside-down crosses and an Arabic script that translated as "The House of Devils." One source told the local newspaper that Lawson's home was filled with "Hot Topic Satan stuff" and that "there was something about him that just made me feel terrible . . . Just his presence made me feel uneasy."[15]

Lawson's satanic activities included mutual bloodletting in local cemeteries and attempted arson of several churches. The man admitted to psychiatrists that he practiced a "Sumerian" religion that required a monthly ritual sacrifice of small animals. He also acknowledged performing this sacrificial ceremony every month during the "black moon."

Yet another source reported that "about once a month, usually on a full moon," Lawson and his wife "sacrificed at least one rabbit and he would eat the heart of it. You could tell when his demons needed something from him, because they took over."[16]

A former high school classmate of Lawson's stated, "After Columbine, he [Lawson] started wearing a trench coat just like the killers. He had a pentagram and *666* tattoos all over his body. He told me he practiced Satanism."[17]

UNHOLY PURSUITS

This death-worshiping spirit did not begin with the Church of Satan and satanic rituals. The spirit of the Antichrist has raised its atrocious head throughout history through the likes of Cain, Haman, Herod, Nero, Stalin, Hitler, Mussolini, Tojo, Mao Tse-Tung, Pol Pot, Kim Il Sung, Saddam Hussein, Al-Assad, Khamenei of Iran, as well as leaders of the newly founded, radically extremist Islamic State.

The spirit of murder was introduced to the world through Satan's manipulative power over Cain, which resulted in the killing of his brother Abel (Genesis 4:1–9). This murderous compulsion can be traced throughout biblical history.

Abimelech coveted the succession of his father's throne and assured his three-year reign over Israel by murdering his seventy brothers (Judges 9).

Herod the Great was the Roman-appointed king of Judea. He was a brutal, paranoid man who killed his father-in-law, nine of his ten wives, and two of his sons. He rebelled against the laws of God to suit his own selfish ambitions and ordered the slaughter of all Israel's male children two years and under because he considered the baby born in Bethlehem a threat to his throne (Matthew 2:16).

Thirty years later the son of Herod the Great, Herod Antipas, entered into Israel's notorious history. Herod was a pathetic and lecherous ruler who openly lived with Herodias, his niece and the ex-wife of his half brother, Philip. When John the Baptist denounced Herod for this incestuous relationship (Leviticus 18:6), Herod had John imprisoned. Then, at the vindictive dictate of Herodias and her daughter (Herod's soon-to-be mistress) Salome, Herod had John the Baptist beheaded (Matthew 14:6–11). Herod Antipas is most remembered, however, as one of the co-conspirators in the conviction and execution of Jesus Christ.

Church history records the persecution and slaughter of innocents under the vicious commands of the maniacal Nero. Eusebius of Caesarea (AD 265–340) chronicled "Nero's plunge into unholy pursuits" in his work *Church History*, Book II, Chapter 25. Eusebius described the Roman despot as an "extraordinary madman" who was responsible for a countless number of murders, including his mother, brothers, and wife.

Nero's lifestyle was marked by lavish self-indulgence and tyranny. His egocentric personality craved acceptance by the people, which drove him to blame the burning of Rome on a new religious sect known as Christians. During his wicked reign, Christians were arrested and thrown to the wild beasts or crucified. Many were also burned to death at night, serving as "lights" in Nero's garden.

This brutal persecution immortalized Rome's ruler as the first antichrist in the eyes of the Christian Church. It was also during Nero's reign that the apostles Peter and Paul were executed, one being crucified upside down and the other beheaded.

Contemporary world history is not exempt from the calculated mass murder of the innocent.

Joseph Stalin, dictator of the Soviet Union from 1922 to 1953, is known as one of history's most prolific killers. Stalin's brutal rule featured so many atrocities (including manufactured famines, torture, acts of mass murder, and massacres) that the actual amount of bloodshed will likely never be known. Several historians have concluded, however, that the death toll attributed to this vicious man who was driven by the spirit of the Antichrist ranges anywhere from forty million to sixty million lives. Stalin's utter disregard for human life is best reflected in his own words: "Death is the solution to all problems. No man; no problem." He also said, "One death is a tragedy; one million is a statistic."[18]

Stalin's regime was the most devastating killing machine ever seen until the rise of Mao Tse-Tung. Mao, the founding father of the People's Republic of China (1949–1976) and the first Chairman of the Chinese Communist Party, was responsible for the disastrous famine that overtook China's millions. This atrocity was the direct consequence of Mao's blind political philosophy and abusive totalitarian power—neither of which held a shred of respect for humanity.

Within a short five-year span, between forty-five million and sixty million men, women, and children died of starvation, disease, or torture—all in the name of Chairman Mao's revolution. This prince of death wrote in his famous *Little Red Book*, which was cherished by many radicals, "Revolution is not a dinner party."

It was said of Mao, "For vast numbers of the people he ruled, dinner was a scraping of corn husks or the bark stripped from trees, and the only party was the one that ruthlessly beat and tortured them into submission and condemned them to a cruel life and a terrible death. They were left, in the words of a much older Chinese aphorism, to 'eat bitterness.'"[19]

The spirit of the Antichrist was also personified through the demonized Nazi leader Adolf Hitler, whose rabid hatred of the Jewish people was fueled by the evil flame of anti-Semitism.

Why does the Devil have such a deep-seated hatred for the Jewish people? The answer lies in the fact that God gave His Word to Moses at Mount Sinai and chose the Jewish people to take the light of God and His message of salvation to the Gentiles. The patriarchs were Jewish, the prophets were Jewish, and Jesus of Nazareth was Jewish. It is this Light that one day soon will conquer the Prince of Darkness for eternity.

Jesus was Abraham's son many generations removed, and today He is the exalted Conqueror of death, hell, and the grave. Every attribute of Christ flies in the face of the Devil!

In His calling of Abraham, the father of the Jewish nation, God made a promise that affects political governments to this day: "I will bless those who bless you, and I will curse him who curses you; and in you all the families of the earth shall be blessed" (Genesis 12:3).

Every nation that comes against the Jewish people will be destroyed by God Himself, for "He who keeps Israel shall neither slumber nor sleep" (Psalm 121:4). All anti-Semitism will come under sentencing at the end-times Judgment of the Nations, and its verdict will be determined by how individuals and nations treated Israel and the Jewish people.

Remember this truth: anti-Semitism is sin, and as with any unrepented sin, it damns the soul.

Hitler was one of the most dominant dictators of the twentieth century. After World War I, he rose through the ranks of the National Socialist German Workers Party and took control of the German government in 1933. Within five years, using deceitful propaganda and deadly pogroms, Hitler intensified the persecution of the Jewish people until initiating his "Final Solution."

In January of 1939, this wicked leader declared that a new world war would lead to the "annihilation of the Jewish race in Europe." Hitler's goal was twofold: to achieve world domination and to exterminate the Jewish people. Even though neither of his objectives was realized, the world lost more than forty-two million lives in combatting this evil dictator. His reign of terror propagated the unprecedented horror of the Holocaust, and as a consequence, six million Jews were systematically slaughtered.

HITLER AND THE OCCULT

Hitler's Nazi ideal was that the German race was superior to all others. He believed that if he could indoctrinate the young in this belief, he could shape them into adults who would be Nazi loyalists.

From their first days in school, German children were brainwashed by "the cult of Adolf Hitler." State educators introduced textbooks that trained students to worship the leader of the Third

Reich, obey state authority, and adhere to militarism, racism, and anti-Semitism.

The following is an oath that ten-year-old boys took in front of the Nazi flag as they dedicated their lives to Hitler:

> In the presence of this blood-banner which represents our Fuehrer, I swear to devote all my energies and my strength to the Savior of our Country, Adolf Hitler. I am willing and ready to give up my life for him, so help me God. One People, one Reich, one Fuehrer.[20]

From its onset, the Nazi Party targeted German youth, considering this vibrant generation the prime market for its propaganda. In January 1933 the Hitler Youth had only fifty thousand members, but by the end of that year the figure had increased to more than two million. By 1936, membership in the Hitler Youth had exponentially grown to 5.4 million members.

Before Hitler's meteoric rise to power, he met a man by the name of Dietrich Eckart. Eckart was the wealthy publisher and editor in chief of an anti-Semitic journal, *In Plain German*. Eckart was also a committed occultist and a master of magic who belonged to the Thule Society. The Thule inner circle believed they could establish contact with "highly intelligent beings" of old through mystical rituals. These beings, or "Ancients," were believed to endow the inner-circle members with supernatural strength and energy. With the help of these "energies," the elect of the Thule Society could supposedly create a race of "Aryan" supermen who would exterminate all "inferior" races.[21]

It is well documented that Hitler was an emotionally charged, expert orator capable of mesmerizing a vast audience. Eckart trained Hitler in self-confidence, projection, persuasive oratory, body language, and ranting discourse. With these tools, Hitler was able to turn an obscure workers' party into a mass political movement that nearly dominated Europe.[22]

One should not underestimate the influence of the occult on Hitler. The root of Hitler's lust for godlike status, his drive for world power, and his twisted philosophies of self-indulgence and anti-Semitism were born of Satan himself.

RADICALIZED OR DEMONIZED

As Christ represents life, the Antichrist spirit represents death. Fanatical extremism has been responsible for a countless number of killings throughout history. This psychopathic, amoral ideal will exist until the return of the Messiah.

Recent headlines depicting "radicalized" individuals carrying out atrocious acts of violence against innocent victims have shocked, saddened, and enraged the world at large.

In May of 2013, an off-duty British soldier was hacked to pieces with a cleaver in the streets of London in broad daylight by two assailants. Government officials concluded that a pair of British citizens—Islamic converts who were known to have been "radicalized"—were responsible for this deliberate attack.

In October of 2014, two separate incidents occurred back-to-back in Canada. The first involved an assailant who was described as "radicalized and classified as a potential important threat to the country." He used his car to run down two members of the Canadian armed forces who were simply walking across a parking lot. One of the soldiers was injured while the other died at the scene.

Three days later, in the heart of the Canadian capital, a lone gunman fatally shot a corporal in the back with a rifle. The corporal was guarding the Tomb of the Unknown Soldier at the National War Memorial. The incident was described as "a lone-wolf assault by a radicalized Canadian."

Within the same time frame, a crazed, "hatchet-wielding man" attacked a group of police officers in New York City. He confessed to converting to Islam and became "self-radicalized" through the propaganda of Al Qaeda and the Islamic State (IS).

In just over a decade, world society has been bombarded with numerous names describing radicalized terrorist organizations, including Al Qaeda, the Taliban, and ISIS (aka ISI and ISIL, which has evolved into the extremist Islamic State). Who are these groups? What do they stand for? And how do they affect us?

Let's first consider what the term *radicalized* means. Radicalization is a practice by which a group or individual adopts extreme political, social, or religious ideals. The goal of the radicalized is to undermine contemporary ideas and stifle the expressions of freedom.[23]

Most radicalization is carried out through violent extremism. This extremism is usually aided by multiple unified networks, which greatly increase a group's resilience and lethal capability.[24] By compromising the individual's ability to blend in with modern society, radicalization further serves as a sociological trap, giving the indoctrinated nowhere else to go to satisfy their material and/or spiritual needs.[25]

The radical extremist Islamic movement gained a foothold during the Islamic revival of the late twentieth century.[26] The first consequence of that revival that we will discuss is *Al Qaeda*, which means "The Base" in Arabic.

The group was founded during the Soviet occupation of Afghanistan (1979–1989). Thousands from around the Middle East came to Afghanistan as *mujahideen* (Islamic warriors) to join the fight against the Soviets.

Renowned Jewish historian Bernard Lewis explained the Islamic resentment of the West and its influence in his writing "The Roots of Muslim Rage":

> The Muslim has suffered successive stages of defeat. The first was his loss of domination in the world, to the advancing power of Russia and the West. The second was the undermining of his authority in his own country, through an invasion of foreign ideas . . . and ways of life and sometimes even foreign rulers or settlers, and the enfranchisement of native non-Muslim elements. The third—the last straw—was the challenge to his mastery in his own house, from emancipated women and rebellious children. It was too much to endure, and the outbreak of rage against these alien, infidel . . . forces that had subverted his dominance, disrupted his society, and . . . violated the sanctuary of his home was inevitable. It was also natural that this rage should be directed primarily against the millennial enemy and . . . draw its strength from ancient beliefs and loyalties.[27]

What became "unnatural" was the manifestation of that rage.

In the mid-1980s, Al Qaeda became recognized as an international terrorist network funded and led by the radical extremist Osama bin Laden. The group's main goal was to purge Muslim countries of direct Western influence and replace it with fundamentalist Islamic regimes. After fighting the Soviets, bin Laden took the ideology of *jihad* (holy war) to other Muslim countries.[28]

The term *Taliban* means "students" in Pashto, which is one of the two official languages of Afghanistan. The Taliban emerged in the southern Afghan city of Kandahar in the fall of 1994 following the withdrawal of Soviet troops.[29] The group was comprised principally of Afghans and former Islamic fighters trained in religious seminaries in Pakistan that were mostly funded by Saudi Arabia. The Taliban professed the hard-line form of the Sunni sect—the first major division of Islam—promising to restore peace and security while enforcing their own extreme form of *Sharia*, or Islamic law.[30]

The world's attention was drawn to the Taliban following the attacks on the World Trade Center in New York City and the Pentagon in 2001. The group was accused of providing asylum to Osama bin Laden and the Al Qaeda movement, who took responsibility for the attacks.

The 2011 killing of bin Laden in Pakistan by a team of US Navy SEALs ended the threat from the evil genius who had orchestrated the 9/11 attacks on American soil a decade earlier. Soon after his death, the Taliban were driven from power in Afghanistan by a US-led military coalition.[31] However, the Taliban vowed to continue to attack foreign targets in a bid to drive out US and international forces from the region. They have kept their word.

In December of 2014, seven Taliban terrorists stormed the Pakistani Army Public School in Peshawar. The assailants went from class to class killing 141 people (including 132 children) and injuring scores more.[32]

Meanwhile, Al Qaeda—the terrorist group that bin Laden formed to usher in global Islam—has greatly expanded. Katherine Zimmerman, senior analyst at the American Enterprise Institute, has stated, "The network remains far from crippled, and there is little evidence indicating that the network on the whole is on the decline. Al Qaeda's affiliates actually strengthened their positions in 2011 despite the death of bin Laden."[33]

Another classic example of a unified, radicalized extremist group is the Islamic State in Iraq and Syria (ISIS). At its outset, ISIS was a splinter group of Al Qaeda whose aim was to create an Islamic state across the Sunni areas of Iraq and Syria. Al Qaeda's target was the Shi'a sect, the second major division of Islam.

The demographic breakdown between the two factions of Islam is approximately 75–80 percent Sunni and 10–20 percent Shi'a.[34] The historic Sunni-Shi'a split occurred when Muhammad died in the year 632.

The word *Sunni* comes from "Ahl al-Sunna," or "people of the tradition." The Sunni Muslims, who regard themselves as the orthodox and traditionalist branch of Islam, believe that Muhammad died without appointing a rightful successor. Therefore, they elected Abu Bakr—Muhammad's father-in-law—as the first Caliph, or temporal and spiritual head of Islam. This contrasts with the Shi'a Muslim belief that Muhammad himself appointed Ali, his son-in-law, as the first Caliph.

However, the more significant difference between the two sects is their fundamental interpretation of the Koran. The Sunni believe in the literal rendering of its writings as well as a strict adherence to its precepts; the Shi'a, on the other hand, abide by a more figurative understanding.

The intense split in Islam between Sunni and Shi'a Muslims is based upon these early questions of leadership and the interpretation of Koranic doctrines.[35] At its essence, this sectarian divide remains a classic family feud that presently involves millions of people and billions of dollars! Once again, the desire for total power and domination is at the center of an extremist religious battle producing murder and mayhem.

The Sunni terrorist group, ISIS, has existed under various names and in multiple forms since 1999. Its exponential growth is a chronicled account of how modern terrorism has evolved from a political and religious ideal into a death cult.

ISIS, formerly known as Al Qaeda in Iraq (or AQI), originated more than two decades ago under the leadership of Jordanian-born Abu Musab al-Zarqawi. He allied with Osama bin Laden, who gave Zarqawi his blessing to establish "The Base" in Iraq.[36]

Zarqawi vehemently opposed the presence of Western military forces in the Islamic world as well as the West's support of Israel. His stated goals were to oust foreign forces from Iraq through beheadings and suicide bombings, and to incite bloody sectarian strife between his fellow Sunni Muslims and members of Iraq's Shiite majority.[37] Zarqawi led the AQI, a group of largely non-Iraqi terrorists, until his death in 2006 during a US airstrike.[38]

Somewhere between 2005 and 2006, as part of a sweeping

roundup of insurgents, one of Zarqawi's associates, Abu Bakr al-Baghdadi, was captured in Fallujah by US forces and detained at Camp Bucca, a facility in southern Iraq, with other future ISIS leaders. Following his release from Camp Bucca, al-Baghdadi resumed his militant activities. In 2006, an umbrella group of terrorist factions, including Al Qaeda, formed the Islamic State in Iraq, which al-Baghdadi joined. He was appointed the organization's leader in 2010 after Zarqawi's successor's death.[39]

By 2011, the newly installed head of ISI transformed it from a mostly foreign group of insurgents to a principally Iraqi operation. Baghdadi then took Zarqawi's murderous tactics and amplified them.

The Shi'a were still ISI's main targets, but Baghdadi escalated efforts with more calculated and effective suicide bombings. In addition, the linking of ISI's growing ranks with the Sons of Iraq (remnants of Iraq's former military) gave the Baghdadi fighters the appearance of a structured army.[40]

Exploiting the chaos of the Syrian War, ISIS took a new form by increasing its influence and expanding its territory. With thousands of armed men now at his command, Baghdadi enlarged his military front against the Iran-backed regime of Syria. Suddenly ISIL's black flags inscribed with "لا آلة إلا الل" ("There is no god but Allah") became universally recognized as the flag of conquest.[41]

Baghdadi's overthrow of the city of Mosul in Iraq (June 2014) marked another phase in ISIL's rapid growth. This conquest led to a domino effect of instability throughout the rest of Iraq and the Middle East. ISIS fighters seized critical weapons from the Iraqi Security Forces in Mosul, which they then used to push their advantage farther into both Syria and western and northern Iraq.[42]

Beyond the use of suicide bombers, they were now seizing control of land, including the rich oil fields of Iraq. These spoils of war produced a strong economic foundation for Baghdadi's military machine.

Original map courtesy of CIA.gov

To reflect his greater fanatical ambition to rule over the entire region from the Mediterranean Sea to the Persian Gulf, Baghdadi renamed the group "the Islamic State."[43] In order to better understand his ruthless yet strategic goals, it is important to note that the combatants in the Islamic State are all Sunni extremist jihadist groups controlling territory in Iraq, Syria, the Sinai, and eastern Libya.

In the process of forming the Islamic State, or "Caliphate" (which had not existed since the Ottoman Empire was dissolved in 1924),[44] Baghdadi declared that all state borders were theoretically removed, making him the de facto spiritual dictator over the world's Muslims.[45]

But what about Iran, whose goal is to *also* be the globally recognized regional power? How is Iran's Supreme Leader responding to Baghdadi's "Caliph" claim? And what makes Iran different from the other Islamic nations?

The Islamic Republic of Iran has its roots in the ancient Persian Empire. This empire, one of the greatest and oldest of biblical civilizations, first appeared on the Old Testament scene in 2 Chronicles and existed throughout Daniel's lifetime.

In 1501, the "Twelver" school of thought—the largest branch of Shi'a Islam—became the official religion of Persia. The term *Twelver* refers to a dozen divinely ordained leaders, known as the Twelve Imams. Shi'a Islamists believe that the returned Twelfth Imam will be the Islamic messiah, or the Mahdi.[46]

Professor Ehsan Yarshater, author of "Persia or Iran," stated that in 1935 the Iranian government changed its name to Iran at the suggestion of the Iranian ambassador to Germany, who came under the influence of Nazi propaganda. This name change would mark a new beginning in Iranian political history, including their separation from Russia and Britain. It would also initiate the Iranian equivalent of the Aryan quest for a "pure society."[47]

Today, Iran is home to the world's largest Shi'a population. The

Shi'a sect represents more than 90 percent of Iranian Muslims, totaling nearly seventy million people.[48]

Since the 1979 revolution that overthrew the ruling Shah, Iran has had two Supreme Leaders, the Ayatollah Ruhollah Khomeini and the current Ali Khamenei. The Supreme Leader is the highest-ranking political and religious authority in the Islamic Republic of Iran. This autocratic position serves as the Commander in Head of the armed forces and the provisional Chief of the three branches of government (judiciary, legislature, and executive).

The headship of the Supreme Leader was established by the new constitution written after the revolution, with the majority of its doctrines based on the writings of the Ayatollah himself.[49]

Khomeini has been described as "a strategic revolutionary [who] created his own Islamic state above Islamic law."[50] After Khomeini's death in 1989, the second Supreme Leader, Ali Khamenei, picked up where his predecessor left off. In his speeches Khamenei regularly mentions themes of the 1979 revolution, including the desire to destroy Israel and the United States. This opposition is at the very core of Iran's current foreign policy.[51]

According to Khamenei, the Islamic Republic has four major foreign policy priorities. The first is war against the United States and Israel, which he sees as a united enemy. Second is the backing of the Hezbollah and Hamas terrorists groups in Lebanon and Gaza respectively. Khamenei's contempt for Israel is consistent; he believes that "supporting the Palestinian and Lebanese people is one of [Iran's] major Islamic duties."[52]

The third foreign policy priority is Iran's nuclear program. For Khamenei, the production of a nuclear bomb embodies the revolution's core themes: the struggle for independence (creating a pure

Muslim world dictatorship), the injustice of foreign powers (the annihilation of America and Israel), and the necessity of self-sufficiency (through the economic control of Middle East oil).[53]

The final priority encompasses the Islamic community. Khamenei envisions Iran as the "vanguard" of the Islamic world while referring to himself as the "Supreme Leader of Muslims." Khamenei believes that none of the critical issues that face the Middle East and the Muslim world of Iraq, Afghanistan, and Lebanon—including the Arab-Israeli conflict and the security of the Persian Gulf—can be fully addressed or resolved without Tehran's input.[54]

Remember this fact: Iran is diligently working to produce a nuclear bomb in order to attain its goal of world dominance.

The problem is that the Shi'a Supreme Leader of Iran (Khamenei) has no intention of allowing a self-appointed Sunni Caliph (Baghdadi) to have Islamic headship. In fact, at the time of this writing, the Pentagon has confirmed that Iran is conducting air strikes in eastern Iraq in a shared desire with the West to defeat the extremist Islamic State.[55]

Make no mistake: Persia is alive and well! Colonel Ralph Peters simplified a very complicated situation with this one statement: "The empires are back, and we are pretending history doesn't matter."[56]

Moreover, we are acting as if prophecy isn't true.

THE WILL AND THE POWER

Islam is currently the world's second-largest religion, with 1.6 billion members.[57] By 2030, the number of people practicing the Islamic faith is expected to grow by twice the rate of the non-Muslim population, bringing the total to nearly 2.2 billion.[58]

persecution in several countries including Egypt, Iran, Iraq, Libya, and Syria.

Father Gabriel Nadaf, a Greek Orthodox priest from Nazareth, recently addressed the United Nations Human Rights Council about the plight of Christians in the Middle East. Father Nadaf, who has campaigned for Christian-Arab rights and for local Christians to support Israel, said, "In the last 10 years, 100,000 Christians have been murdered each year . . . because of their faith. Those who can escape persecution at the hands of Muslim extremists have fled. Those who remain exist as second-, if not third-class, citizens to their Muslim rulers."[63]

The ravaging death toll of the radical Islamic extremists continues: the Islamic State (ISI, ISIL, and ISIS), Boko Haram of the African continent, Al Qaeda, and the Taliban are responsible for the majority of all terrorist murders worldwide.[64] Many of these horrific murders are carried out through public executions, crucifixions, and beheadings. In fact, there are reports of "a park in Mosul, where they [ISIS] actually beheaded children and put their heads on a stick."[65]

In February 2015, Islamic State militants beheaded twenty-one Egyptian Christians who had been taken hostage in the Libyan city of Sirte.[66] As of this writing, the Islamic State and other radicalized jihadist groups have also claimed responsibility for the beheadings of several Westerners, and they have sent video proof for the world to see.[67]

It has been nearly impossible to keep up with the number of worldwide radical Islamic attacks that have occurred since my research began for this book. In January of 2015, Prime Minister Manuel Valls of France declared that his country was at war with radical Islam after the murderous attacks that killed seventeen people: twelve at a local magazine office, a policewoman, and four hostages in a Jewish market.[68] These stories, however, don't include the thousands of unreported innocent victims who are butchered in cold blood on a daily basis—all in the name of religion and world domination.

The demonized, radical, megalomaniacs discussed in this chapter were and are obsessed with total power at all costs, just like their Evil Mentor, who has come to rob, kill, and destroy (John 10:10). The devastation they have left in their wake has already cost multiple millions of innocent lives—and the numbers are only rising.

You may ask, "What can I do?" Saint Paul gives the answer: we are to put on the whole armor of God and engage the enemy in spiritual combat until the victory comes! The *only* way Christians can attain victory is to separate ourselves from all forms of evil.

Finally, my brethren, be strong in the Lord and in the power of His might. Put on the whole armor of God, that you may be able to stand against the wiles of the devil. For we do not wrestle against flesh and blood, but against principalities, against powers, against the rulers of the darkness of this age, against spiritual hosts of wickedness in the heavenly places. Therefore take up the whole armor of God, that you may be able to withstand in the evil day, and having done all, to stand. (Ephesians 6:10–13)

CHAPTER 10

DELIVER US FROM THE EVIL ONE

I must confess that writing these past few chapters was arduous and challenging. The more I researched, the more I concluded that Satan's agenda is prospering on all fronts. Every form of wickedness is escalating. Our world is filled with bedlam, terrorism, murder, blasphemy, depravity, deception, and occult activity.

I sought the Lord's peace many times as I plowed through these unspeakable accounts of evil. I grieved over the deadly cancer that we have allowed to consume the innocent of our society. As I prayed, the Lord brought to my mind a very special memory that once again anchored me in the promise that no matter how dark the evil becomes, Jesus Christ is the Light who causes darkness to flee!

That memory was of the day that Derek Prince taught on the subject of deliverance at Cornerstone Church.

EXPELLING DEMONS

I invited Derek to San Antonio to present his insights on demonology to my congregation. His teachings were in such high demand that it was several months before he could come to us. It was well worth the wait; my church was about to experience a spiritual explosion the likes of which I had never seen.

Derek Prince was educated as a scholar of Greek and Latin at Eton College and Cambridge University, England. Derek also held a Fellowship in ancient and modern philosophy at King's College and studied several languages, including Hebrew and Aramaic at Hebrew University in Jerusalem. While serving in the British army during World War II, he began to study the Bible as a philosophical work. The unexpected result was a life-changing encounter with Jesus Christ.

Brother Derek was internationally known for presenting solid biblical foundations in an unemotional, point-by-point, precept-upon-precept style. He methodically taught our congregation for two nights on the basic doctrines concerning demonology.

The people hung on his every word as he told the story of a woman in his church who collapsed while he was teaching on the subject of demons. In his very proper British way he explained, "I could not ignore her and continue my sermon; I simply had to address the problem and deliver her from the demon that held her hostage."

At the conclusion of the second night, Derek announced in a matter-of-fact manner, "I have taught you the fundamental Bible truths of expelling demons, and tomorrow night we will have a deliverance service."

No one, including myself, was prepared for what was to take place.

On the third night, the sanctuary and the overflow wings were at capacity. When Derek began the deliverance service, he calmly presented a brief review of the biblical confirmations of the existence of the Kingdom of Darkness, the presence of the demonic legions that do Satan's bidding, and the authority of the believer to expel demon spirits. Derek then warned our congregation, "If you or anyone with you does not believe in demon spirits, I ask you to leave the sanctuary at this time." He made it clear that as demons were expelled from their hosts, they would enter another human body that was not protected by the blood of Jesus Christ. There was a shuffling of feet as several attendees quickly walked out of the service. You could feel the tension mounting.

Next, Derek said, "The first area of demonic activity that we will come against is the spirit of witchcraft." He then quietly and resolutely declared, "In the authority of Jesus' name and by the power of the blood of His Cross, I command every spirit of witchcraft to leave."

What happened next was beyond belief. About a dozen women instantly and in unison jumped to their feet and let out blood-curdling screams. I quickly glanced across the sanctuary; some of my members were looking at the back door like it was a city of refuge.

While the women screamed, a man in his mid-twenties ran up the aisle, pushed aside the Communion table, and charged toward Derek, who was standing on the platform behind the pulpit. It took three of our strongest ushers to intercept the young man and wrestle him to the floor. Derek never skipped a beat.

He continued to pray for the women, who were still on their feet screaming to high heaven. A freelance reporter was covering our service and taking pictures as quickly as his fingers could snap the camera. Some in attendance hurried to the exits, the demonic manifestation being more than they could handle.

Looking over my congregation, I witnessed a worldwide wrestling match taking place on the platform, twelve women screaming like fire trucks going to a five-alarm call, and the dearly departed running for the back door. It was a night to remember. I laughed out loud! Who said church was a boring place?

After two hours of intense spiritual combat, Derek had completed his list of targets. There was a momentary silence—and then the congregation erupted with a thunderous explosion of joy! The spontaneous, Holy Spirit–anointed celebration lasted for thirty minutes. We all knew our church had experienced a new dimension of spiritual warfare, and the victory was ours.

Forty years later we employ the same biblical principles of deliverance on a regular basis to combat and conquer the Kingdom of Darkness. Satan is relentless in his efforts to destroy the home, the church, and the nations of the world. However, the Word of God, the name of Jesus, and the power of His blood have ultimate authority over any satanic attack.

It is obvious that we live in a world that personifies the culture of death, but we do not have to accept this destructive philosophy. The Lord mandates us to separate ourselves from evil. We are encouraged to choose blessings over curses, life over death, and to lead a life of victory.

I call heaven and earth as witnesses today against you, that
I have set before you life and death, blessing and cursing;
therefore choose life, that both you and your descendants

may live; that you may love the LORD your God, that you may obey His voice, and that you may cling to Him, for He is your life and the length of your days. (Deuteronomy 30:19–20)

SETTING THE CAPTIVES FREE

The topic of deliverance is not a widely accepted part of Christian ministry. In my years of study and research, I have discovered that the Catholic Church has the only established course for exorcism.

Many respond to the subject of demons with apathy, superstition, or fear, while others categorize these forces as hallucinations, ghosts, hyped exaggerations, or phobias. Do not be deceived: Satan prefers to conceal the actual objective of his evil activities to better accomplish his agenda.

The Church of Jesus Christ can no longer ignore this diabolical presence in our society. It is time to remove the veil of deception that has blinded us to satanic influence for far too long. We are called to be Christlike by following the examples that the Lord set before us (1 Peter 2:21–25). Like Christ, we must take a bold and fearless stand against the Prince of Darkness!

I have attempted to expose a sliver of Satan's massive inroads to our society. It is now time to take the next step and learn from Scripture how believers can be free from the Deceiver's attempts to influence our lives, our families, and our nation.

The Old Testament cites many miracles performed by God and His people, but it does not contain the expulsion of demons. It was not until Jesus began His earthly ministry that we read of several deliverance accounts. New Testament Scripture testifies that Jesus

Christ successfully dealt with evil spirits time and time again. One of the first chronicled accounts of Jesus' deliverance ministry is in the Gospel of Luke.

> Now in the synagogue there was a man who had a spirit of an unclean demon. And he cried out with a loud voice, saying, "Let us alone! What have we to do with You, Jesus of Nazareth? Did You come to destroy us? I know who You are—the Holy One of God!"
>
> But Jesus rebuked him, saying, "Be quiet, and come out of him!" And when the demon had thrown him in their midst, it came out of him and did not hurt him. Then they were all amazed and spoke among themselves, saying, "What a word this is! For with authority and power He commands the unclean spirits, and they come out." And the report about Him went out into every place in the surrounding region. (4:33–37)

I think it is worth noting that this man was tormented by demon spirits while *in* the synagogue! He was the equivalent of a modern-day church member. Do not be deceived; the Devil's forces are active *in* and *beyond* the walls of the church house!

After Jesus left the synagogue, He went directly to Simon Peter's home, rebuked the fever that was making Simon's mother ill, ate supper, and before the sun set, cast out even more demon spirits (Luke 4:38–41). Deliverance was a normal part of Jesus' ministry.

There are some theological skeptics who suggest that demonic activity was exclusive to the time of Christ. I beg to differ, for I have personally witnessed present-day satanic manifestations, their destructive consequences, and their successful expulsion.

To convey the importance of deliverance in the life of today's Christian, I challenge you to study the number of times that Jesus Christ cast out demons and taught His disciples to do the same. More than sixty times in the New Testament, "demons," "evil spirits," or "devils" are referenced when describing a demonically tormented person.[1]

I must caution, not every disturbed individual is affected by a demon. As a trained counselor and minister of the gospel for more than fifty-seven years, I can testify that there are some similarities between demonic influences and mental disorders. A proper diagnosis of the problem is absolutely critical. By the same token, not all mental conditions have physical causes; some indeed have spiritual roots.

The more you study the Word of God, the more the Holy Spirit reveals the areas in your life that need to come under the total authority of God's Word. Once revealed, it is essential that you take action. However, if you choose not to separate yourself from these destructive influences, you allow the evil forces to grow even stronger (Matthew 12:45). Remember this truth: You cannot change what you will not confront. What you do not conquer will conquer you!

THE GATES OF EVIL

At this point you may be thinking, *I don't listen to satanic music, I don't play with Ouija boards or hold séances, I don't watch horror movies or read occultic books, and I don't ascribe to "Antichrist" doctrines or seek world domination . . . so I don't need to worry about deliverance!* Once again, Satan in his own very subtle way has deceived you!

Just as we must recognize and obey traffic signals to safely arrive at our destination, we must recognize the warning signals that God clearly defines in His Word to avoid the Devil's entrapments. Through many years of ministry I have come to identify certain "gates" or points of entry by which Satan and his demonic goons relentlessly try to gain access into our lives. What follows are some of the portals by which the Evil One's legions invade.

THE MIND GATE

Satan and his minions relentlessly strive to oppress our thoughts. Once he takes the mind captive, the whole person inescapably becomes a prisoner of war, including the soul. Saint Paul warned us of Satan's intent to contaminate our thoughts: "But I fear, lest somehow, as the serpent deceived Eve by his craftiness, so your minds may be corrupted from the simplicity that is in Christ" (2 Corinthians 11:3).

Make no mistake: the battleground is the mind! Among the weapons of war used by Satan's demonic forces to attack your thoughts are doubt, confusion, indecision, compromise, humanism, and excessive fear or worry. The people most vulnerable to these types of demonic assaults are those who rely on their own intellect rather than those who have faith in God's Word to take them through the storms of life.

Our thoughts will determine our destiny. Tell me what a man thinks on all day, and I'll tell you where he is going in life. The wisdom of the Holy Spirit has recorded, "As he thinks within himself, so he is" (Proverbs 23:7 NASB).

One of my mother's personal proverbs was, "While you may *not* be responsible for the birds that fly over your head, you certainly *are* responsible for those you allow to build a nest in your hair." Translation: An ungodly thought should be recognized for what it is—an attempt by the Devil to gain a stronghold in your mind. These fleeting attacks should be immediately resisted. If not, you will allow the root of your destruction to take hold.

Since Satan's primary target is our mind, we must guard against thoughts that are contrary to Scripture and submit them to the dictates found in God's Word.

> For the weapons of our warfare are not carnal but mighty in God for pulling down strongholds, casting down arguments and every high thing that exalts itself against the knowledge of God, bringing every thought into captivity to the obedience of Christ. (2 Corinthians 10:4–5)

Satan does not care whether you attend church, as long as your thoughts don't become Christ-centered. He doesn't mind if you serve in the church, as long as he is the Master of your thoughts. In fact, he takes sinister delight in having demonically influenced people involved in church because he uses them to spread his doctrines of strife, doubt, and discord like a deadly virus.

John 10:12 says, "The wolf catches the sheep and scatters them." Imagine this scene every Sunday, when a pack of wolves disguised as harmless sheep invades your church. They do not rush in announcing their predatory intentions; instead, they subtly prowl among the unsuspecting flock, planting divisive thoughts of dissension.

The apostle Paul, a soldier of the Cross of Jesus Christ, issued a standing order for all Christians to follow:

Brethren, whatsoever things are true, whatsoever things are honest, whatsoever things are just, whatsoever things are pure, whatsoever things are lovely, whatsoever things are of good report; if there be any virtue, and if there be any praise, think on these things. (Philippians 4:8 KJV)

We must ask ourselves: Where is my thought life leading me? The answer to this critical question will impact your life for good or for evil, now and forevermore.

THE EMOTION GATE

Derek Prince taught that a person who has an outburst of anger or of sudden fright, for example, is not necessarily under the influence of the demon of anger or fear; however, if these emotions become uncontrolled, obsessive, habitual, or harmful, then quite possibly a demon spirit is at work.[2]

I have come to the conclusion that extreme negative emotions or destructive attitudes potentially open the gate for an equivalent spirit to come into your life. Demons tend to operate in groups or legions (Mark 5:9). As an example, a spirit of rejection will open the gate of the mind and hold it open to allow other demons of like character to enter. These invasive spirits, once they take up residence, may manifest themselves passively through self-pity, loneliness, depression, or despair; or more aggressively through chronic anger or hatred or through physical violence, rebellion, or witchcraft. Once the gate to your mind is opened to evil thoughts, your emotions and attitudes will begin to reflect specific demonic influences.

Consider the spirit of death. This spirit will manifest itself in various tormenting ways such as deep depression, a desire to inflict personal harm (cutting), or an obsession with mortality (which in extreme cases could eventually manifest as murder or suicide).

Demon spirits are no respecter of persons; they will viciously attack anyone they are assigned to, including you and me. No one is immune, even those of us who are covered by the blood of Jesus Christ. The blood of Christ totally protects the redeemed from demonic *possession*, but we are still subject to demonic *attack*.

As human beings we all struggle with certain emotions from time to time. However, when these feelings seem to spin out of control—when they seize your ability to think clearly and they obsessively dominate your everyday life—then you need to recognize them as a demonic attack, reject them in the authority of Jesus' name, and separate yourself from them. Here are a few to be especially aware of.

Doubt

"Has God indeed said . . . ?" (Genesis 3:1). This was the first question the Serpent asked Eve in the Garden. It sounds innocent enough, but this question laid the foundation for all forms of doubt.

At first this spirit manifests as the simple questions we all occasionally ask ourselves. But once the seed of disbelief is planted by the Evil One and allowed to take root, it cultivates uncertainty about God's existence. Doubt was the open gate through which disobedience and rebellion entered the mind of Adam and Eve. Doubt is still a powerful weapon employed by the ancient foe against mankind. To doubt is to disbelieve.

Recently a man left my office whose life had been dominated by uncertainty. He questioned his wife's loyalty even though she loved him dearly; he questioned his ability to make an adequate living even though he was very qualified; he questioned his self-worth even though he had accomplished great things. Ultimately he doubted himself and God's influence over his life. He had a blessed life but he was tormented because he allowed the spirit of doubt to destroy his peace of mind.

We are who we are by the genius of the Master Creator who is in total control. Yet the spirit of doubt distrusts everything He has done for us in the past, is doing for us in the present, or will do for us in the future. Doubt challenges God's existence and supernatural power!

Recognize doubt when it attempts to open the gate to your mind. Refuse this critical spirit, and reject any thought that challenges your ability to reach your goals or accomplish your divine destiny. Instead, listen to the words of Jesus; He declares that you can accomplish the impossible: "Whoever says to this mountain, 'Be removed and be cast into the sea,' and does not doubt in his heart, but believes that those things he says will be done, he will have whatever he says" (Mark 11:23).

Take in this simple truth: If your thoughts do not bring you peace, joy, and hope, they are not of God!

Worry

To worry is to fret or torment yourself with disturbing thoughts. A wise person once said, "Most of the problems I've had in life never happened."

Is the emotion of anxiety consuming you? Is it attacking someone in your family? Do you dwell on "what will happen if" more than you abide in God's Word and promises of divine provision? "Worry is a thin stream of fear trickling through the mind.

If encouraged, it cuts a channel into which all other thoughts are drained."[3]

Ultimately, worry is faith in fear and not in God!

We all experience various trials in this life. It's normal to be concerned about the crisis you or a member of your family may be facing. But excessively worrying about a situation will not change it; only by taking your concerns to the Lord in prayer and leaving them at the altar can your outcome be different.

Anxiety will fruitlessly occupy your mind. It is like a rocking chair: it will give you something to do, but it will not take you anywhere.

Many of you have opened the gate to the spirit of worry and have become consumed by its presence. Jesus preached an entire sermon to His disciples concerning this mind-set, and it is worth sharing in its entirety.

Place yourself on the side of the mountain with the multitudes that have come to hear the Rabbi who has been teaching and preaching in the synagogues as well as healing the sick and delivering the oppressed throughout Galilee.

> Therefore I tell you, stop being perpetually uneasy (anxious and worried) about your life, what you shall eat or what you shall drink; or about your body, what you shall put on. Is not life greater [in quality] than food, and the body [far above and more excellent] than clothing?
>
> Look at the birds of the air; they neither sow nor reap nor gather into barns, and yet your heavenly Father keeps feeding them. Are you not worth much more than they? And who of you by worrying and being anxious can add

one unit of measure to his stature or to the span of his life?

And why should you be anxious about clothes? Consider the lilies of the field and learn thoroughly how they grow; they neither toil nor spin.

Yet I tell you, even Solomon in all his magnificence [excellence, dignity, and grace] was not arrayed like one of these . . .

Therefore do not worry and be anxious, saying, What are we going to have to eat? or, What are we going to have to drink? or, What are we going to have to wear?

For . . . your heavenly Father knows well that you need them all.

But seek (aim at and strive after) first of all His kingdom and His righteousness (His way of doing and being right), and then all these things taken together will be given you besides. (Matthew 6:25–33 AMP)

Don't forget: When worry knocks, send faith to answer. This will guarantee that no one will be on the other side of the door.

Worry and faith cannot coexist; you can choose to pray, believing God will answer, or you can choose to worry about your situation . . . but you can't do both. Worry results in anxiety, frustration, helplessness, and defeat. Faith leads to reassurance, success, confidence, and victory.

Fear

The Bible uses the phrases "Fear not" or "Do not be afraid" more than one hundred times. Our merciful heavenly Father knew Satan would often use fear to imprison hearts and minds. Fear paralyzes the mind; it weakens the will and destroys the dream within each of us.

President Franklin D. Roosevelt, in an attempt to comfort a frightened and grieving America following the bombing of Pearl Harbor, made this powerful declaration: "The only thing we have to fear is fear itself." This is profoundly true in the life of a believer. Once we allow the spirit of fear to control us, we are bound by an all-consuming emotion that will destroy our lives and our future.

Jesus, who is the Prince of Peace and not the author of fear, said, "Don't be afraid; I am the First and the Last. I am He who lives, and was dead, and behold, I am alive forevermore. Amen. And *I* have the keys of Hades and of Death" (Revelation 1:17–18).

Fear is the antithesis of faith, for great faith casts out fear. Fear is one of the daunting weapons that Satan uses to destroy our peace. Hold on to God's promise to you: "Fear not, for I am with you; be not dismayed, for I am your God. I will strengthen you, yes, I will help you, I will uphold you with My righteous right hand" (Isaiah 41:10).

Resentment

Resentment is anger toward a person whom you perceive has offended you. You can't be responsible for what happens to you, but you are eternally accountable for how you respond to what happens to you.

Pastor Brian Houston of Hillsong Church made this insightful comment: "No mature Christian who is seasoned in the Word has any reasonable excuse to live their life offended." So I ask you this question: Are you routinely offended and habitually resentful?

Some of us have truly been wounded by the remarks or deeds of others. King David often cried out to the Lord to heal him from the offenses of others (i.e., Psalms 17; 27; 35; 109; 143). It is when we permit the insult or injury to breed resentment that we have fallen into Satan's trap.

Resentment will ultimately take your joy and peace and ruin your relationships. Consistently begrudging anyone—for their material or professional success, for failing to include you in a social event, or for committing even the most minor of slights—is all part of Satan's scheme to fill your mind with an emotional poison that can lead to unrighteous bitterness!

Resentment has to be allowed in before it can gain control. It was resentment that fueled the first murder when Cain killed Abel. Resentment caused Jacob to covet his brother's birthright. Resentment motivated King Saul to chase David across the hills of Israel in an attempt to prevent him from becoming king.

Resentment is the cyanide of the soul. Recognize it and remove it!

Rebellion

Why are America's cities filled with anarchy and lawlessness, which oppose civil authority? Why is there a generation that is senselessly gratified by looting or burning homes, churches, and places of business under the guise of "the right to protest"? Why are students rioting in the classrooms instead of seeking knowledge in preparation for their future? Why are children challenging their parents' authority while submitting to the leadership of gangs in the streets?

The answer is the spirit of rebellion. It is running rampant in our country.

This spirit resists or defies any form of authority. When is the last time you heard a sermon in your church on the topic of submission to authority? The preaching of the gospel in our churches has become more New Age than New Testament, more self-pleasing than God-pleasing. We are failing to teach the basic precepts found in the Word of God.

One of these essential precepts is submission to righteous authority. It's time for those in authority in our homes, churches, schools, and within our government to close the gates of rebellion that have allowed demonic influences to corrupt our society.

God has a more exhaustive depiction of this emotion: "Rebellion is as the sin of witchcraft, and stubbornness is as iniquity and idolatry" (1 Samuel 15:23).

You don't have to wear a black pointed hat and recite incantations around a boiling cauldron to be influenced by the spirit of witchcraft. More subtle invasions of this vicious spirit—such as domination, intimidation, and manipulation—seek to undermine us. They are strongholds that have infiltrated our lives and the lives of our loved ones.

How can we be delivered from the death grip of these spirits?

First, we must acknowledge that this detrimental demonic spirit is from Satan (Lucifer), who is the first source of rebellion. Next, we must examine ourselves to recognize how the spirit of rebellion has manifested itself within us. Like all other demonic spirits, it slithers into our minds and takes hold, often without our awareness.

Domination is the act of towering over someone's life or feelings for the purpose of control. People seek to master others through abusive or condescending remarks, mockery, and a host of other ploys. A dominating spirit demands attention and power.

The spirit of intimidation forces people to do what they don't want to or deters them from doing what they want to do by inducing fear. Bullying and exploitation are two primary tactics.

The news is riddled with accounts of young people committing suicide due to relentless harassment through cyber-bullying. Sex trafficking has reached epidemic proportions, ruining the lives of countless young men and women. Even parents are victimized by this destructive, manipulative spirit. A recent study revealed that parents are reluctant to discipline their children for fear of what they may post on Facebook or Twitter.

Manipulation is the act of managing someone's actions or emotions in an unfair manner. Whether employing subtle or confrontational methods, manipulators entice or seduce others to achieve their own end results. Women often use sex, men can use finances, and children may use temper tantrums to get their way. The spirit of manipulation is self-gratification.

Ultimately, the spirit of rebellion makes idols of *our* wills, opinions, and lusts. However, there is one truth we must consider: God will share His Kingship with no one—man or spirit.

You shall worship no other god, for the LORD, whose name
is Jealous, is a jealous God. (Exodus 34:14)

It is only through repentance and submission to the will of God that we can be freed from rebellion's grasp.

The gate to our emotions must be carefully guarded to protect our supernatural peace—what the Bible describes as "the peace of God, which surpasses all understanding." This is what will "guard your hearts and minds through Christ Jesus" (Philippians 4:7).

THE SPEECH GATE

The presence of demonic influence can also be reflected in the content of a person's speech, such as compulsive lying, gossip, vulgar language, and destructive declarations.

The tongue is a powerful tool for good or for evil. It is, according to James 3:6, "a fire, a world of iniquity. The tongue is so set among our members that it defiles the whole body, and sets on fire the course of nature; and it is set on fire by hell."

Any person who compulsively misrepresents the truth is motivated by a spirit contrary to God's Word. King David warned us, "Keep your tongue from evil, and your lips from speaking deceit" (Psalm 34:13).

Paul listed the sin of gossip with adultery, murder, and unrighteousness (Romans 1:29–32). Few church members would consider participating in adultery or murder, but far too many indulge in gossip. In the Lord's eyes, to murder another person's character with your tongue (slander) is just as grave as taking his life. God will not tolerate either.

A perverse man sows strife, and a whisperer [a gossip] separates the best of friends. (Proverbs 16:28)

Whoever secretly slanders his neighbor, him I will destroy. (Psalm 101:5)

Indecent or vulgar language is a breeding ground for spiritual viruses. It can cultivate lewd thoughts and lustful behaviors that ultimately lead to sinful actions.

His mouth is full of cursing and deceit and oppression; under his tongue is trouble and iniquity. (Psalm 10:7)

Crude, explicit, offensive language is not a badge of honor but a shroud of disgusting demonic deviance.

Now you yourselves are to put off all these: anger, wrath, malice, blasphemy, filthy language out of your mouth. Do not lie to one another, since you have put off the old man with his deeds, and have put on the new man who is renewed in knowledge according to the image of Him who created him. (Colossians 3:8–10)

Making destructive statements such as "I hate you!" "I wish I was never born!" or "I wish I was dead!" is another way that our speech lets evil in.

Death and life are in the power of the tongue, and those who love it will eat its fruit. (Proverbs 18:21)

Once you make a verbal declaration, you have set your destiny into motion. If your speech is affirmative, your actions will soon reflect it: "I can do all things through Christ who strengthens me" (Philippians 4:13). If your words are negative, you will act out on that proclamation as well:

If anyone . . . does not consent to wholesome words, even the words of our Lord Jesus Christ, and to the doctrine which accords with godliness, he is . . . *obsessed with disputes and arguments over words, from which come envy, strife, re-viling, evil suspicions, useless wranglings of men* of corrupt minds and destitute of the truth, who suppose that godliness is a means of gain. From such withdraw yourself. (1 Timothy 6:3–5)

The root source of your words is either God or Satan, and what flows out of your mouth reflects the content of your heart.

Out of the abundance of the heart the mouth speaks. A good man out of the good treasure of his heart brings forth good things, and an evil man out of the evil treasure brings forth evil things. (Matthew 12:34–35)

Your speech has the power to bring blessings into your life and the lives of your loved ones. Or it can open the gate of hell through curses, adversely affecting your future for generations to come.

THE CARNAL GATE

To be carnally minded is death, but to be spiritually minded is life and peace. (Romans 8:6)

Christians are commanded to be in control of their physical habits: "Those who are Christ's have *crucified the flesh with its passions and desires*. If we live in the Spirit, let us also walk in the Spirit" (Galatians 5:24–25). Are you in control of your carnal desires? Have you taken inventory of your negative habits? Do they feed the spirit man or the carnal man? Do your desires lead to life or destruction?

The same forces that drive drug addicts to obsessively ravage themselves with a needle also compel millions to destroy themselves with other, less obvious habits. If you have "no control," then you could be under the influence of destructive, demonic powers. A proper diagnosis is critical.

Are you a compulsive eater? Do you excessively drink alcohol? Are you a chain smoker? Are you addicted to pornography? Do you engage in sex outside of marriage? If you answered yes to any of these questions, ask yourself: "Does God want this for my life, or have I chosen a poison that will eventually destroy me?" These compulsive habits have filled penitentiaries, psychiatric wards, hospitals, and divorce courts, and have provided an endless supply of guests for reality television.

Ignoring the root cause of these abusive behaviors will lead to certain ruin. Satan and his demons are sadistic monsters who delight in this human wreckage, constantly promoting the "virtues" of vice, bombarding our generation with false promises of acceptance, significance, and escapism. The enemy entices, deceives, defiles, torments, enslaves, and will destroy everyone who invites these demon powers to invade their lives.

We must acknowledge that our body is the temple of the Holy Spirit, and Jesus our Redeemer—who paid the ultimate price for our abundant life—takes no pleasure in witnessing God's creation self-destruct.

God the Father has a divine plan for our lives.

Saint Peter presented a profound dissertation, warning us about the threats of the flesh as well as describing the promised gifts of God:

His divine power has given to us all things that pertain to life and godliness, through the knowledge of Him who called us by glory and virtue, by which have been given to us exceedingly great and precious promises, that through these you may be partakers of the divine nature, having escaped the corruption that is in the world through lust.

But also for this very reason, giving all diligence, add to your faith virtue, to virtue knowledge, to knowledge self-control, to self-control perseverance, to perseverance godliness, to godliness brotherly kindness, and to brotherly kindness love. For if these things are yours and abound, you will be neither barren nor unfruitful in the knowledge of our Lord Jesus Christ . . .

Therefore, brethren, be even more diligent to make your call and election sure, for if you do these things you will never stumble; for so an entrance will be supplied to you abundantly into the everlasting kingdom of our Lord and Savior Jesus Christ. (2 Peter 1:3–11)

The perfect defense against the Prince of Darkness and His legions of demons can't be accomplished without divine assistance. Satan will whisper in your ear that you are defeated and your future is utterly hopeless. Saint Paul gave us the counterattack: "But thanks be to God, who gives us the victory through our Lord Jesus Christ" (1 Corinthians 15:57).

Let every discouraged heart, every worried and tormented mind, every depressed and defeated spirit, cry out: there is deliverance in Jesus Christ!

RECOGNIZE, REJECT, AND REMOVE

I recall Derek Prince sharing a sobering truth about demonic activity:

> I wish it were true that Christians were immune to demonic invasion. Unfortunately, our corruptible has not yet "put on incorruption," and our mortal has not yet "put on immortality," as it says in 1 Corinthians 15:43. Until that happens, our minds and bodies will still be vulnerable to the enemy. A demon can go anywhere that sin can go.

Remember this truth: Where there is no sin, there is no offense; where there is no offense, there is no guilt; where there is no guilt, there is no shame.

Demons cannot be expelled with pious phrases and frivolous formulas; they must be defeated on a spiritual field of battle. You don't negotiate with demons; you cast them out! Jesus proclaimed in Matthew 12:28, "If I cast out demons by the Spirit of God, surely the kingdom of God has come upon you."

It requires spiritual power and scriptural truth to resist Satan and His insidious temptations.

> Then Jesus, being filled with the Holy Spirit, returned from the Jordan and was led by the Spirit into the wilderness, being tempted for forty days by the devil. (Luke 4:1–2)

> Then Jesus returned in the power of the Spirit to Galilee. (Luke 4:14)

When He arrived in Nazareth, He read from the book of Isaiah:

The Spirit of the LORD is upon Me . . . to proclaim liberty to the captives . . . [and] to set at liberty those who are oppressed. (Luke 4:18)

Jesus Christ, who knew all things, testified by His words and actions that Satan is only defeated by the power of the Holy Spirit.

The believer has been given the authority to cast out demons (Mark 16:17). When Jesus sent out the seventy believers to minister, they returned to Him and said, "Lord, even the demons are subject to us in Your name" (Luke 10:17). When Paul was confronted with a demonized woman at Philippi, he spoke in the power of Jesus' name: "I command you in the name of Jesus Christ to come out of her" (Acts 16:18).

The Bible clearly states, "Submit to God. Resist the devil and he will flee from you" (James 4:7). Once we have *recognized* the Evil Intruder, we must *reject* his influence and *remove* ourselves from his presence. If for some reason you feel inadequate to do so, then go to your designated spiritual authority (pastor or priest) who has sound knowledge of the biblical doctrine of demons and deliverance, and ask for help. Either way, believers have both the authorization *and* the ability to be victorious over the powers and principalities of the Devil.

THE JOURNEY TO FREEDOM

Allow me to guide you on the same journey to freedom that Derek Prince first led my congregation on some forty years ago.

First, surrender your life to Jesus Christ and acknowledge His Lordship. You cannot expect deliverance without yielding to Christ and His Word.

Holy brethren, partakers of the heavenly calling, consider the Apostle and High Priest of our confession, Christ Jesus. (Hebrews 3:1)

Second, you must humble yourself and crucify the sin of pride. Pride will make you choose your ego over your liberty.

"God resists the proud, but gives grace to the humble." Therefore humble yourselves under the mighty hand of God, that He may exalt you in due time. (1 Peter 5:5–6)

According to Scripture, the following promises are guaranteed to believers who humble themselves:

- redemption (Philippians 2:5–8)
- riches and honor (Proverbs 22:4)
- sweet fellowship (Isaiah 57:15)
- peace (Matthew 11:29)
- greatness (Matthew 23:11)
- exaltation (Luke 14:11)
- unity (Ephesians 4:1–3)
- a victorious Christian life (Romans 12:9–21)

Third, you must make a full and honest confession of the sins that have allowed Satan and his demonic forces into your life. This is no time to hide behind the veil of secrets! God knows! He is aware of every sin you have committed and are presently committing: "For nothing is secret that will not be revealed, nor anything hidden that will not be known and come to light" (Luke 8:17). The only sins God will not remember are those that have been confessed and covered by the blood of Jesus Christ.

> He who covers his sins will not prosper, but whoever confesses and forsakes them will have mercy. (Proverbs 28:13)

> I will be merciful to their unrighteousness, and their sins and their lawless deeds I will remember no more. (Hebrews 8:12)

Fourth, we must repent of our sin by taking responsibility for our actions and turning away from them (2 Peter 3:9). Just like King David, we need to cry out to God and admit that we have sinned against Him and Him alone (Psalm 51:4). We must learn to despise sin as much as our Father does (Proverbs 6:16–18).

The fifth step on the journey to deliverance is forgiving those who have offended you or brought you harm. Before you receive forgiveness from God, you must first be willing to extend forgiveness to others. The Lord's Prayer confirms this truth, "Forgive us our debts as we forgive our debtors" (Matthew 6:12 KJV).

Scripture further explains why this is so important:

> If you forgive men their trespasses, your heavenly Father will also forgive you. But if you do not forgive men their trespasses, neither will your Father forgive your trespasses. (Matthew 6:14–15)

Harbored hatred toward others will hinder, and ultimately prevent, your deliverance. Complete forgiveness is imperative in order for you to experience sweet communion with Jesus Christ.

Forgiveness sometimes seems impossible because we consider the offense too grievous. It is in these times that we must ask God to give us the willingness to forgive. One of the best examples of this kind of willful action was demonstrated by a remarkable woman I had the high honor to meet at an author's banquet.

Corrie ten Boom, the author of the international bestseller *The Hiding Place*, survived the hellish and incomprehensible horrors of the Holocaust, enduring brutality and heartbreaking loss on a scale that overwhelms the mind.

One of the guards in the Ravensbruck concentration camp personally committed vicious, inhumane acts against her and her fellow prisoners as well as causing the death of her only sister, Betsie.

After Corrie spoke on forgiveness at one of her many engagements after the war ended, a man from the audience approached her. She immediately recognized him as her "offender" from Ravensbruck even though he did not remember her.

He came up to Corrie and told her that he had been a guard at a camp, but since then he had become a Christian. Knowing that God had forgiven him, he was still desperate to receive forgiveness from those who had been in his concentration camp.

There he was, the one whom she had felt such hatred toward for all these years, asking for forgiveness. Corrie stood there, speechless and practically paralyzed for a brief moment, which seemed like hours.

Memories and thoughts ran crazily through her mind as she

wondered how she could ever forgive someone like this, someone who had played a part in her sister's death. But she also thought of how many times God had forgiven her of her sins.

In that moment her obedience to the Holy Spirit overtook her fleshly desire to rebel:

> I had to do it . . . I knew that. The message that God forgives has a prior condition: that we forgive those who have injured us . . .
>
> "Help!" I prayed silently. "I can lift my hand. I can do that much. You supply the feeling" . . .
>
> "I forgive you, brother!" I cried. "With all my heart!"[4]

For a long moment, the former guard and prisoner—the former oppressor and the oppressed—grasped each other's hands. She said that in this moment she felt God's love more intensely than ever before.

I cannot imagine a more beautiful display of forgiveness between two people. We must conquer and command our will before forgiveness can become a part of our spiritual deliverance and emotional healing.

The next crucial step is to break ties with all forms of occultic activities, false religions, and idols; there are *no* exceptions!

> Nor shall you bring an abomination into your house, lest you be doomed to destruction like it. You shall utterly detest it and utterly abhor it, for it is an accursed thing. (Deuteronomy 7:26)

The seventh and final step is to prepare your heart, mind, and spirit to be released from the bondage of hell itself. You have lived under the curse of Satan long enough; it's time to step into the Light of God's blessing and be forever free!

A great exchange occurred at the time of Christ's death on the Cross. Paul described that miraculous freedom this way:

> Christ has redeemed us from the curse of the law, having become a curse for us (for it is written, "Cursed is everyone who hangs on a tree"), that the blessing of Abraham might come upon the Gentiles in Christ Jesus, that we might receive the promise of the Spirit through faith. (Galatians 3:13–14)

THE ACT OF DELIVERANCE

We have come full circle and are now ready to submit to God and His Word and demand that the Devil flee from us (James 4:7)! We must speak the name of Jesus, for demons tremble at the mere mention of it (James 2:19).

Once you have fulfilled each step, identify the enemy by name—whatever it is—reject it from your life, and then pray the prayer of deliverance, and the demon spirit that has held you hostage has no choice but to leave.

I offer this simple yet powerful prayer as an example you can use to complete your journey to freedom:

> Satan, in the name of Jesus and by the power of His shed blood and by the authority I have through the Word of God, I renounce you and your Kingdom. I reject your

demon spirits of [call them by name] and their influence over my life. No longer will I be dominated by any stronghold that has held me captive. I receive my deliverance in the name of Jesus Christ. I am free! Amen.

Derek declared the following promise over my congregation after a deliverance service, and I now declare it over your life: "Every prayer of a Christian, prayed in faith, according to God's Word, based on His promises, prayed in the name of Jesus Christ, inspired by the Holy Spirit, whether for temporal or spiritual blessing, will be fully answered."

PROTECTING YOUR FREEDOM

After you have experienced God's deliverance, it is imperative that you immerse yourself in His Word, attend a Bible-centered church that preaches the uncompromised gospel of Christ, and stay in fellowship with like-minded believers (Psalm 133:1; Philippians 1:5–6).

Jesus warned that we must

1. guard our minds, hearts, and spirits after we receive deliverance;
2. stay separated from Satan and his Kingdom of Darkness.

If we fail to do both, then remember: we are susceptible to an attack seven times greater than before (Luke 11:24–26)!

You are in control of your destiny. Do not give Satan a foothold in your life that will steal your peace, your joy, your hope. God promises to never leave or forsake us. He has presented His Word for our instruction, His Son for our redemption, and the Holy Spirit for our comfort and guidance. God also created a heavenly host to protect and defend us: "He shall give His angels charge over you, to keep you in all your ways" (Psalm 91:11).

Let us now take a journey into the invisible world of angels and discover their power to protect and defend you and those you love. There are angels standing beside you right now . . .

CHAPTER 11

WHY I BELIEVE IN ANGELS

*To which of the angels did He ever say: "You are My Son, today
I have begotten You"? And again: "I will be to Him a Father, and
He shall be to Me a Son"? But when He again brings the firstborn into
the world, He says: "Let all the angels of God worship Him."
And of the angels He says: "Who makes His angels spirits and
His ministers a flame of fire." . . . But to which of the angels has
He ever said: "Sit at My right hand, till I make Your enemies
Your footstool"? Are they not all ministering spirits sent forth
to minister for those who will inherit salvation?*

Hebrews 1:5–7, 13–14

I believe in God's angels, not because of a Renaissance artist's inspirational painting depicting winged cherubs playing harps while floating on fluffy white clouds; not because Hollywood has made mystical blockbuster movies on the subject; not because of someone's testimony of an angelic vision or because I have seen one (I have not). I believe in angels because the Bible tells me they exist!

The Bible is the inerrant Word of God, and it is *absolute* truth (John 17:17). The Word is a wellspring of life for the believer (John 4:14); it is milk for infants (1 Peter 2:2) and meat for men (Hebrews 5:14); it is our perpetual source of blessings (Deuteronomy 28:2); it is our guiding light through life's journey (Psalm 119:105) and our eternal promise of redemption for tomorrow (Psalm 111:9).

WHAT ARE ANGELS?

To fully appreciate the reality of angels and their importance in a believer's life, one must first study the Holy Scriptures, which present detailed accounts of their existence, their characteristics, their office and ranks, their power to protect and defend, and their assignments given by God Almighty.

According to the apostle Paul, angels are created beings: "For by Him all things were created that are in heaven and that are on earth, visible and invisible" (Colossians 1:16). Angels are also spiritual beings (Psalm 104:4) that appear and disappear at will with unimagined speed.

Angels are purely spirit but can assume the form of humans (Genesis 19:1–3). Angels live in the Third Heaven (Mark 13:32; Revelation 10:1), but they are not bound to any specific location; they serve in the heavens or on the earth depending on God's mission (Daniel 10:13; Hebrews 1:14). Angels are obedient; they fulfill their commissions without question or hesitancy (Psalm 103:20; 1 Peter 3:22; Jude 6).

Angels are alive (Ezekiel 1:1–5), they are immortal (Luke 20:34–35), and they present the Lord's proclamations (Luke 2:10–11). Angels offer God praise (Luke 2:13) and worship (Hebrews 1:6). Angels are meek; they are neither resentful nor critical (2 Peter

2:11; Jude 9). Angels are set apart by and for God, for they are holy (Luke 9:26; Revelation 14:10), they see His face (Matthew 18:10; 1 Timothy 3:16), and they guard His throne.

> Then I looked, and I heard the voice of many angels around the throne, the living creatures, and the elders; and the number of them was ten thousand times ten thousand, and thousands of thousands. (Revelation 5:11)

ANGELIC CHARACTERISTICS

Angels are under God's authority (1 Peter 3:22). Their nature (Hebrews 2:7) and knowledge (2 Samuel 14:20) are superior to that of man's. They also have supernatural power and strength (2 Peter 2:11). Angels can fly (Isaiah 6:6), they can speak (Hebrews 2:2), and they reflect God's joy (Luke 15:10 AMP). Angels never marry or die (Luke 20:35–36). The angels of God can discern between good and evil (2 Samuel 14:17) and are our holy escorts in life (Hebrews 1:14) and in death (Luke 16:22).

Angels are without number!

Daniel 7:10 reports, "A thousand thousands ministered to Him; ten thousand times ten thousand stood before Him." Jesus referred to more than "twelve legions of angels" (Matthew 26:53); Luke 2:13 describes the "multitude of the heavenly host"; and Hebrews 12:22 states there is "an innumerable company of angels."

Think on that. As children of God we are surrounded by an immeasurable, invisible, and invincible order of intelligent supernatural beings sent on a special mission by God Himself for our defense, our comfort, and our protection!

Angels are God's messengers who convey His commands and carry out His judgments; they perform God's bidding.

> Bless the LORD, you His angels, who excel in strength, who do His word, heeding the voice of His word. Bless the LORD, all you His hosts, you ministers of His, who do His pleasure. Bless the LORD, all His works, in all places of His dominion. (Psalm 103:20–22)

ANGELIC OFFICES

The office of an angel is fourfold.

The first is to worship and adore the living God, the Creator of Heaven and Earth and Jesus Christ His Son. John the Revelator wrote, "I heard the voice of many angels . . . saying with a loud voice: 'Worthy is the Lamb that was slain to receive power and riches and wisdom, and strength and honor and glory and blessing'" (Revelation 5:11–12).

Second, angels are God's servants sent to minister (Hebrews 1:14), to sustain (1 Kings 19:5; Matthew 4:11; Luke 22:43), to preserve (Genesis 16:7; 24:7; Exodus 23:20; Revelation 7:1), to deliver (Genesis 48:16; Numbers 20:16; Psalm 34:7; 91:11; Isaiah 63:9; Daniel 6:22; Matthew 26:53), to intercede (Zechariah 1:12; Revelation 8:3), and to attend to the righteous after death (Luke 16:22).

Third, angels are God's messengers. The word *angel* actually means "messenger" in both Greek (*angelos*) and Hebrew (*mal'ach*). Through His angels, God sends annunciations (Matthew 1:20- 21;

Luke 1:11–20), warnings (Daniel 4:13–17; Matthew 28:2–6; Acts 10:3), encouragement (Acts 27:23), and revelation (Daniel 9:21; Acts 7:53; Galatians 3:19; Hebrews 2:2; Revelation 1:1).

The fourth office of angels is to be God's agents and the executors of His decrees and judgments regarding mankind (Genesis 3:24; 19:1; Numbers 22:22–27; 2 Samuel 24:16; 2 Kings 19:35; Matthew 13:39, 41, 49; 16:27; 24:31; Mark 13:27; Acts 12:23; and throughout the book of Revelation).

ANGELIC RANKS AND ASSIGNMENTS

The angels are the dispensers and administrators of the Divine beneficence toward us; they regard our safety, undertake our defense, direct our ways, and exercise a constant solicitude that no evil befall us. (John Calvin)

Angels are referenced in thirty-four books of the Bible, from Genesis to Revelation, and occupy specific positions and duties. God created the earth out of nothing, and since "order is the first law of heaven,"[1] it is only logical that angels are classified in order of rank and assignment. Angels are organized in terms of authority, power, and glory. Their ranks consist of archangels, seraphim, cherubim, principalities, power, thrones, and dominion (Ephesians 1:21; Colossians 1:16; 1 Peter 3:22).

The Angel of the Lord

It is important to note that the Lord Himself appeared as an angel in the Old Testament—which is an angelic category in itself. When this took place, the expression "Angel of the Lord" or "Angel of God" was used. God the Father also sent His Son to man in the form of an angel.

> Behold, I [God the Father] send an Angel [Jesus the Son] before you [Moses] to keep you in the way and to bring you into the place which I have prepared. Beware of Him and obey His voice; do not provoke Him, for He will not pardon your transgressions; for My name is in Him. But if you indeed obey His voice and do all that I speak, then I will be an enemy to your enemies and an adversary to your adversaries. For My Angel will go before you. (Exodus 23:20–23)

This Angel of the Lord led Moses and the children of Israel through the wilderness. He is not a "created being" and is distinguished above all other angels in His power to pardon or retain transgressions. The name of God *is in* Him!

Exodus 33:14 says, "My Presence [My face] will go with you, and I will give you rest." Exodus 32:34 states, "My Angel shall go before you." Bible scholar and author Myer Pearlman compared the verses in Exodus with Isaiah 63:9: "In all their affliction He was afflicted, and the Angel of His Presence [God's face] saved them; in His love and in His pity He redeemed them."

Pearlman made two conclusions about the Angel referenced in these verses. First, Jehovah's name (His revealed character) is *in Him*. Second, the face of Jehovah (His holy Presence) can also be seen *in Him*. This Angel is identified by Jacob in Genesis 32:30: "For I have seen God face to face"; and again in 48:16: "the Angel who has redeemed me from all evil." Pearlman concludes that "this mysterious Angel referenced in all of these verses is none other than the Son of God, the Messiah, the Deliverer of Israel and the Savior-to-be of the world."[2] Derek Prince said of this Angel, "He was the same Person who later was manifested in history as Jesus of Nazareth."[3]

The Angel of the Lord appeared to Hagar when she was first cast out by a jealous Sarah (Genesis 16:9–10). He once again appeared to Hagar when she and her son were banished to the blazing desert with only a flask of water and a measly loaf of bread. The Angel took her to a well and blessed her and prophesied that her son would become a powerful and rich nation (Genesis 21:17–19).

Her son was Ishmael, the son of Abraham and the father of the Arab nations who today represent the awesome wealth and power of OPEC (Organization of the Petroleum Exporting Countries). Only God Himself could make and fulfill such promises: "I will multiply his descendants exceedingly," and "I will make him a great nation."

On a personal note, if you are a single mother going through a difficult time, be assured the eye of God is upon you. He will personally provide what you need, when you need it, and your seed will be blessed above and beyond all you can ask or imagine.

Moses received a visit: "The Angel of the LORD appeared to him in a flame of fire from the midst of a bush" (Exodus 3:2). Two verses later the same Angel is referred to as God: "God called to him from the midst of the bush," and in verse 6 God specifically identifies Himself: "I am the God of your father—the God of Abraham, the God of Isaac, and the God of Jacob." This visitation was the beginning of the extraordinary relationship between God and Moses that initiated the written account of God's Word through the Pentateuch, the first five books of the Bible.

Gideon was also visited: "The Angel of the LORD appeared to him, and said to him, 'The LORD is with you, you mighty man of valor!'" (Judges 6:12). So was Samson's mother: "The woman came and told her husband, saying, 'A Man of God came to me, and His countenance was like the countenance of the Angel of God, very awesome; but I did not ask Him where He was from, and He did not tell me His name" (Judges 13:6).

This Angel appeared to Balaam: "Then the LORD opened Balaam's eyes, and he saw the Angel of the LORD standing in the way with His drawn sword in His hand; and he bowed his head and fell flat on his face" (Numbers 22:31). Then God personally met with Balaam (Numbers 23:4), and as a result of this unique encounter, Balaam spoke forth four prophecies revealing God's destiny for Israel and the Jewish people.

The first prophecy (Numbers 23:9–10) is the fulfillment of God's promise to Abraham found in Genesis 13:16:

I will make your descendants as the dust of the earth; so that if a man could number the dust of the earth, then your descendants also could be numbered.

The second (Numbers 23:21–24) refers to Jacob's prophecy concerning the tribes of Israel in Genesis 49:9:

Judah is a lion's whelp; from the prey, my son, you have gone up. He bows down, he lies down as a lion; and as a lion, who shall rouse him?

In this case, Judah (from which the word *Jew* is derived) stands for the whole nation of Israel, which was eventually ruled by King David.

Balaam's third and fourth prophecies are in Numbers 24:7–9, 17–19. They are the revelation of the Messiah and His coming Kingdom on earth (Isaiah 9:6–9) and include the blessings of the nations concerning Israel found in Genesis 12:3.

The Archangel

> Michael the archangel, in contending with the devil, when he disputed about the body of Moses, dared not bring against him a reviling accusation, but said, "The Lord rebuke you!" (Jude 9)

Arch is the Greek term for "ruling" or "chief"; therefore, an archangel is a top-ranking angel. The word *archangel* is mentioned twice in the Bible (1 Thessalonians 4:16; Jude 9), and only Michael is specifically associated with this title. Michael is also represented as "one of the chief princes" in Daniel 10:13 and as a leader over other angels ("his angels") in Revelation 12:7.

The Hebrew meaning of the name Michael is "Who is like God?" and his main assignment is to guard over the State of Israel and the Jewish people: "At that time Michael, the great prince who stands guard over the sons of your people, will arise" (Daniel 12:1 NASB).

There are three places in the Bible that depict Michael as the defender of Israel (Daniel 10:13, 21; 12:1). Let's review the first recorded incident where the angel Gabriel, God's messenger, had a world-changing communiqué from God for Israel's prophet Daniel.

Gabriel left the Third Heaven and couldn't advance past the Prince of Persia and his principalities (fallen angels assigned by Satan) in the Second Heaven to complete his mission. Michael, "the chief prince" of Israel, entered this supernatural battle in the heavenlies and cleared the path for Gabriel to reach Daniel with God's revelation for the future of Israel and the nations of the world.

By verse 21 of chapter 10, the message from the Lord is delivered to Daniel by Gabriel: "But I will tell you what is noted in the Scripture of Truth. No one upholds me against these [principalities] except Michael your prince."

The third reference in the book of Daniel (12:1) further confirms Michael's position as the protector of the Jewish people through a prophecy of the end time.

At that time [of the end] Michael shall arise, the great [angelic] prince who defends and has charge of your [Daniel's] people. And there shall be a time of trouble, straitness, and distress such as never was since there was a nation till that time. But at that time your people shall be delivered, everyone whose name shall be found written in the Book [of God's plan for His own]. (AMP)

Israel has faced many battles and wars throughout her rich history, and the Lord has always surrounded His people with supernatural protection—from their first battle to their latest. The nation of Israel recently engaged in a fifty-day war with Gaza called Operation

Protective Edge. The following are some of the miraculous stories of God's supernatural protection over the people of Israel, which He has assigned to the archangel Michael.

The Protector of Israel: An Israeli Defense Force (IDF) unit identified the home of a wanted Hamas terrorist in Gaza and made preparations to arrest their target by daybreak. As the soldiers were about to enter the building, they saw a white dove hovering overhead. This was a most unusual sight in such an active battle zone, so they momentarily stopped to watch the dove alight on a tiny string.

A second after the dove landed, there was a huge explosion and the house was destroyed with everyone in it. The building was booby-trapped; the string that was connected to the door was detonated by the dove.

As one of the soldiers later testified in his synagogue, "Had it not been for God's protection, our entire army unit would have been killed."[4]

A Prayer of Blessing: Another young IDF soldier tells this miraculous story. He had received permission from his commanding officer to pack and carry some chocolate cookies sent by the Israelis as their unit entered Gaza.

After a day and a half of constant fighting with minimal amounts of food, we were . . . in a house and I recalled that I had cookies packed with my gear. I opened the box and noticed a note stuffed in the package from a child . . . : "I know that you are protecting me, and this is a small token of my appreciation to you. I am still young, but I have one request, that you say a blessing over the food."

I am a secular Jew and I did not know how to make a blessing. A soldier friend of mine was observant, but he was sitting in the opposite corner of the house. I crawled toward my friend and asked him to show me how to say a blessing . . .

As he [finished] . . . an RPG rocket was shot directly into the house and exploded exactly in the place where I had been sitting moments before . . . I was only slightly wounded instead of being killed. The angel of God was with me![5]

Psalm 30: Here's another miraculous story of angelic protection. On the day Operation Protective Edge began, Avraham was preparing to leave the IDF and return to his *yeshiva* (school of Torah study). Instead, he was sent from his position on the Golan Heights to fight the war in the Gaza Strip.

Amid the battles, during brief missions to the rear for tank repairs or ammunition, Avraham would contact his parents on the unit commander's phone. Every conversation was a gift from heaven. Avraham's mother asked him to observe all safety regulations, and his father asked him to read from the book of Psalms every day.

The clashes were fierce as snipers fired a barrage of bullets from underground tunnels and the enemy sustained its attack using anti-tank missiles. During one such skirmish there was a powerful flash of light that surrounded Avraham's tank, followed by the sound of a deafening explosion. The tank filled with smoke as the commander announced over the radio, "Tank No. 3 has been destroyed."

They were Tank No. 3!

Avraham was disoriented by the explosion and didn't know if he or his companions had been wounded. Within seconds he heard their commander shout, "Are you all alive?" They all responded affirmatively and instantly received the order to return fire, scoring a direct hit on the terrorist who had fired the missile at their tank.

Avraham describes in his own words what happened next—an even greater miracle than the first.

There was a cease-fire, and we retreated to a safe position to rest. The commander gave us permission to leave the tank. We had spent 48 hours inside; it was very hot and we were exhausted and shaken by the near miss. However, I decided to remain inside and read the Psalms as I had promised my father.

The psalm for that day was Psalm 30, "I will extol Thee, O LORD, for Thou hast raised me up, and hast not suffered mine enemies to rejoice over me." . . . My fellow crew members remained with me to hear the Scripture reading.

Even though we were hidden inside an olive grove, the Hamas lookouts spotted us. They shot at us with a Sagger guided anti-tank missile and made a precise hit to the rear of our tank.

We emerged from the tank and looked in amazement at the exact spot where we would have stood during our rest period. All of the equipment was totally charred . . . the missile had passed within one meter of the rear of the tank.

Upon returning from war, Avraham told his parents of the miracle he had experienced thanks to the psalms of King David and to the Guardian of Israel sent by God.[6]

God's Special Messenger

I am Gabriel, who stands in the presence of God, and was sent to speak to you and bring you these glad tidings. (Luke 1:19)

Gabriel is the Hebrew name *Gavri'el,* meaning "God is my strong man," and is one of only four angels mentioned by name in the Bible. The first is Lucifer (Isaiah 14:12), the second is Michael (Jude 9), and the last is Abaddon (Revelation 9:11), the fallen angel out of the Abyss.

Gabriel has a higher position than the other "messengers" based on the type of supernatural communications he is ordered to deliver to mankind. He is God's personal emissary.

Gabriel is referenced at least four distinct times in Scripture.

First, he was sent by God (Daniel 8:15–16) to give the prophet Daniel the interpretation of his vision of world events that would lead to the end times (Daniel 8:1–14). Second, Gabriel explained to Daniel the events of the "seventy weeks" concerning Israel and the holy city of Jerusalem (Daniel 9:21–27). Third, the angel Gabriel announced the birth of John the Baptist to Zacharias (Luke 1:11–20). And finally and most importantly, Gabriel carried God's message to Mary as recorded in the first chapter of the Gospel of Luke (1:26–33).

Cherubim

> He drove out the man; and He placed cherubim at the east
> of the garden of Eden. (Genesis 3:24)

Cherubim stood guard at the gate of the Garden of Eden, preventing sinful man from entering (Genesis 3:24). These angels were created with indescribable powers and beauty as portrayed by the prophet Ezekiel in chapter 1. In Israel's ancient temple, cherubim were the golden figures covering the mercy seat above the Ark of the Covenant in the Holy of Holies (Exodus 25:17–22).

King David describes the Lord coming down from the Third Heaven riding a cherub "upon the wings of the wind" (2 Samuel 22:11). King Solomon used the likeness of cherubs to adorn the inner and outer sanctuaries of the temple (1 Kings 6). And in the vision Ezekiel was given, he witnessed the cherubim escorting the glory of the Lord from the temple (Ezekiel 1:4–5; 10:15–20).

Lucifer was a cherub and was the wisest and most beautiful of all God's created beings (Ezekiel 28:14, 16). God placed him in a position of authority over the cherubim surrounding the throne of God. Pride caused his fall from the Third Heaven as fully described in chapter 4 of this book. The angels that did not follow Lucifer and his fallen angels (Matthew 25:41) but remained true to God are all referred to as the "elect angels" (1 Timothy 5:21).

Cherubs are described as having lion-like strength, man-like intelligence, eagle-like speed, and ox-like service (Ezekiel 1:10).[7]

These four symbols also represent the four characteristics of righteous servants of God on earth.

Believers are to possess divine boldness:

The righteous are bold as a lion. (Proverbs 28:1)

The Church of Jesus Christ in the twenty-first century needs to remember this! Live for Christ fearlessly! When the wicked defame you, roar back by "rejoicing and being exceedingly glad"! When you are persecuted, press on! When you are attacked, put on the whole armor of Christ and *fight* back! When you feel like giving up, remember the message of the Lion of Judah: endure!

He who endures to the end shall be saved. (Matthew 24:13)

The second characteristic of the righteous is that of a man:

All men shall fear, and shall declare the work of God; for they shall wisely consider His doing. (Psalm 64:9)

I am a fifth-generation pastor who sat around the dining table as a child listening to my father and his minister friends grieve over the lives of men and women, called of God, who had fallen from grace and had given up their heavenly assignment.

What happened?

They forgot they were fatally flawed humans. They failed to acknowledge that man's wisdom is from God and meant to be used according to His purpose. They tried to walk in their own strength rather than God's. It's His Kingdom . . . His power . . . His glory!

We are servants; He is Savior! We are called, anointed, chosen, equipped, set apart, and given the favor and wisdom of God by our Holy Father.

We are *human*; therefore, we *will* fail! Failure is not a sin; falling down is not a sin; but staying down is missing the mark. Get up! Dust yourself off! Failure is not fatal, but quitting is!

The third characteristic of the righteous is that of an eagle:

Those who wait on the LORD shall renew their strength; they shall mount up with wings like eagles. (Isaiah 40:31)

Eagles effortlessly fly on the adverse winds of the storm. Are you facing the winds of adversity? Soar higher . . . higher . . . higher . . . until you touch the face of God!

The fourth characteristic is that of an ox. Oxen are plodders. They pull the plow at a steady pace from dawn till dusk, day after day, until their task is completed.

Saints of God, the winners in this life are not those full of dash and flash. The winners are those who plod and plow, day after day, until the assignment is completed! After over fifty-seven years of ministry—fifty-seven years of plodding and plowing—I've passed many of the bones of those who thought life was a sprint. It's not. The blue ribbon always goes to those who put their hand to the plow and plod!

I have fought the good fight, I have finished the race, I have kept the faith. (2 Timothy 4:7)

Seraphim

> I saw the LORD sitting on a throne, high and lifted up, and the train of His robe filled the temple. Above it stood seraphim; each one had six wings: with two he covered his face, with two he covered his feet, and with two he flew. (Isaiah 6:1–2)

The word *seraph* comes from the Hebrew root-verb *sarap*, meaning "to burn." Seraphim stand in the direct presence of God. They are seen surrounding the throne of God and exclaiming, "Holy, holy, holy" in Isaiah 6:3. Their assignment is to praise, proclaim, and protect the perfect holiness of God. Anyone who desired access to God had to pass through the fire that these angelic creatures emitted.

An example of seraphim guarding God's holiness is demonstrated in Isaiah:

> And the posts of the door were shaken by the voice of him [seraphim] who cried out, and the house was filled with smoke.
>
> So I [Isaiah] said: "Woe is me, for I am undone! Because I am a man of unclean lips, and I dwell in the midst of a people of unclean lips; for my eyes have seen the King, the LORD of hosts."
>
> Then one of the seraphim flew to me, having in his hand a live coal which he had taken with the tongs from the altar. And he touched my mouth with it, and said: "Behold, this has touched your lips; your iniquity is taken away, and your sin purged." (6:4–7)

The live coal symbolizes the purification from sin by blood sacrifice *and* the fire of the Spirit, which anointed Isaiah's message to men. In essence, the prophet Isaiah experienced his personal day of atonement. Furthermore, this purging was a type and shadow of the ultimate redemptive sacrifice of Christ our Savior at the Cross and the power (fire) in which believers can share His divine Word.

There is a procession of angels in Scripture that are sent forth with special duties. God charges His heavenly agents to guide, protect, defend, and minister, and to serve Him in the final judgments. We will read of their service in the next chapter.

CHAPTER 12

WHERE ANGELS TREAD

Angels delight to be known as the servants of God, heeding the voice of His Word and completing His mandates. They tread where He leads. These "servant messengers" and their divine assignments help us better appreciate the very nature of God.

The following are but a few of the many examples of biblical and contemporary angelic interventions.

PETER'S ESCAPE

The most famous jailbreak in the history of the world was not the escape from Alcatraz but that of the apostle Peter in the book of Acts (12:7–11). Herod was persecuting the Church and had just killed James, the brother of John. This evil ruler then arrested Peter and was determined to have him executed.

Picture Peter chained between two prisoners in a Roman jail as "four squads of four soldiers each" watch over him day and night. Guards stood by his bed and at the cell door. Escape was impossible! Then it happened . . .

And behold, an angel of the Lord suddenly appeared and a light shone in the cell; and he struck Peter's side and woke him up, saying, "Get up quickly." And his chains fell off his hands. And the angel said to him, "Gird yourself and put on your sandals." And he did so. And he said to him, "Wrap your cloak around you and follow me." (Acts 12:7–8 NASB)

This Bible text bears evidence of how little the followers of Christ believed in the power of angels. The angel led Peter to the house where his church members were intensely praying for his supernatural release from prison. He knocked, and a young woman answered. She was shocked to see him and ran to tell these "prayer warriors" that Pastor Peter was at the door.

Their response?

They said unto her, Thou art mad. But she constantly affirmed that it was even so. Then said they, It is his angel. (Acts 12:15 KJV)

The miracles that occur in this brief drama are enough for a six-sermon series centered on God's angel, who delivered and guided this anointed New Testament pastor out of Herod's prison.

THE LIONS' DEN

The story of Daniel and the lions' den is one of history's most celebrated narratives of God's angelic protection of the righteous against all odds. Daniel faithfully served King Darius, but because of the accusations and plots of evil men, the king had no choice but to send Daniel into a den of ravenous lions.

Because of Daniel's faithful testimony of God's power, even King Darius believed that God would protect His man: "Your God whom you constantly serve will Himself deliver you" (Daniel 6:16 NASB).

Daniel 6:22–23 records what took place:

My God sent His angel and shut the lions' mouths, so that they have not hurt me, because I was found innocent before Him; and also, O king, I have done no wrong before you.

Now the king was exceedingly glad for him and commanded that they should take Daniel up out of the den. So Daniel was taken up out of the den, and no injury whatever was found on him because he believed in his God.

Remember this truth: the angels of the Lord will protect you at your greatest time of need, no matter your circumstance.

THE CHARIOTS OF FIRE

The king of Syria sent a great army to surround the city of Dothan to capture the man of God who was sabotaging his war plans (2 Kings 6:12–14). Elisha's servant was terrified, but the prophet prayed that his servant could see what was revealed to him: angels sent by God to protect and deliver them.

Elisha prayed, and said, "LORD, . . . open his eyes that he may see." Then the LORD opened the eyes of the young man, and he saw. And behold, the mountain was full of

horses and chariots of fire [spirit beings] all around Elisha.
(2 Kings 6:17)

I know that some Christians believe God's miracles were reserved for ancient times. I disagree. Just as God's angels delivered
and guided Peter, protected Daniel, and defended Elisha, so is it
with every one of us. Allow me to share a few among the countless
number of modern-day miracles performed by angels sent by God
to protect His own.

THE INVINCIBLE SOLDIER

My mother adopted Psalm 91 as her own. It helped her raise four
boys, guided her as she served in the ministry at my father's side for
fifty-three years, and its divine declarations protected her through
her successful battle with cancer.

Diana and I and our children have taken her legacy and relied
on King David's prayer through many trials, finding it a great comfort in the time of trouble. This psalm has likewise been known
to shield many who have relied on its powerful promises of divine
protection while abiding in the presence of God.

Psalm 91 is often referred to as the "Soldier's Psalm." Though
by no means limited to soldiers, many a combatant has been the
recipient of God's supernatural protection. George Washington was
one such recipient.

During the French and Indian War (1754–1763), the British
army, along with the American colonists and their Indian allies,
fought against the French. In 1755, twenty-three-year-old Colonel
George Washington led a contingent of one hundred Virginia
Buckskins to join forces with British General Edward Braddock,

who had 1,300 troops under his command. Their mission was to drive the French out of western Pennsylvania.

Braddock's soldiers were veterans of European warfare, trained to fight in column formation and on open fields, not in the dense woods like they were encountering in Pennsylvania. When Braddock's army came under fire near the French fort, his men lined up shoulder-to-shoulder along the bottom of the ravine and, not surprisingly, were slaughtered as they marched directly into a waiting ambush.

Of the eighty-six British and Colonial officers involved in the battle, sixty-two were killed or wounded. However, George Washington remained untouched. He was subjected to constant gunfire while riding back and forth along the frontlines: two horses were shot out from under him; he was attacked with bayonets, tomahawks, and arrows, and four bullets ripped through his coat. Yet he was shielded by the angels of Psalm 91.

The word of God's supernatural protection over George Washington swept the colonies. The Reverend Samuel Davis, considered one of the greatest pulpit preachers of his time, suggested that the manner in which God had directly intervened to preserve the colonel indicated "providence has preserved him for some important service to his country."

George Washington did indeed have a special call upon his life. He became the father of America, which was founded on godly principles and unwavering faith in the Bible. The United States of America became a refuge—a "city that is set on a hill" (Matthew 5:14)—for all the oppressed peoples of the world who were in search of life, liberty, and happiness. More than 150 years later, many of the seed of Abraham came to America to escape the horrors of the Holocaust and received refuge until they could reclaim their homeland at the rebirth of Israel in 1948.

Surely the angels of God were the divine protectors of George Washington, whose enemies deemed him the "soldier who could not die."[1]

He shall give His angels charge over you, to keep you in all your ways. In their hands they shall bear you up, lest you dash your foot against a stone. (Psalm 91:11–12)

THE FLAMING SWORDS

Missionary Morris Plotts reported the following miraculous story of angelic protection during the tribal uprisings in East Africa.

A band of roving Mau Mau warriors surrounded the village of Lauri and killed all three hundred inhabitants. Not more than three miles away was the Rift Valley Academy, a private Christian boarding school where children were educated while their missionary parents served the Lord elsewhere in Africa.

Immediately after the carnage at Lauri, the bloodthirsty Mau Mau advanced toward the school with bows, arrows, spears, clubs, and torches, bent on continuing their murderous rampage. News of the utter slaughter in Lauri had already reached the teachers and students, and they were terrified. With no place to hide, they prayed to God, their highest refuge and protection.

As the schoolchildren peered out their windows into the blackness of the night, they could see the blazing torches coming toward them. Soon they were surrounded by a horde of terrorists who cut off all possible avenues of escape.

The Mau Mau's shrieking curses could be heard as they

approached their prey. Their menacing circle tightened, and when they were near enough to throw their razor-sharp spears, they suddenly halted, inexplicably stepped back, and turned away in a terror-driven retreat.

An army that had been dispatched to the school captured the entire band of raiding Mau Mau in the surrounding jungle. Later, while standing before a judge at trial, the Mau Mau leader was called to the witness stand. The judge asked him, "Did you kill the inhabitants of Lauri?"

"Yes" was his reply through an interpreter.

"Was it your intent to do the same to the children of the Rift Valley Academy?"

"Yes," he said unrepentantly.

"Well then," asked the judge, "why did you not complete the mission? Why didn't you attack the school?"

The leader, who had never read the Bible and never heard the gospel, answered, "We were on our way to destroy all the people there. But as we came closer, suddenly between us and the school were many huge men, dressed in glowing white with flaming swords. We became afraid and we ran to hide!"[2]

King David wrote in Psalm 34:7, "The angel of the LORD encamps all around those who fear Him." The word *encamp* means "to constantly encircle."

God's agents are always on duty!

GUARDIAN ANGELS

Several years ago Diana and I decided to take our children on one of my speaking engagements in Washington, DC, so we could show them our nation's capital. We visited the monuments that memorialized Washington, Jefferson, and Lincoln, as well as other historic sites. After a very lengthy visit to the Smithsonian, we made our way to the airport and boarded our flight to Texas. This would be a day we would never forget!

Before I go any further, you should know: Diana is a nervous flier.

Every time there's any form of turbulence, she seizes my forearm with a vise grip. At these times, as the plane begins to bounce through the choppy air, she urges me, "Go ask the pilots if everything is okay." I dutifully pat her hand and confirm that "all is well."

All our children are sky kings with the exception of Sandy, our youngest daughter. She inherited her mother's propensity for the "Nervous Flier Club."

Diana and I were in first class on that trip back from DC, and our children were traveling in coach. Sandy wanted her mother to change seats with her because flying next to Dad made her feel safer. Her mother pulled rank and told Sandy to go back and sit with her calm siblings.

We prayed with Sandy and assured her, "Everything is going to be fine!" She skeptically rolled her big, dark-brown eyes at me and reluctantly walked back to her seat.

The jet engines of the massive aircraft roared as the plane lurched forward with its wheels clicking along the concrete runway. We were airborne and all was running smoothly. Diana released her grip, smiled, and reached for a book.

After a short time I realized something was out of the ordinary, for we were not gaining the proper altitude. I said nothing, hoping we were in a holding pattern for other jets coming in and out of

DC. However, after several minutes, it was obvious something was wrong. Diana read my face like a book; one glance and she was asking, "John, what's wrong?"

I calmly replied, "We are not gaining altitude; I believe we are going in circles!"

"How can you tell?" she asked with concern.

"We have just passed the Washington Monument for the third time," I responded.

Within seconds the pilot's voice came over the intercom: "Ladies and gentlemen, we are experiencing mechanical difficulties. Please stay in your seats and make sure your belts are securely fastened."

Diana's hand was instantly digging into my forearm, and I knew Sandy was on the verge of absolute panic. The atmosphere on the plane was immediately transformed from one of laughter to stone-cold silence. You could hear the snap of seatbelts up and down the aisle.

It was about to get worse . . . much worse!

The pilot came back with new instructions that were less than comforting. "Ladies and gentlemen . . . we are forced to return to Dulles Airport. Tighten your seatbelts and put your heads on your knees as the crew prepares for an emergency landing."

My heart sank. By the actions of the crew, I sensed we were being prepared for an imminent crash.

I didn't put my head down but instead began to pray to the Almighty God; the Creator of heaven and earth; the God who scooped up a handful of dirt, breathed into it, and produced a living soul. I called out to the God who flung the glittering stars into the heavens to sparkle like diamonds against the velvet of the night.

I petitioned the God who is the Commander of every angel in the Third Heaven: "Heavenly Father, send Your angels to escort this plane to a safe landing. Amen!"

Desperate people were sobbing unashamedly, crying, "I don't want to die!" Others sat in the silence of shock, denial, and disbelief.

The plane repeatedly rolled right and left. It was obvious the skilled pilots were using all their training to stabilize the aircraft. As the plane came closer and closer to the runway, I saw fire trucks and ambulances lined up on both sides, their lights flashing and their engines running, prepared for our emergency landing.

As our aircraft neared the ground, the emergency vehicles raced beside us with sirens blaring. Terrified voices continued to fill the plane . . . and then suddenly there was the sweet sound of the wheels screeching on the concrete runway.

We had safely landed.

The plane taxied into the receiving gate to the thunderous applause of the relieved and grateful passengers. You could hear the declarations of "Thank You, God!" and "God bless the pilots!"

Sandy came charging down the aisle while a flight attendant tried to get her to return to her seat, but our daughter prevailed. She threw her arms around my neck and started sobbing. I held her until the terror in her heart subsided.

I prayed as I held my wife and baby girl: "Father God, thank You for sending Your angels to escort this plane to the ground. We are alive and well because Your guardian angels went before us to prepare our way."

The next greatest miracle of the day was getting Sandy on another plane bound for Texas.

ANGELIC ESCORTS

The Bible records: "Precious in the sight of the LORD is the death of His saints" (Psalm 116:15) and "Blessed are the dead who die in the Lord" (Revelation 14:13). When the righteous die, they are escorted from this life into the Third Heaven by angels, who take them to their mansions of splendor created by the Architect of the Ages (John 14:2).

The following are a few illustrations concerning the precious "death of His saints," one of which is very personal to me regarding my father, Bythel Hagee.

My father was the second of eleven children. He survived his premature birth, the flu epidemic of the 1900s, and the Depression of the early 1930s. He was the second son of the second son who became the fourth generation of Hagee men to preach the gospel, serving the Lord as an ordained minister and evangelist for fifty-three years.

My father became ill in his late seventies, and as his final days drew near, my mother and three brothers gathered around his bed for our last prayer with him. I thanked the Lord for my dad's years of faithful service, the thousands of souls who had been saved, the healings and restored marriages that were made possible through his ministry. Then I prayed for the angels of God to come and carry him from his bed of suffering to his home in the Third Heaven. When I finished praying, my father was escorted into glory.

For David, after he had served his own generation by the will of God, fell asleep, was buried with his fathers. (Acts 13:36)

Many years prior to my father's death, a member of his church was about to pass away while the town was enduring a bitter winter ice storm. I was only eight years old at the time, and my dad woke me up to "go sing for Mrs. Moy as she's dying."

As we sang, her ninety-year-old face became radiant. "God's angels have arrived!" she exclaimed. "Two are standing at the foot of my bed! I'm going home!" While we sang, "I will meet you in the morning; just inside the eastern gate," she extended her hand to the visitors we could not see.

It was the first time I was privileged to witness a saint of God being escorted from this earth to her heavenly home.

Missionary journalist Carl Lawrence, in his book *The Church in China*, wrote of a miraculous story involving a seventy-year-old Chinese woman. The godly matriarch was the only person with knowledge of most of the daily operations of her family as well as the activities of an underground house church in her village. She alone knew where the Bibles were, who the messengers were, and who could or could not be trusted.

She died suddenly of a heart attack.

Her family was lost without her. What's more, she'd had no opportunity before her untimely end to share the information that was critical to so many, so the family began to pray for a miracle: "Lord, restore our mother to life with time enough to enlighten us with the information we need to carry on Your work."

Suddenly, after being dead for two days, this woman of God came back to life!

She scolded her family for calling her back from heaven. They let her know that God had answered their prayer and allowed her to return so she could set all matters straight. They also promised her that they would pray that she could return to the Lord within two days.

As promised, exactly two days later, with all their questions answered, the family and friends began to sing hymns and pray that the Lord would take her back to glory. The mother's final words before she returned to heaven were, "They're coming! Two angels are coming."

This miraculous incident caused the entire village to repent.[3]

Be mindful of this: if angels can comfort Hagar in the desert of her days; if they can comfort Elijah by the brook Cherith as he ran from Jezebel; if the angels of God can comfort Jesus Christ in the Garden of Gethsemane . . . angels can surely comfort you *now*!

God still sends His angels to minister to the righteous, empowering them to carry out their divine assignments.

Look up and celebrate, child of God! You are not alone! Rejoice and be exceedingly glad, for God's angels are watching over you! They are God's heavenly army on the battlefront!

ANGELS ON THE BATTLEFRONT

There are two fundamental groups of angels: those who are in obedience to God, and those who are in rebellion against Him. Both participate in spiritual warfare and are assigned specific areas of responsibility by their masters—one faction for good and the other for evil.

Good cannot coexist with evil; subsequently, the angels of God and the angels of Satan are always in direct conflict with each other. These battles are not to be taken lightly—they can determine the future of nations (Esther) and the divine destiny of mankind (Daniel).

When engaged in battle, angels take a stand. The archangel Michael stood against the prince of Persia (Daniel 10:13; 12:1). Paul colorfully described spiritual warfare in Ephesians 6:10–20, instructing believers to stand, stand, and finally, to stand again against the plans of the Devil and over the principalities of darkness.

If you are a committed Christian, then you will encounter warfare; there is no avoiding it. God is not afraid of the battle and we shouldn't be either. We are promised the victory, for the battle is not ours—it belongs to the Lord (1 Samuel 17:47)!

Moses described the Lord as a "man of war" (Exodus 15:3). Joshua conquered the city of Jericho with the help of the "Commander of the Lord's army" (Joshua 5:13–15). King David identified Him: "Who is this King of glory? The Lord strong and mighty, the Lord mighty in battle" (Psalm 24:8). Isaiah was given a vision of the judgment of Babylon and he saw a great army coming against the city.

> The noise of a multitude in the mountains, like that of many people! A tumultuous noise of the kingdoms of nations gathered together! The Lord of hosts musters the army for battle. (Isaiah 13:4)

The Lord is the Commander, and He leads a great army!

In taking up our position during warfare, we affirm the authority that God has committed to us, and we empower Him to release His angels to help us win the battle. Believers make this spiritual stand through the Scriptures, through biblical proclamations, by offering praise, and by worshiping God.

Keep in mind: your greatest weapon in warfare is the Word of

God. Jesus stood His ground and proclaimed this infallible truth when He was battling the Tempter in the desert:

> Then Jesus said to him, "Away with you, Satan! For it is written, 'You shall worship the Lord your God, and Him only you shall serve.'" Then the devil left Him, and behold, angels came and ministered to Him. (Matthew 4:10–11)

King David praised the Lord during and after his time of battle:

> The LORD is my rock and my fortress and my deliverer; my God, my strength, in whom I will trust; my shield and the horn of my salvation, my stronghold. I will call upon the LORD, who is worthy to be praised; so shall I be saved from my enemies. (Psalm 18:2–3)

God hears the cries of those who worship Him, and He will give His angels charge over them: "Now we know that God does not hear sinners; but if anyone is a worshiper of God and does His will, He hears him" (John 9:31).

Wrap your mind around the miraculous promise of protection and victory that the God of Abraham, Isaac, and Jacob has afforded His children. Picture Him on His throne in the Third Heaven, surrounded by multiplied thousands and thousands of angels. He waits for you to call on Him, and He anticipates hearing you proclaim His Word over your situation.

At that very moment He releases His angels, saying, "My people are calling My name. They are declaring My Word over their battle, and they need our help! Go to their aid. Go before them to safeguard their path, walk beside them to comfort them in the fight, and stand behind them to protect them from the arrows of the Evil One! Bring them the victory, angels, for they are Mine and they are made righteous by the blood of My Son!"

The Lord is waiting to move His sovereign hand on your behalf and send His angels in your defense.

> Fear not, for I am with you; be not dismayed, for I am your God. I will strengthen you, yes, I will help you, I will uphold you with My righteous right hand. Behold, all those who were incensed against you shall be ashamed and disgraced; they shall be as nothing, and those who strive with you shall perish. You shall seek them and not find them— those who contended with you. Those who war against you shall be as nothing, as a nonexistent thing. For I, the LORD your God, will hold your right hand, saying to you, "Fear not, I will help you." (Isaiah 41:10–13)

ANGELS IN BIBLE PROPHECY

Angels have been given the highest honor of announcing the birth of Christ (Luke 2:10–11); of witnessing His resurrection (Luke 24:4–7); of escorting Him at His ascension and declaring the Redeemer of mankind's imminent return to earth.

> Men of Galilee, why do you stand gazing up into heaven? This same Jesus, who was taken up from you into heaven, will so come in like manner as you saw Him go into heaven. (Acts 1:11)

When the Son of Man comes in His glory, and all the holy angels with Him, then He will sit on the throne of His glory. (Matthew 25:31)

And it will be the angels' solemn assignment at the command of Almighty God to distinguish the righteous from the sinful.

So it will be at the end of the age. The angels will come forth, separate the wicked from among the just, and cast them into the furnace of fire. There will be wailing and gnashing of teeth. (Matthew 13:49–50)

The book of Revelation records the elect angels' final tasks as assigned by God Almighty: to execute His final judgments on the earth.

THE ANGELS OF REVELATION

In chapter 5 of Revelation the Lion of the tribe of Judah, Jesus Christ, will open the scroll and "loose its seven seals" (v. 5). The first four seals represent the horsemen of the Apocalypse—the white horse of the Antichrist, the red horse of war, the black horse of famine, and the pale horse of death. The fifth represents the martyrs under the altar who were slain for their faith. The sixth seal is the natural and physical calamities marked by a great earthquake, the sun turning black, and the moon becoming like blood. The final seal introduces a time of silence. And then the angels of prophecy will execute their assignments.

Of all the books in the Bible, none illustrate the office, ranks, and assignments of angels more vividly than the book of Revelation. I will briefly share the duties faithfully carried out by God's heavenly hosts.

> And I saw the seven angels who stand before God, and to them were given seven trumpets. (Revelation 8:2)

THE ANGELS AND THE SEVEN TRUMPETS

The first seven angels will blow seven trumpets to announce the first of the seven judgments on the earth during the Great Tribulation.

> The first angel sounded . . . And a third of the trees were burned up, and all green grass was burned up. (Revelation 8:7)

For those of you who believe global warming is coming, you're absolutely right! But this is only the beginning.

> Then the second angel sounded: And something like a great mountain burning with fire was thrown into the sea, and a third of the sea became blood. And a third of the living creatures in the sea died, and a third of the ships were destroyed. (Revelation 8:8–9)

Here is how this could happen. Scientists have warned of the real probability that a massive meteor would in time strike the earth. This colossal impact could send a mega-tsunami racing across the world's oceans, destroying everything in its path while snapping oil rigs like twigs, causing millions upon millions of gallons of oil to gush into the seas.

There was a photo taken of a comparatively infinitesimal oil slick caused by the British Petroleum catastrophe in the Gulf of Mexico a few years ago. The oil made the water appear to be covered with blood. This could happen on a much more epic scale.

When the third angel sounds, a great star will fall from heaven and make one-third of the drinking water of the world so bitter that people will die from it (Revelation 8:10–11). If this isn't bad enough, imagine an angel in heaven crying out and agonizing over the fate of mankind; not for what has already occurred but for what is to come!

> The fourth angel sounded: And a third of the sun was struck, a third of the moon, and a third of the stars, so that a third of them were darkened; and a third of the day did not shine, and likewise the night.
>
> And I looked, and I heard an angel flying through the midst of heaven, saying with aloud voice, "Woe, woe, woe to the inhabitants of the earth, because of the remaining blasts of the trumpet of the three angels who are about to sound!" (Revelation 8:12–13)

The fifth angel will be given the key to the bottomless pit, and out of this pit will come locusts the size of horses that sting like scorpions. They will wound all who do not have the seal of God on their forehead. Unimaginably, the pain from the sting of these massive scorpions will last for five months without relief (Revelation 9:1–12).

The sixth angel sounded, and John the Revelator heard a voice saying, "Release the four angels who are bound at the Great River Euphrates."

So the four angels, who had been prepared for the hour and day and month and year, were released to kill a third of mankind. Now the number of the army of the horsemen was two hundred million; I heard the number of them. And thus I saw the horses in the vision: those who sat on them had breastplates of fiery red, hyacinth blue, and sulfur yellow; and the heads of the horses were like the heads of lions; and out of their mouths came fire, smoke, and brimstone. By these three plagues a third of mankind was killed—by the fire and the smoke and the brimstone which came out of their mouths. (Revelation 9:15–18)

Incredibly, one-third of humanity will be destroyed in one day! Think of it! There are currently more than seven billion people on the earth; one-third would be approximately 2.5 billion people. This staggering figure equates to the total populations of Afghanistan, China, France, Germany, Italy, Japan, Pakistan, Russia, Saudi Arabia, Syria, the United Kingdom, and the United States of America. Yes, *all* their inhabitants *destroyed* in twenty-four hours!

Doesn't seem possible, does it? But with an all-out nuclear war . . . it is *very* possible!

A series of natural disasters such as massive volcanoes exploding beneath the earth, similar to the one recently documented under

Yellowstone National Park, could also contribute to this global destruction.

> Scientists have considered Yellowstone as merely the skin on top of a super volcano; a giant pool of magma sitting just under the Earth's surface.
>
> However, a recent discovery has shown that Yellowstone's magma chamber is 2.5 times larger than previously thought.
>
> It is an underground cavern that measures some 55 miles by 20 miles and runs between 3 and 9 miles below the earth.
>
> If it erupts it will wipe out the North American continent and have enormous impact on the rest of the world.[4]

Yet even after all of these severe judgments, John the Revelator recorded:

> But the rest of mankind, who were not killed by these plagues, did not repent of the works of their hands, that they should not worship demons, and idols of gold, silver, brass, stone, and wood, which can neither see nor hear nor walk. And they did not repent of their murders or their sorceries or their sexual immorality or their thefts. (Revelation 9:20–21)

The seventh angel will announce the magnificent triumph of God over Satan and his Kingdom. This event is not actually fulfilled until later in the book of Revelation (11:15).

THE ANGELS AND THE SEVEN BOWLS
OF JUDGMENTS

John also saw seven angels with seven bowls filled with the seven last plagues that release the wrath of God upon the earth.

The first angel will pour out his bowl upon the earth, and every person who has taken the mark of the Beast will be covered with boils (Revelation 16:1).

The second angel will pour out his bowl, and all the seas will become as the blood of a dead man. Every living thing in the seas and oceans of Planet Earth will die (Revelation 16:3).

The third angel will pour out his bowl upon the rivers and springs (freshwater sources), and they too will become blood (16:4).

People say, "God would never do this!" The truth is, He did exactly that in Egypt during the time of the plagues, when the Nile River was turned to blood and every creature in its waters died (Exodus 7:19)!

The fourth angel will pour out his bowl on the sun, and power is given to him to scorch men with fire (16:8).

Scientists are now concerned with solar flares coming from the sun. If just one of these is released toward the earth, it will become a ball of fire hurtling through space.

In mid-December of 2014 the sun fired off a massive solar flare after days of intense storms from our nearest star. The huge solar flare registered as an X1.8-class event, one of the most powerful types of flares possible.

The flare triggered a strong radio blackout for parts of the world sparking a high-frequency radio blackout over

Australia and the South Pacific. This enormous solar flare capped an active week of sun storms.

X-class solar flares are the strongest the sun can unleash. When aimed directly at Earth, they can disrupt communications and GPS navigation systems, and even pose a threat to satellites and astronauts in space.[5]

The fifth angel will pour out his bowl "on the throne of the beast [the Antichrist]." Men will gnaw their tongues because of their severe pain and sores. What will be their reaction? They will blaspheme the God of the highest heaven and refuse to repent of their deeds (Revelation 16:10–11).

The sixth angel will pour out his bowl on the great river Euphrates so that the kings of the East (China and its allies) can march their army of two hundred million to the battle of Armageddon.

Why is China rapidly becoming a global superpower while America is weakening? Why have we entered a dimension of history where America's friends do not trust us and our enemies do not fear us? Why is America reducing its military might when China and Russia are expanding theirs? The answer is painfully clear! The world as we know it is about to come to an end.

Everything in God's Word is coming into alignment. John the Revelator prophetically recorded the headlines that the world will soon read, "Nations Gather for War at Armageddon."

And they [demon spirits] gathered them [kings of the earth] together to the place called in Hebrew, Armageddon. (Revelation 16:16)

Then it will be over . . .

The seventh angel poured out his bowl into the air, and a loud voice came out of the temple of heaven, from the throne, saying, "It is done!" (Revelation 16:17)

Instantly there will be a global earthquake far greater than anything ever seen before. The islands of the sea will sink into the ocean, and mountains will be reduced to dust. Every city on the face of the earth will be lying in rubble, bridges will crumble, and gas lines will rupture and explode with raging fires sweeping the countryside. People around the globe will be burned and buried alive, and there will be no one left to come to their rescue.

In the Old Testament, the signature of God against sin was stoning; it remains the same in the book of Revelation, for God Himself will cast hailstones from heaven upon any survivors.

Revelation 18:1 records "another angel coming down from heaven" who illuminates the earth with his glory. And later a "mighty angel" rejoices over Babylon's destruction (Revelation 18:21).

Revelation 19:17–18 reports an angel standing in the sun calling for the buzzards of Planet Earth to come and "eat the flesh of kings, the flesh of captains, the flesh of mighty men, the flesh of horses and of those that sit on them, and the flesh of all people, . . . small and great." All who come against Israel in the Battle of Armageddon will be totally destroyed by the two-edged sword that comes out of the mouth of Jesus Christ—the spoken Word of God. The Lord our Commander and the armies of heaven that follow Him will utterly destroy all who lift their hand against His beloved (Revelation 19:15–16).

The next angel of prophecy comes from heaven with the key to the bottomless pit and a great chain in his hand (Revelation 20:1). This angel will arrest the Prince of Darkness, place him in chains, and cast him into the bottomless pit for one thousand years.

The last angel of prophecy is one of the seven who poured out a bowl of God's wrath. This angel reveals to John a glimpse of the New Jerusalem:

> "Come, I will show you the bride, the Lamb's wife." And he carried me away in the Spirit to a great and high mountain, and showed me the great city, the holy Jerusalem, descending out of heaven from God, having the glory of God. (Revelation 21:9–11)

The battle for Jerusalem will be over forever! Presidents, prime ministers, and the queens and kings of earth will stand in line in the streets of Jerusalem to bow before the Nazarene, the carpenter's son. The King of kings and the Lord of lords, the Son of David (Luke 1:32), will sit on the throne of His Father, and of His Kingdom there shall be no end! This fulfills the promise God made to King David three thousand years ago. Hallelujah!

Our supernatural journey has taken us through the First and Second Heavens, and it is now time to explore the final and most indescribable destination of all: the Third Heaven and its wonders.

SECTION THREE

THE THIRD
HEAVEN

CHAPTER 13

THE THRONE ROOM OF GOD

If I find in myself a desire which no experience
in this world can satisfy, the most probable explanation is
that I was meant for another world.[1]

C. S. Lewis

Most people believe in heaven as a place to spend life beyond the grave. It's my opinion that this divine instinct is planted in the human soul by our Creator. However, these same people who believe in heaven have various opinions of what it is.

We have discussed the First Heaven, the heaven we see, and the Second Heaven, where Satan has his throne. We will now take a scriptural journey into the Third Heaven.

Solomon referenced the Third Heaven in his prayer for the dedication of Jerusalem's ancient temple: "Who is able to build Him [the Lord] a temple, since heaven and the heaven of heavens [the Third Heaven] cannot contain Him?" (2 Chronicles 2:6).

Job further confirmed there is a *highest* heaven: "Is not God in the height of heaven?" (Job 22:12). The highest heaven is literally the Third Heaven, which John the Revelator (Revelation 4:1) and the apostle Paul visited. As we previously discussed, Paul established that there are three distinct heavens and that the Third Heaven is also known as Paradise (2 Corinthians 12:2–4).

THE NAMES OF HEAVEN

Paradise

When Jesus was on the Cross, one of the thieves hanging next to Him said, "Remember me when You come into Your kingdom." Jesus responded, "Today you will be with Me in Paradise" (Luke 23:42–43). The "Paradise" Jesus spoke of is the Third Heaven. It is a real place, where God has His throne (Revelation 4:2) and where the righteous go when they pass from this life into eternity.

Remember: Paradise and the Third Heaven are one and the same place! As we take our last breath on earth, we will take our first breath in Paradise. There is no place of waiting for the righteous when they die!

Saint Paul saw himself in Paradise (the Third Heaven):

> He [Paul] was caught *up into Paradise* [Third Heaven] and heard inexpressible words, which it is not lawful for a man to utter. (2 Corinthians 12:4)

John described Paradise as a place of reward.

> To him who overcomes I will give to eat from the tree of life, which is in the midst of the Paradise of God [Third Heaven]. (Revelation 2:7)

The Father's House

Jesus spoke of His Father's home and referred to the "many mansions" that are in the Third Heaven. He also promised to return and take the righteous to live with Him in the place that He has personally prepared for us!

> In My Father's house are many mansions; if it were not so, I would have told you. I go to prepare a place for you. And if I go and prepare a place for you, I will come again and receive you to Myself; that where I am, there you may be also. (John 14:2–4)

A Heavenly Country

> These [Abraham, Isaac, and Jacob] all died in faith . . . were strangers and pilgrims on the earth . . . But now they desire a better, that is, a heavenly country. Therefore God is not ashamed to be called their God, for He has prepared a city for them. (Hebrews 11:13–16)

Knowing that the Lord made the earth on which we live in just six days, with all its breathtaking beauty, can you imagine how glorious our heavenly country must be?

Christians need to stop thinking of heaven as an invisible place where the righteous are floating on fluffy white clouds. Instead, we should imagine the Third Heaven as God sees it. The Architect of the Ages, in the highest heaven, created a spectacular city with beautiful mansions of splendor on streets of purest gold since before the beginning of time!

WHERE IS THE THIRD HEAVEN?

Isaiah gives the clearest answer in all of Scripture on the location of the Third Heaven. The prophet recorded these words from the Lord:

> How are you *fallen from heaven*, O Lucifer, son of the morning! . . . For you have said in your heart: "I will *ascend into heaven*, I will exalt my throne *above the stars* of God; I will also sit on the mount of the congregation on the *farthest sides of the north*." (Isaiah 14:12–13)

The Third Heaven is located upward (Ephesians 4:10); it is above the stars (1 Kings 8:23) and in the most northern part of the universe (Luke 2:14) when pointing from the earth. Job declared, "He [God] stretches out the north over empty space; He hangs the earth on nothing" (26:7). Man cannot even hang a feather on "nothing," yet God effortlessly hurled the brilliant stars into position and the earth in place, all upheld by the power of His Word!

King David, a warrior-statesman, poet, and prophet, also pinpointed the location of the Third Heaven:

> For promotion [lifting up] cometh neither from the east, nor from the west, nor from the south. (Psalm 75:6 KJV)

The law of reasoning dictates that if promotion does not come from three of the four compass points, then it comes from the remaining point, the north. Therefore, if God's throne is in the Third Heaven and His promotion comes from the north, then the location of the Third Heaven is in the north.

I've always wondered why every compass on earth is magnetically attracted to due north. I believe it is because God, who reigns from His throne in the Third Heaven, is directing the way to our eternal home!

THE CHARACTERISTICS OF HEAVEN

A Place of Unimaginable Beauty

When Paul was given a guided tour through the Third Heaven, the man whose descriptive powers exceeded Shelly, Keats, Milton, and Shakespeare simply said:

> Eye has not seen, nor ear heard, nor have entered into the heart of man the things which God has prepared for those who love Him. (1 Corinthians 2:9; reference Isaiah 64:4)

A Place of Brilliant Light

There is no need of a physical sun or moon in the Third Heaven, for the redeemed will walk in the light and glory of the Lamb. John the Revelator described the Third Heaven thusly:

> The city had no need of the sun or of the moon to shine in it, for the glory of God illuminated it. The Lamb is its light. (Revelation 21:23)

A Place of Service

The God who created man and woman and placed them in His perfect Garden to tend it will also be served by the redeemed in the Third Heaven.

Therefore they [the redeemed] are before the throne of God, and serve Him day and night in His temple. And He who sits on the throne will dwell among them. (Revelation 7:15)

A Place of Joy

As we abide in the presence of the Lord, we will find no strife, disappointment, worry, or mourning.

You will show me the path of life; in Your presence [Third Heaven] is fullness of joy; at Your right hand are pleasures forevermore [eternity]. (Psalm 16:11)

The Third Heaven is a place of rejoicing. The apostle John described the angels and elders among thousands singing, "Worthy is the Lamb who was slain to receive power and riches and wisdom, and strength and honor and glory and blessing!" (Revelation 5:12).

The New Testament opens with angels singing over Bethlehem's manger, "Glory to God in the highest" (Luke 2:14), and it ends with the saints of God standing on the sea of glass singing the Song of the Redeemed.

We began with a song, and we end with a song! We are a joyful Church because we are a victorious Church!

WHAT WILL WE SEE IN HEAVEN?

There are so many beautiful treasures stored up in the Third Heaven awaiting the saints of God (Matthew 6:20)!

We know from Scripture that in the Third Heaven we will see rivers and trees producing fruit-yielding good health (Revelation 22:1–3). There will be animals (2 Kings 2:11–12), including the horses that Jesus Christ and the armies of heaven will ride to the final battle of Armageddon (Revelation 19:11–14).

We will see a city (Revelation 21:2) with mansions (John 14:1–3) and twelve gates of pearls, and we will walk the streets of gold (Revelation 21:21). We will hear musical instruments and glorious singing (Revelation 5:8–9). And the redeemed of the Lord will sit at the banquet table prepared for the marriage supper of the Lamb (Revelation 19:7–10).

WHO IS IN THE THIRD HEAVEN?

God the Father is in the Third Heaven sitting on His throne (Revelation 4:2), surrounded by angels singing His praise (7:11). The Third Heaven is His dwelling place.

> Look down from Your holy habitation, from heaven [Third Heaven], and bless Your people. (Deuteronomy 26:15)

The twenty-four elders will be there (Revelation 4:4). We will see Enoch and Elijah as well as those who have died in the faith. Abraham, Isaac, and Jacob, King David, and the prophets *all* will be there. Those who have been washed in the blood of the spotless Lamb will be in the Third Heaven, in their immortal and incorruptible bodies (1 Corinthians 15:42–54), and *Jesus* will be there, for He promised, "Where I am, there you may be also" (John 14:3).

The Third Heaven is an actual place, as real as the country in which you were born. It is even called a "better . . . heavenly country" (Hebrews 11:16). It is above the earth (1 Kings 8:23), and it is where God the Father dwells (Matthew 5:16). Heaven is where

God's throne is located (Matthew 5:34), and the Lord Jesus Christ is there, seated with His Father (1 Peter 3:22; Revelation 3:21), waiting for the arrival of the redeemed.

THE WONDERS OF THE THIRD HEAVEN

For generations, the Hagee family has produced a line of preachers and singers. When I was a child, my mother would play the piano every Saturday night, and like magnets, we were all drawn to the music. My dad would grab his Gibson guitar, my brother would take up his bass fiddle, and I would get my saxophone. We would play and sing until the wood shingles on the roof hummed with joy.

Our singing brought much comfort to our family. World War II had just ended, leaving America reeling at the loss of life and our sense of security. Communism had begun to rear its ugly head, casting the shadow of an atomic cloud over our country's horizon. We'd sing mostly about heaven. Songs like "When We All Get to Heaven," "Heaven's Jubilee," and "How Beautiful Heaven Must Be."

I apologize to God, His holy angels, and to you in advance for falling short of describing the breathtaking beauty and wonders of heaven. There are no earthly words that can help me convey its magnificent splendor.

Saint Paul, the brilliant author of thirteen books of the New Testament, was given a guided tour of the celestial city. And when he put his pen to parchment, he still could not describe what God had prepared for those who love Him. I will attempt, however, to paint a word picture of the majesty of the Third Heaven by portraying a few of its countless wonders.

The Wonder of What Won't Be There

I'm reminded of the story of a young man who longed to enter the military service but didn't want to march. He went to the Marines and asked, "Do you people march?"

"Absolutely, about twenty miles a day!" they answered.

"This is not for me!" he replied.

Then he went to the Army. "Do you march?"

"Every day of the week!" they said.

"Then I don't want this either!" he muttered.

Finally, some smooth-talking Air Force recruiter told him, "Son, all you have to do for us is get in a plane, jump out, and pull the rip cord. When you land on the ground, a truck will be there to carry you back to the base. That's what life in the Air Force is all about."

"That's for me!" the young man said. "I'll sign up!"

The day finally came for his first jump. He got in the plane, his heart pounding as it climbed to the proper altitude. The "jump" light came on, and the sergeant pushed him out the door. Gripped by fear, the new recruit pulled his rip cord. Nothing happened! He frantically pulled his emergency cord. Nothing happened! As he was hurtling through the air, speeding down toward the earth, he screamed, "I'll bet that truck won't be down there either!"

Based on God's Word, there are certain things you won't find in the Third Heaven.

There will be no death, no parting, no sorrow or sickness. Saint John said in Revelation 21:4–5, "And God will wipe away every tear from their eyes; there shall be no more death, nor sorrow, nor crying. There shall be no pain, for the former things have passed away . . . Behold, I make all things new."

The Third Heaven will have no cancer wards, no cardiac intensive care units, no wheelchairs, no crutches, and no twisted limbs. You will not be able to find a blind eye, a deaf ear, or a mind consumed by disease.

The silence of the night will not be shattered by screaming sirens. The Third Heaven is a perfect world.

There will be no separation in heaven.

While on the Isle of Patmos, the exiled John recorded the vision God gave him of the Third Heaven and the end times. In Revelation 21:1 he wrote, "There was no more sea."

What was he describing?

John was considered "an enemy of the state" by Rome. He was removed from his church at Ephesus, where he was pastor. John was apart from everyone he cherished. He was isolated, forsaken, and homesick.

When John beheld the Aegean Sea that surrounded him, he saw a vast body of water keeping him from everything that was precious to him. John was saying that when we get to heaven, we will never be separated from those we love again.

When our loved ones leave this world, we are parted from them for a time and our hearts and spirits are filled with grief and loneliness. However, our Lord Jesus Christ promised that one day soon, the faithful will be gathered together from all directions of the earth into the Third Heaven and will never be separated again.

Then He will send His angels, and gather together His elect from the four winds, from the farthest part of earth to the farthest part of heaven. (Mark 13:27)

Heaven is the one place that has never seen a tear fall from the face of the brokenhearted, for no good-byes are ever spoken there.

In this earthly life we seem to go from one storm to another. Like lightning out of a clear-blue sky, trouble strikes. Dreams are crushed. Hopes are shattered. Lifelong plans are changed instantly and forever. But there is coming a day for the righteous in eternity when there will be no more heartache and no more crying to dim the eyes because the storms of life will be left behind.

Troubles will be replaced by a peace that surpasses all understanding, a peace that will flood our hearts and minds forever and ever. How beautiful heaven must be!

There will be no sin in heaven.

What is sin? James has the answer: "One who knows the right thing to do and does not do it, to him it is sin" (4:17 NASB).

The world we live in is so infested by self-indulgence and humanism that the true meaning of sin is lost. Sin sears mankind's conscience, clouding our ability to distinguish between right and wrong. Secular humanism has taught us to rationalize our sin and call it "a mistake, a social blunder, a weakness." Sin is a cancer that eats away at the soul; we either get the cancer, or the cancer gets us.

So the LORD said to Cain, "Why are you angry? And why has your countenance fallen? If you do well, will you not be accepted? And if you do not do well, sin lies at the door. And its desire is for you, but you should rule over it." (Genesis 4:6)

Some people who watch our ministry program on television will write me and say, "Pastor Hagee, I wish you were more progressive; you need to have a more positive attitude toward sin." All right, I'm going to be absolutely, positively progressive!

I am positive that sin exists (Genesis 4:7). I am positive that if we say we have no sin, we deceive ourselves (1 John 1:8). I am positive that your sins will find you out (Numbers 32:23). I am positive that the wages of sin is death (Roman 6:23). And I am absolutely positive that the soul that sins, without repentance, will surely die (James 5:20).

I recognize that our society wants a feel-good theology that's bright, brotherly, and breezy. "Don't remind us about our sin. Instead, tell us how to feel good without being good. Give us the cotton-candy gospel about how to adjust to our sin rather than confess it. Equip us to be the masters of our own fate!"

I am a Bible-preaching pastor who straightforwardly inspires people with the principles found in God's Word. In the 1930s, *Webster's Dictionary* defined *inspiration* as "the supernatural influence of the Holy Spirit of God on the human mind, by which prophets and apostles and sacred writers were qualified to set forth Divine Truth without any mixture of error."[2] By that definition, the only power that Christians should be imbued with is the power found in the Holy Spirit (Acts 1:8).

We must come back to the Bible! Back to the God of Abraham, Isaac, and Jacob! Back to morality, truth, integrity, and individual responsibility! Back to the work ethic and to holiness, without which no man shall see the Lord!

Know this truth: sin is missing the mark; it ultimately separates man from God.

The Wonder of the Rewards

Jesus specifically spoke to His Church about rewards:

> Rejoice and be exceedingly glad, for great is your reward in heaven [Third Heaven]. (Matthew 5:12)

> Behold, I am coming quickly, and My reward is with Me, to give to every one according to his work. (Revelation 22:12)

A reward is an honor in recognition of service. God Himself will reward His saints with special crowns. People ask, "Pastor, won't we all have the same reward when we get to heaven?" Absolutely not! Your reward in heaven will be directly predicated by your service on earth.

Crown of Glory:

> Shepherd the flock of God which is among you, serving as overseers, not by compulsion but willingly, not for dishonest gain but eagerly; nor as being lords over those entrusted to you, but being examples to the flock; and when the Chief Shepherd appears, you will receive the crown of glory that does not fade away. (1 Peter 5:2–4)

The Lord Jesus Christ is the Chief Shepherd, and every mature believer has the opportunity of being an under-shepherd (anyone who teaches the Word of God in their respective ministries).

The crown of glory is not merely given to those who consider themselves such. Peter clearly stated that how you execute your ministry to the sheep, and the spirit in which you perform it, will determine whether or not you receive this special crown.

> Therefore, my beloved brethren, be steadfast, immovable, always abounding in the work of the Lord, knowing that your labor is not in vain in the Lord. (1 Corinthians 15:58)

Crown of Rejoicing: Jesus spoke of heaven's response to man's salvation:

> Likewise, I say to you, there is joy in the presence of the angels of God over one sinner who repents. (Luke 15:10)

Saint Paul addressed his converts in Philippi with these words: "My beloved and longed-for brethren, my joy and my crown." (Philippians 4:1)

If you have ever led someone to the saving knowledge of Christ, you will experience this type of rejoicing. One day their earthly journey will end and they will stand in absolute perfection in the presence of God! Once they were dead, and now they are alive in eternity forever!

> What is our hope, or joy, or crown of rejoicing? Is it not even *you* in the presence of our Lord Jesus Christ at His coming? For you are our glory and joy. (1 Thessalonians 2:19–20)

Charles Haddon Spurgeon, one of the greatest ministers to walk the path of evangelical history, had this to say about winning the lost to Christ:

> If sinners be damned, then at least let them leap into hell over our dead bodies. And if they perish, let them perish with our arms wrapped about their knees imploring them to stay. If hell must be filled, let it be filled in the teeth of our exertions; and let not one go unwarned and unprayed for![3]

I encourage you, if you have a song to sing, sing it now. If you have a gift to give, give it now. If you have a prayer to pray, pray it now. If you have a soul to win, win it now . . . while you still can!

Those who win the lost to Christ will be rewarded with the crown of rejoicing, which is the soul-winner's crown!

Crown of Righteousness: I teach my congregation that when they study Scripture, they should ask themselves the following questions:

1. Who was the author?
2. To whom was it written?
3. Under what circumstances was it written?
4. What was the purpose of the writing?

While Paul was imprisoned in Rome, he addressed his disciple Timothy with these words:

Finally, there is laid up for me the crown of righteousness, which the Lord, the righteous Judge, will give to me on that Day, and not to me only but also to all who have loved His appearing. (2 Timothy 4:8)

Paul had just stood before Nero, the unrighteous judge, and knew that his execution was near. Paul was telling Timothy that his race was over, that he wanted his work to continue, and that soon he would stand before his *Righteous Judge*, who would reward him with the crown of righteousness.

We are not made righteous by what we do; we are made righteous by what Christ imputed to us at the Cross. Every person who accepts Christ as Savior, who obeys His Word and looks forward to His return, will receive the crown of righteousness. Because of Paul's martyrdom, this crown is also referred to as the martyr's crown.

The Imperishable Crown:

Do you not know that those who run in a race all run, but one receives the prize? Run in such a way that you may obtain it. And everyone who competes for the prize is temperate in all things. Now they do it to obtain a perishable crown, but we for an imperishable [incorruptible] crown. (1 Corinthians 9:24–25)

Paul was instructing the Church that if we expect to gain our reward, we must do all that we do for Christ with the same discipline the world exhibits when they enter into competition for a prize. The believer is to faithfully run the race of life, deny the flesh, and point others to the Redeemer. An earthly prize is a wreath that withers in time, but our heavenly reward will last for eternity.

Crown of Life:

> Blessed is the man who endures temptation; for when he has been approved, he will receive the crown of life which the Lord has promised to those who love Him. (James 1:12)

Those of us who love the Lord will do all that is possible to *please Him*, not because we *fear Him* but because we *love Him*.

This crown will be given to those who go through severe hardship, testing, tribulation, and even death because of their love and devotion to Christ. Christians who are martyred for their faith today, as well as those who have died in the faith throughout history, will be given the crown of life.

> Do not fear any of those things which you are about to suffer. Indeed, the devil is about to throw some of you into prison, that you may be tested, and you will have tribulation ten days. Be faithful until death, and I will give you the crown of life. (Revelation 2:10)

Yes, we are in the battle, but when we have endured and the battle is over, we shall wear the crown! Yes, "many are the afflictions of the righteous, but the Lord delivers him out of them all" (Psalm 34:19).

In the darkest and deepest valley you can sing the sweetest song because the God of the valley is the God of the mountain.

THE WONDER OF HOW FEW PEOPLE
ARE GOING THERE

Years ago Diana and I were driving through the Texas hill country. We were thoroughly enjoying the rolling hills and lush green valleys; the scenery was beautiful. As we rounded a bend in the road, there was the most stunning mansion I had ever seen. I don't know how many millions of dollars it took to build, but it was breathtaking. It looked like the Greek Parthenon.

It had a massive fence surrounding about fifty acres, and it literally looked like Paradise had been dropped into the middle of the countryside. I drove up the driveway and triggered some kind of sensor as we neared the front gate. Suddenly we heard a recorded monotone voice announce, "Get out of the driveway . . . Get out of the driveway . . . Get out of the driveway . . . Get out of the driveway."

I turned to Diana and said, "I don't think they want us here!"

What's my point? Here was a property owner who built a mansion that cost millions of dollars, and he wanted to make sure no one got close to it. But God the Father, the Creator of all things, has invited everyone to join Him in the Third Heaven:

And the Spirit and the bride say, "Come!" And let him who hears say, "Come!" And let him who thirsts come. Whoever desires, let him take the water of life freely. (Revelation 22:17)

Most people want to go to heaven for the same reason they want to go to Florida: the weather is good, and they think most of their relatives are there.

An amazing fact in a recent Pew Poll stated that 92 percent of Americans say, "We believe in heaven." However, based on their other answers to the survey, they're not making preparations to go there!

We sing the song "When We All Get to Heaven." But you need to know: you can sing a lie as well as tell a lie.

Matthew 7:22 says, "Many will say to Me in that day, 'Lord, Lord, have we not prophesied in Your name, cast out demons in Your name, and done many wonders in Your name?'" Jesus' response? "I never knew you: depart from me, ye that work iniquity" (Matthew 7:23 KJV).

All who stand before God in the Great White Throne Judgment will be lost for all eternity.

First Peter 4:18 is a shocking verse.

If the righteous scarcely be saved, where shall the ungodly and the sinner appear? (KJV)

What does this mean? Noah's family and the Flood clearly answer this question.

This one man preached for 120 years without one convert. His divine commission was to build a boat in a society that had never seen rain. The public's response was laughter, mockery, and scorn, and the local media reported, "Noah is feeble-minded. We have never seen rain, yet he actually believes his God is going to judge the earth through a massive flood!"

As the skies threatened, Noah and his family got on board that boat, and God closed the door so that no one could open it. The rains began to fall and the fountains of the deep opened up, gushing water out of the ground. Those who had mocked Noah now ran screaming for the ark. Those who laughed were now trembling in terror. Noah's boat was the only means of salvation.

People pounded and clawed the sides of the huge vessel, screaming Noah's name in terror. As the raging waters rose, the weak drowned in a watery grave while the strong ran to higher ground. When the waters covered even the tops of the mountains, those who were still alive swam until exhaustion sucked them into an eternity without God. Meanwhile, the lone survivors sailed on in the safety of the ark.

There is a twenty-first-century application. As the ark was the only way of rescue, so is Jesus Christ the only way to heaven, for He declares, "No one comes to the Father except through Me" (John 14:6).

You will not be saved by philanthropy. You will not be saved by your good works. You will not be saved by your superior intelligence or your economic or political power. You may be able to move governments with your monetary might or influential associations, but heaven couldn't care less. You can only be saved by the blood of Jesus Christ and the blood of Jesus Christ alone!

The author of Hebrews wrote, "Without the shedding of blood there is no remission [of sin]" (9:22). Noah preached of the judgment to come, and his generation laughed. In our generation, we are surrounded by people who scoff at the gospel of repentance, the gospel of morality and integrity, and the gospel of holiness. In the end, they are mocking God!

My warning is that a day of judgment is coming. A day will come very soon when the wrath of the Lamb of God will be poured out on the earth. John the Revelator said the mighty men and the captains of war, the rich and the powerful, will run to the rocks in the mountains and say, "Fall on us and hide us from the face of Him who sits on the throne and from the wrath of the Lamb!" (Revelation 6:16).

Just as the people in Noah's time pounded the sides of the ark, so will those who are left behind pound the doors of a church house in terror, crying out for mercy as they recognize that Jesus Christ has come and gone and the Antichrist is on his way. By that time there will be only two options: take the mark of the Beast, or be executed by those who believe the Antichrist is their messiah (Revelation 13:16).

We will all answer to God someday. With the eyes you are using to read this book, you'll see Him face-to-face, either as Savior and Lord or as your Righteous Judge. Your eternal home is your choice. Choose wisely and choose now!

THE WONDER OF ETERNAL REST

God set the example of rest in the Bible when He finished His work of creation. He mandated that humans do the same; six days we labor, and one day we rest from our physical work and devote our time to God (Genesis 2:2–3). The biblical context of "rest" is both a release of and a reward for man's work.

Scripture presents examples of physical rest (Exodus 23:12), social rest (1 Kings 5:4), and spiritual rest (Matthew 11:28).

Ahhh, rest. We long for it, but our lives here on earth are dominated by calendars, clocks, and computers. Phones and twenty-four-hour newsfeeds guarantee there is no rest. If I wake up in eternity and hear a phone ring, I'll know I died and went to hell!

The Third Heaven, however, is a place of perfect, eternal rest, and the saints who die in the Lord will receive their reward for their good deeds.

"Blessed are the dead who die in the Lord from now on."

"Yes," says the Spirit, "that they may rest from their labors, and their works follow them." (Revelation 14:13)

When we've been in the Third Heaven for "ten thousand years, bright shining as the sun, we've no less days to sing God's praise than when we first begun."[4]

How long is eternity? Let me describe it for you very simply. If a sparrow could carry a handkerchief one time every ten thousand years over Mount Whitney, should the sparrow not die and the handkerchief not wear out, then when that fourteen thousand feet of granite rock is worn smooth with the sands of the ages, the first second of eternity will not have begun.[5]

Be aware: the righteous will experience eternal rest in the wonders of the Third Heaven, and the lost will spend eternity in the torments of the Lake of Fire.

He who believes in the Son has everlasting life; and he who does not believe the Son shall not see life, but the wrath of God abides on him. (John 3:36)

A PLACE PREPARED

I have attempted to portray a few of the wonders of the celestial city, though there are an infinite number yet to be discussed. But the question is, are you ready for heaven?

We will all leave this world one day and walk into eternity;

what then? Will you open your eyes in the majesty of the Third Heaven and be with your heavenly Father, or will you be lost forever in outer darkness without God?

Jesus Christ has prepared a place for every born-again believer, and it is located in the Third Heaven. The Lord has assured us that heaven is where He and the Father are, and He has even given us directions on how to get there:

I am the way, the truth, and the life. No one comes to the Father except through Me. (John 14:6)

CHAPTER 14

YOUR ETERNAL HOME

I feel within me that future life. I am like a forest that has been
razed; the new shoots are stronger and brighter. I shall most
certainly rise toward the heavens . . . the nearer my approach
to the end, the plainer is the sound of immortal symphonies of
worlds which invite me. For half a century I have been translating
my thoughts into prose and verse: history, philosophy, drama,
romance, tradition, satire, ode, and song; all of these I have tried.
But I feel I haven't given utterance to the thousandth part of what
lies with me. When I go to the grave I can say, as others have said,
"My day's work is done." But I cannot say, "My life is done."
My work will recommence the next morning. The tomb is not
a blind alley; it is a thoroughfare. It closes upon the twilight
but opens upon the dawn.[1]

Victor Hugo

Death is a rendezvous, a universal appointment. It is the
parting of the spirit—from the body and the ultimate
path to eternity.

Man has diverse opinions on this topic of death and the afterlife.

Derek Prince was nearly ninety years of age when he wrote the book *The End of Life's Journey*. (Derek Prince Ministries continues to publish this scholar's profound, archived teachings even years after his passing.) In it, he discussed some of humanity's views toward death.

There is the cynical perspective. This mocking view espouses that since man can do nothing to avoid death, why not do all you can to enjoy the journey toward it? This attitude is reflected in Isaiah 22:13: "Let us eat and drink, for tomorrow we die!"

Pessimism is another attitude toward death. This perspective approaches the end of life with fear, and often leads to deep depression. King David personally experienced the effect of this belief:

My heart is severely pained within me, and the terrors of death have fallen upon me. (Psalm 55:4)

Another is the morbid preoccupation with death. Notice the titles and subject matter of popular films, television series, and bestselling books, and it is apparent that our culture is engrossed in a dark obsession with death. King Solomon referred to this fascination in Proverbs 24:11: "Deliver those who are drawn toward death."

Then there is the escapist view, found in many mystical and cult philosophies, that plunges man from the responsibility of this life to a vague "nirvana-like" existence in the next life.[2]

God's Word clearly speaks of the certainty of death and the reality of eternity. The most important fact about these two experiences centers on Christ's death and resurrection. As soon as He died and rose again, death merely became the believer's doorway to Paradise. Christ forever abolished death as a sentence of condemnation and instead made it a promotion (Philippians 1:21). Death was the first visible consequence of sin, and it is the last effect of sin from which we can be saved.[3]

There are two paths that a person can take after death: one is for those who have received Christ as Savior and Lord, and the other is for those who have rejected Him.

> If it seems evil to you to serve the LORD, choose for your-
> selves this day whom you will serve, whether the gods
> which your fathers served that were on the other side of
> the River, or the gods of the Amorites, in whose land you
> dwell. But as for me and my house, we will serve the LORD.
> (Joshua 24:15)

TWO PATHS TO ETERNITY

Charles Haddon Spurgeon described the profound difference between the experience of death for the redeemed and for the lost:

> Death comes to the ungodly man as a penal infliction, but
> to the righteous as a summons to his Father's palace. To the
> sinner it is an execution, to the saint an undressing from
> his sins and infirmities. Death to the wicked is the King of
> terrors. Death to the saint is the end of terrors, the com-
> mencement of glory.[4]

The "commencement of glory" is eternity. *Webster's* measures eternity as a "time without an end; an endless life after death." We will all die, and we will all enter our eternal home; the issue is, *which one?*

Our journey has taken us through the Three Heavens, where I made a fleeting attempt to describe the Third Heaven. I feel it is only fair to also describe the place called hell and another place known as the Lake of Fire as portrayed in the Word of God.

THE PLACE CALLED HELL

Hell is a real place; in fact, I know many people who spend much of their time telling other people how to get there!

The best example of hell in the New Testament is the story Christ told of a man named Lazarus.

Now there was a rich man, and he habitually dressed in purple and fine linen, joyously living in splendor every day. And a poor man named Lazarus was laid at his gate, covered with sores, and longing to be fed with the crumbs which were falling from the rich man's table; besides, even the dogs were coming and licking his sores. Now the poor man died and was carried away by the angels to Abraham's bosom; and the rich man also died and was buried. In Hades he lifted up his eyes, being in torment, and saw Abraham far away and Lazarus in his bosom. And he cried out and said, "Father Abraham, have mercy on me, and send Lazarus so that he may dip the tip of his finger in water and cool off my tongue, for I am in agony in this flame." But Abraham said, "Child, remember that during your life you received your good things, and likewise Lazarus bad things; but now he is being comforted here, and you are in agony. And besides all this, between us and you there is a great chasm fixed, so that those who wish to come over from here to you will not be able, and that none may cross over from there to us." (Luke 16:19–26 NASB)

Through His teaching, Jesus identified Hades (hell) as a place of torment and agony; a place of recognition (the rich man recognized Abraham); a place of remorse and consciousness (the rich man cried out for mercy from the misery he was in); a place of flames; and a place of ultimate separation from which there is no possibility of reunion with the righteous.

The agony of the rich man cried out in hopelessness, which is the heartrending destiny of all who will spend eternity in hell.

When a wicked man dies, his expectation will perish, and the hope of the strong man perishes. (Proverbs 11:7)

Death is a physical condition that claims man's body; Hades is an actual place that claims man's soul.

THE LAKE OF FIRE

Hell and the Lake of Fire are two different places. The Lake of Fire is named four times in Scripture, and only within the book of Revelation (19:20; 20:10, 14–15). It is the place of eternal punishment for the devil, his fallen angels, the Antichrist, the false prophet, and all who have rejected Jesus Christ on this earth. The Gospel of Matthew refers to it in this way:

Then He will also say to those on the left hand, "Depart from Me, you cursed, into the everlasting fire prepared for the devil and his angels." (25:41)

The Lake of Fire is described as a place of eternal "fire and brimstone" (Revelation 20:10). Those who are sentenced there will experience relentless, horrifying misery and excruciating torment forever and ever and ever and ever.

All who have rejected Christ will be temporarily sentenced to hell until they are condemned to the Lake of Fire for eternity following their day of reckoning at the Great White Throne Judgment. Of that throne, Spurgeon remarked, "[It] is said to be white. What other throne can be so described? The thrones of mere mortals are often stained with injustice, or bespattered with the blood of cruel wars; but Christ's throne is white, for He doeth justice and righteousness, and His name is truth."[5]

Only those who have received Christ as Savior and Lord will escape both hell and the Lake of Fire, because they have been redeemed through the power of His blood. Their names are written in the Book of Life at the very moment they accept the Lamb of God's sacrifice for their sins.

Upon their death, this divine record will allow them immediate entry into the Third Heaven and into the presence of God the Father, Christ His Son, His Holy Spirit, the elect angels, and the redeemed Church of Jesus Christ.

It has been said that you may have missed every appointment you ever made, but there are two that you will keep: the first is death, and the second is the judgment. People often get confused about the "judgments" described in Scripture, so allow me to simplify them.

The judgment of *believers* takes place at the Judgment Seat of Christ (2 Corinthians 5:10), and it occurs before Christ's millennial Kingdom. The judgment for *unbelievers* takes place at the Great

White Throne and happens at the close of the millennial Kingdom.

Noted Baptist theologian and scholar Clarence Larkin (1850–1924) described death, hell, and the Lake of Fire:

> In this Judgment [at the Great White Throne] "Death" and "Hell" are personified. By "Death" we are to understand the "Grave" which holds the "body" until the Resurrection; by "Hell," the Compartment of the "Underworld" or "HADES," where the "souls" of the Wicked Dead remain until the Resurrection of the Wicked. That both "Death" and "Hell" are cast into the "LAKE OF FIRE" signifies that Death and Sin will not be found on the New Earth.[6]

John vividly described what happens at the Great White Throne Judgment:

> Then I saw a great white throne and Him who sat on it, from whose face the earth and the heaven fled away. And there was found no place for them. And I saw the dead, small and great, standing before God, and books were opened. And another book was opened, which is the Book of Life. And the dead were judged according to their works, by the things which were written in the books. The sea gave up the dead who were in it, and Death and Hades delivered up the dead who were in them. And they were judged, each one according to his works. Then Death and Hades were cast into the lake of fire. This is the second death. And anyone not found written in the Book of Life was cast into the lake of fire. (Revelation 20:11–15)

Derek Prince called Satan the "life-taker" and Christ the "Life-giver." It's that simple! Satan kills; he murders and he lies. Accept him and his Kingdom of Darkness and you will receive a sentence of eternal damnation from the Righteous Judge. Or . . . you can choose to accept God's offer of salvation through repentance and faith in Jesus Christ, live a life in accordance with His Word, joyfully anticipate His return, and receive everlasting life.

Judgment for the believer does not result in condemnation.

[Jesus said,] "Most assuredly, I say to you, he who hears My word and believes in Him who sent Me has everlasting life, and shall not come into judgment, but has passed from death into life." (John 5:24)

There is therefore now no condemnation to those who are in Christ Jesus, who do not walk according to the flesh, but according to the Spirit. (Romans 8:1)

The life of a Christian from its beginning is in Christ alone; not any portion of it is sourced from one's self. The continuation of that life is equally the same: Jesus is not only the resurrection *to begin with* but the life *to go on with*.[7]

FOUR BLOOD MOONS

In my book *Four Blood Moons: Something Is About to Change*, I describe in great detail the supernatural connection of celestial events to biblical prophecy—the future of God's chosen people and that of the nations of the world.

The book centers on three Tetrads (four consecutive Blood

Moons as identified by NASA) that have appeared in the past five hundred years of recorded history. Each of the three has coincided with historical events concerning the Jewish people and the Feasts of the Lord according to the Hebrew calendar:

- 1492: The discovery of America (which provided a haven for the Jewish people escaping the persecution of The Inquisition)
- 1948: The rebirth of the nation of Israel
- 1967: The reunification of the city of Jerusalem with the Jewish people

Four Blood Moons was published in the late summer of 2013, and in April 2014, the last Tetrad in this century began during the Feast of Passover. The final Blood Moon of the Tetrad will happen in September of this year, 2015.

It is interesting to note some of the world headlines concerning Israel and the Jewish people since the appearance of the first Blood Moon on April 15, 2014.

- June 23, 2014: "Iraq Invaders Threaten Nuke Attack On Israel: ISIS focuses on destroying 'Zionist regime' to 'liberate Palestine'"[8]
- July 24, 2014: "Iran Supreme Leader: The Only Solution for Crisis Is Israel's Destruction"[9]
- August 26, 2014: "Iranian General Threatens Surprise Attack on Israel"[10]
- October 17, 2014: "Iran Arms Palestinians for New War with Israel"[11]

The second Blood Moon took place on October 8, 2014, during the Feast of Tabernacles.

- November 10, 2014: "Ayatollah Publishes Plan to 'Eliminate' Israel"[12]
- December 10, 2014: "Iran Launches 'We Love Fighting Israel' Campaign on Social Media"[13]
- January 12, 2015: "Four Jewish Hostages Killed in Paris Grocery Store Attack"[14]
- February 1, 2015: "Hostage's Apparent Beheading by ISIS Stirs Outrage in Japan"[15]
- February 3, 2015: "Jordan Pilot Hostage Moaz al-Kasasbeh 'Burned Alive'"[16]

This book, *The Three Heavens*, was completed in early February 2015. The third Blood Moon will occur on April 4, 2015, at Passover. The fourth and final Blood Moon in this century that will coincide with the Jewish Feasts will appear on September 28, 2015, during the Feast of Tabernacles.

To say that the past several months have been historically significant is an understatement. Israel succeeded in protecting her people in the war against Hamas in Gaza, even though Hamas was funded and equipped by Iran. However, the Israeli Defense Force has warned that Hezbollah will try to take territory inside Israel as well as damage strategic facilities within the country by firing more than a thousand rockets per day.

America's withdrawal from Iraq has spawned the most vicious and radical terrorist organization in the history of the world, ISIS (the Islamic State of Iraq and Syria). Christians are being crucified, journalists are being decapitated, and innocent children are being murdered for their confession of faith in Jesus Christ.

Russia has invaded the Ukraine, and a renewed anti-Semitism has exploded in America and Europe. Our administration is releasing known radical terrorists from prison as well as allowing thousands of undocumented aliens to enter our country; we have become a nation without borders.

The world has changed as we know it, but the one thing that has never changed is the character and faithfulness of God and the majesty of His creation.

> The sun shall be turned into darkness, and the moon into blood, before the coming of the great and awesome day of the LORD. (Joel 2:31)

> There will be signs in the sun, in the moon, and in the stars; and on the earth distress of nations, with perplexity, the sea and the waves roaring; men's hearts failing them from fear and the expectation of those things which are coming on the earth, for the powers of the heavens will be shaken. Then they will see the Son of Man coming in a cloud with power and great glory. Now when these things begin to happen, look up and lift up your heads, because your redemption draws near. (Luke 21:25–28)

WE SHALL SEE HIM

Beloved, now we are children of God; and it has not yet been revealed what we shall be, but we know that when

He is revealed, we shall be like Him, for we shall see Him
[Jesus] as He is. (1 John 3:2)

How do you see Jesus? Mary first saw Jesus as a baby in Bethlehem's manger. John the Baptist initially saw Him as a candidate for baptism in the river Jordan. The disciples saw Him as a rabbi and master teacher. Rome saw Him as an insurrectionist too dangerous to live. The citizens of Jerusalem saw Him hanging from Calvary as a common thief. The recognized religious leaders saw Him as a drunkard, a heretic, and a liar.

But when the redeemed get to heaven, "we shall see Him as He is"—as the Lord of glory, high and lifted up, full of grace and truth. As the Alpha and the Omega, the First and the Last! We shall see Him as the Lamb of God, the Light of the world, the Lord of glory, the Lion of Judah!

We shall see Him as the fairest of ten thousand, the Bright and Morning Star! We shall see Him as heaven's hope and hell's dread! We shall see Him as the Great I AM, and the Great Shepherd, and the Great Physician! We shall see Him as our Rock, our Shield, our Buckler, our Redeemer, the Horn of our salvation, and our Righteous Judge!

My purpose in writing this book is to whet your appetite for the Third Heaven. Many of you are not ready to stand before God in the judgment and be numbered among the righteous, as sons and daughters of the Father's royal family. You think about heaven; you talk about heaven; you sing about heaven . . . but are you going there?

There's a story about a prince who longed for a bride who would love him for who he was and not for what he had, so he went out into the world disguised as a commoner. Soon he found a job with a farmer. He fell deeply in love with the man's daughter and asked his permission to marry her.

"Absolutely not!" the father said. "My daughter deserves better than you; you're nothing but a commoner!"

The couple ran away and got married anyway, and decided to go to the royal city on their honeymoon. The prince's father knew they were coming and prepared a proper reception. The king's carriage met them at the city gates, and thousands of citizens lined the streets, applauding their celebratory procession. The royal guards surrounded them; the king's musicians played for them. It was a magnificent event.

In seeing all of this, the bride asked, "What does this mean?"

The prince answered, "I am the king's son. You married me in obscurity; you loved me as a common man. Now all the wealth and the honors and power of the kingdom are yours. You are a member of the royal family!"

The application is this: Jesus Christ is the crowned Prince of the Third Heaven. He came to this earth in obscurity as a common man, born in a manger as the son of a carpenter. He came to take for Himself a bride called the Church.

When you confess Jesus Christ as Savior and Lord, you receive the gift of eternal life and join the royal family alongside Him. The Lord gives you a mansion in the suburbs of heaven just because you are His and He is yours. You become an heir and joint-heir with Jesus Christ!

I ask, are you a member of the royal family? If the answer is no, you can be . . . and God wants you to be. He knows all your faults and failures and yet He loves you unconditionally. God's greatest gift to all of us is eternal life through Jesus Christ, His Son.

You might ask, "What must I do to be saved?" All any of us need to do is receive Him as our Savior and Lord. I have, and I encourage you to do the same.

We all have a date with death *someday*, and we will all spend eternity *somewhere*. If you were to die within the next sixty seconds and open your eyes in eternity, where would you be? If you are not absolutely certain, I ask that you pray the following prayer and allow the angels of heaven to record your name in the Lamb's Book of Life:

> Heavenly Father, I come to Your throne in the name of Jesus Christ. I ask You to forgive me of my sins and come into my life as Savior and Lord. I confess that "the wages of sin is death, but the gift of God is eternal life." I now receive Your gift of everlasting life as I become a part of Your royal family. Amen.

Do you hear what I hear? It's the sound of angels rejoicing in heaven because you have made the wisest decision a mortal can make.

> Likewise, I say to you, there is joy in the presence of the angels of God over one sinner who repents. (Luke 15:10)

Welcome to the family of God! Your name has been written in

the Lamb's Book of Life, and a mansion has been reserved for you in the Third Heaven! I look forward to seeing you around the throne of God as we sing the Song of the Redeemed forever and ever.

ACKNOWLEDGMENTS

With grateful appreciation to my wife, Diana; my executive assistant, Jo-Ann; my typist, Melissa; editor Kris Bearss; and the fabulous staff at Worthy Publishing.

NOTES

Chapter 1: "Mommy, God Is Alive"

1. Told with the permission of David and Sherry Kreye via personal correspondence with the author, January and February 2015.
2. North Central Baptist Hospital video, *Mission Moment: The Jackson Kreye Story* (2008); https://docs.google.com/file/d/0ByeoS4kB6d21UjBPV2hYXzV3d0E/ edit?pli=1, accessed March 3, 2015.
3. Told with the permission of Sam Zuckerman, MD, via personal correspondence with the author, January 2015.

Chapter 2: The Heaven We See

1. "How Great Thou Art" © 1949 and 1953 by the Stuart Hine Trust. USA print rights administered by Hope Publishing Company.
2. J. Vernon McGee, "Tower of Babel," chap. 11 in *Thru the Bible*, vol. 1 (Nashville: Thomas Nelson, 1983), 52–53.
3. J. Vernon McGee, *Thru the Bible*, vol. 4 (Nashville: Thomas Nelson, 1983), 14.
4. Charles Q. Choi, "Earth's Sun: Facts about the Sun's Age, Size, and History," Space. com, November 20, 2014.
5. Ibid.
6. Traci Watson, "NASA Confirms 715 Planets outside Solar System," *USA Today*, February 27, 2014.
7. John Hagee, *Four Blood Moons: Something Is About to Change* (Nashville: Worthy, 2013), 224–225.

Chapter 3: Journeys into the Supernatural

1. Derek Prince, *The End of Life's Journey: Sharing Christ's Victory over Death* (Charlotte, NC: Derek Prince Ministries International, 2004), 114.
2. Mrs. A. S. Bridgewater, "How Beautiful Heaven Must Be," 1920. Public domain.
3. Told by permission of the attending doctor, who has asked to remain anonymous, via personal correspondence, February 2015.
4. Johnny Cash, *Man in Black: His Own Story in His Own Words* (Grand Rapids, MI: Zondervan, 1975), 177.
5. Multiple sources: Mary C. Neal, *To Heaven and Back: A Doctor's Extraordinary Account of Her Death, Heaven, Angels, and Life Again* (Colorado Springs: WaterBrook Press, 2012); Mark Galli, "Mary Neal Describes Her Visit to the Gates of Heaven," *Christianity Today*, December 6, 2012, ChristianityToday.com; Mary C. Neal, MD, "A Sneak Peek of Heaven," *Guideposts*, June 4, 2012, guideposts.org.

Chapter 4: The Midst of Heaven

1. Derek Prince, *War in Heaven: God's Epic Battle with Evil* (Grand Rapids, MI: Chosen Books, 2003), 61–62.
2. C. S. Lewis, *Mere Christianity* (New York: McMillan, 1952), 121.
3. Charles H. Spurgeon, "Evening – June 3," in *Morning and Evening: Daily Readings*, vol. 1 (Charleston, SC: BiblioBazaar, 2008), 362–363.
4. Myer Pearlman, *Knowing the Doctrines of the Bible* (Springfield, MO: Gospel Publishing House, 1937), 87.

Chapter 5: The Clash of Two Kingdoms

1. Finis Jennings Dake, *God's Plan for Man* (Lawrenceville, GA: Dake Bible Sales, 1949), 559.
2. Pearlman, *Knowing the Doctrines*, 79.
3. J. Vernon McGee, *Thru the Bible*, vol. 1 (Nashville: Thomas Nelson, 1983), 13.
4. Colin S. Smith, *Unlocking the Bible Story*, vol. 1 (Chicago: Moody, 2002), 27.
5. Ibid., 32–34 (adapted).
6. Finis Jennings Dake, *Dake Annotated Reference Bible* (Atlanta: Dake Bible Sales, 1963), 4.
7. Ibid., 94.
8. Watchman Nee, *Ye Search the Scriptures* (New York: Christian Fellowship, 1974), 149–56.
9. Martin Blumenson, "Rommel," in *Hitler's Generals*, ed. Correlli Barnett (New York: Grove Press, 2003), 293–316.
10. John C. Hagee, *Invasion of Demons* (Old Tappan, NJ: Fleming H. Revell, 1973), 108.
11. Definition and usage of the terms *devil* and *demons*: Dake, *Dake Annotated Reference Bible* (Atlanta: Dake Bible Sales, 1963), 632; Derek Prince, *They Shall Expel Demons* (Grand Rapids, MI: Chosen Books, 1998), 93–94.

Chapter 6: Invasion of Demons in Society

1. Jim Daly, "Are Cartoons Bad for Children?," *Daly Focus* (blog), Focus on the Family, September 14, 2011.
2. Marian T. Horvat, PhD, "Secret Spells Barbie and the Tendencial Revolution," Tradition in Action, November 21, 2003.
3. Hephzibah Anderson, "Obama's 'Dreams,' Meyer's Vampires Capture 'Nibbie' Book Awards," Bloomberg.com, April 3, 2009.
4. Lev Grossman, "It's Twilight in America: The Vampire Saga," *Time*, November 13, 2009.
5. Suzanne Collins, *The Hunger Games* (New York: Scholastic Press, 2008).
6. Mike Rose, "*The Walking Dead* sells 28M episodes, third season on the way," Gamasutra, July 28, 2014.
7. Eddie Makuch, "*Grand Theft Auto* Series Sales Climb to 185 Million Units—How Many

Do You Own?: GTA V Alone Has Shipped 32.5 Million Copies," GameSpot.com, May 27, 2014.

8. Rebecca Leung and Ed Bradley, "Can A Video Game Lead to Murder?: Did *Grand Theft Auto* Cause One Teenager to Kill?," *60 Minutes*, CBS, March 4, 2005.

9. Ibid.

10. Ibid.

11. Ibid.

12. Dana Beyerle, "Conviction Upheld in '03 Fayette Slayings: Video Game Defense Used in Officers' Slayings Spurred National Debate," *Tuscaloosa News*, February 18, 2012.

13. Robert DeWitt, "Judge stands by Fayette decision," *Tuscaloosa News,* 2005-11-22. Jay Reeves, "Court rejects appeal in Alabama suit blaming game for slayings," Associated Press, March 29, 2006.

14. "Arizona Man Sang Eminem Songs While Stabbing Family; Thought Wife Was a Demon, Police Say," Fox News, June 22, 2009. Michael Miller, Arizona Man, Sang Eminem While Stabbing Family: Police," *Huffington Post*, July 23, 2009, updated May 25, 2011. Dustin Gardiner, "Glendale Man Admits to Stabbing Wife, Daughter to Death," AZCentral.com, October 10, 2009. Dustin Gardiner, "Glendale Man Gets Life Term for Murdering Wife, Daughter," AZCentral.com, December 10, 2009.

15. Ice-T and Douglas Century, "Freedom of Speech," part 4 in *Ice: A Memoir of Gangster Life and Redemption—From South Central to Hollywood* (New York: Random House, 2011), 127–140.

16. Jon Pareles, "POP VIEW; Dissing the Rappers Is Fodder for the Sound Bite," *New York Times*, June 28, 1992.

17. "Memory Training from US Military," Improve Memory by Ron White (website), February 13, 2011.

18. "Number of TV Households in the United States from Season 2000–2001 to Season 2014–2015," The Statistics Portal, Statista (website).

19. "Television Watching Statistics," BLS American Time Use Survey, A.C. Nielsen Co., on Statistic Brain (website), verified December 7, 2013.

20. "About the Series," *Dexter*, Showtime website.

21. "*Dexter* (2006–2013): Awards," IMDb.com.

22. James Hibberd, "*Dexter* Finale Is Showtime's Most-Watched Episode of Anything Ever," *Entertainment Weekly*, September 23, 2013.

23. Jessica Best, "Teen Obsessed with TV Serial Killer Dexter Jailed for Murdering and Dismembering Girlfriend," *Mirror*, October 2, 2014.

24. Ibid.

25. Ibid.

26. Ibid.

27. Roger Ebert, review of *The Omen*, by David Seltzer, directed by Richard Donner, Twentieth Century Fox, RogerEbert.com, June 28, 1976.

28. Ebert, review of *The Omen*.

Chapter 7: Invasion of Demons in the Church

1. Winston Churchill, "Blood, Toil, Tears and Sweat" (first speech as Prime Minister, House of Commons, May 13, 1940).
2. Fictitious name.
3. Voodoo is an occultic practice characterized by sorcery and spirit possession.
4. John Hagee, *Invasion of Demons* (Ada MI: Revell, 1973), 26–32.
5. Wright Barton and Evelyn Roat, *This is a Hopi Kachina* (Flagstaff, AZ: Museum of Northern Arizona, 1965), 4.
6. Wright Barton, "Hopi Kachinas: A Life Force," chap. 4 in *Hopi Nation: Essays on Indigenous Art, Culture, History, and Law*, ed. Edna Glenn, John R. Wunder, Willard Hughes Rollings, and C. L. Martin (Lincoln, NE: University of Nebraska Digital Commons, 2008).
7. Dennis Gaffney, "Collecting Kachina Dolls," Tips of the Trade, *Antiques Roadshow*, PBS, March 1, 2004.
8. They are made from cottonwood, which typically burns very quickly.
9. Told with the permission of this couple, who choose to remain anonymous, via personal correspondence with the author, February 2015.

Chapter 8: The Evolution of Evil

1. Linda Rodriguez McRobbie, "The Strange and Mysterious History of the Ouija Board," Smithsonian.com, October 27, 2013.
2. Brent Lang, "Box Office: 'Nightcrawler,' 'Ouija' Tied for First in Deadly Halloween Weekend," Variety.com, November 2, 2014.
3. "*Ouija*," Storyline, IMDb.com.
4. Sophie Jane Evans, "Three American Friends Hospitalised after Becoming 'Possessed' Following Ouija Board Game in Mexican Village," DailyMail.com, June 23, 2014.
5. Ibid.
6. Ibid.
7. Ibid.
8. *Dake Annotated*, 330
9. "Top 10 TV Shows 2013," Rotten Tomatoes website.
10. "Top 100 Songs of 1973 – Billboard Year End Charts," Pop Culture, Bobborst.com.
11. Alan di Pirna, "Dangerous Creatures: Marilyn Manson Have Come for Your Children," *Guitar World*, December 1996, Internet Archive.
12. Ibid.
13. Ibid.
14. Jen Chaney, "Nicki Minaj's Grammy Performance Has Angered the Catholic League," *Celebritology* (blog), *Washington Post*, February 13, 2012.
15. Brent Staples, "Nicki Minaj Crashes Hip-Hop's Boys Club," *New York Times*, July 8, 2012, New York edition.

16. Kevin Rutherford, "Katy Perry Reveals 'Prism' Influences, Adds Stripped-Down Performances at Album Release Event," *Billboard*, October 22, 2013.

17. *E! Online* tweet quoted in "The 2014 Grammy Awards: Still Pushing the Illuminati Agenda," Vigilant Citizen, January 28, 2014.

18. Keith Caulfield, "Beyonce Leads for Third Week at No. 1 on Billboard 200 Chart," *Billboard*, January 2, 2014.

19. "1973 in Film," *Wikipedia*, last modified January 25, 2015.

20. David Lister, "Natural Born Killers?," Television, *Independent* (London, UK), October 24, 1994.

21. "Police Seize Suspect Obsessed by Movie," *New York Times*, November 4, 1994; Jason N. Swensen, "Bluffdale Teen Pleads Guilty to '94 Slayings," *Deseret News* (Salt Lake City, UT), November 15, 1995.

22. "Gunman Kills 2, Injures 21," *New York Times*, April 15, 2001; "Bar Shooting Suspect Obsessed with Guns," *Los Angeles Times*, April 16, 2001; Mickey Ciokajlo, "Elgin Spree Killer Gets Death," *Chicago Tribune*, January 4, 2002.

23. *Murderpedia*, s.v. "Barry Dale Loukaitis," by Juan Ignacio Blanco, accessed February 14, 2015.

24. Julie Grace, "When the Silence Fell," *Time*, June 24, 2001.

25. "Media Companies Are Sued in Kentucky Shooting," *New York Times*, April 13, 1999.

26. "15 Films That Inspired Real Life Crimes," Brainz.org.

27. John Grisham, "Unnatural Killers," http://facstaff.gpc.edu/~jbusbee/Grisham.htm, originally published in *Oxford American*, April 1996, 2–5.

28. "15 Films That Inspired Real Life Crimes," Brainz.org.

29. Ibid.

30. "Timeline: Colorado Theater Shooting," CNN, accessed February 14, 2015.

31. Sean Higgins, "Was the Batman Movie Shooting Imitated from Scene in 1986 Comic?" *Washington Examiner*, July 20, 2012.

32. "Colorado Shooting Suspect's 'Batman' Obsession Examined," 10News.com.

33. Ibid.

34. Craig Kapitan, "Mother: Slain Daughter More Than Victim," MySA, *San Antonio Express-News*, July 21, 2012.

35. Geoff Boucher, "'Dark Knight Rises': Christopher Nolan Opens Up about Bane Choice," Hero Complex, *Los Angeles Times*, December 12, 2011.

Chapter 9: The Spirit of the Antichrist

1. Adapted from Pearlman, *Knowing the Doctrines*, 391.

2. Anton Szandor LaVey, *Die Satanische Bible* [Satanic Bible], (Berlin: Second Sight Books, 1999).

3. Blanche Barton, "Church of Satan History: The Magic Circle/Order of the Trapezoid," Church of Satan website.

4. Nicholas Pileggi, "The Age of Occult," *McCall's*, March 1970 63–74.

5. "The Satanic Mass," track A9 (Zeena's Baptism), on "The Satanic Mass: Recorded Live at the Church of Satan," Murgenstrumm, 1968, vinyl LP.

6. Pileggi, "Age of Occult."

7. "Archdiocese of OKC Comments on Upcoming Black Mass," broadcast news report by Andrew Donley, in "Archdiocese of OKC Pleads with the City to Cancel Upcoming Satanic Ritual," News Channel 4, KFOR.com, August 11, 2014.

8. Ibid.

9. "The Satanic Temple Crowdsources Effort to 'Adopt-a-Highway' in New York City," official website of the Satanic Temple, August 5, 2013.

10. Christopher Behnan, "Satanist Group Mounts Capitol Display to Little Fanfare," *Lansing* (MI) *State Journal*, January 2, 2015.

11. "Woman Arrested after Damaging Satanic Display at Florida Capitol," FoxNews.com, December 24, 2014.

12. Jim Kouri, "Satanic or Ritualistic Crime and Murder," Examiner.com, April 14, 2009; "Elyse Pahler: Killed in Nipomo in 1995," SLO Homicides, *San Luis Obispo Tribune*, April 14, 2010.

13. Phil Archer and Jill Courtney, "Prosecutors: Girl's Murder Part of Satanic Ritual," Click2Houston.com, February 11, 2014.

14. Alex Heigl, "Three Suspects Arrested after Skeletal Remains Found in North Carolina Backyard," *People*, October 10, 2014; "John 'Pazuzu' Lawson . . . The Boogey Man Cometh," *Camel City Dispatch* (Winston-Salem, NC), October 6, 2014.

15. "John 'Pazuzu' Lawson," *Camel City Dispatch*.

16. Michael Hennessey, "Clemmons Murder Suspect Sacrificed Animals, Spoke 'As Though He Were Possessed, According to Source," Fox8, October 8, 2014.

17. Jeff Truesdale, "Satanists Next Door: House of Horrors," *People*, October 27, 2014.

18. Palash Ghosh, "How Many People Did Joseph Stalin Kill?," *International Business Times*, March 5, 2013.

19. Tony Rennell, "Madman Who Starved 60 Million to Death: Devastating Book Reveals How Mao's Megalomania Turned China into a Madhouse," *Daily Mail*, July 22, 2011.

20. "Hitler Youth: Principles and Ideology," Historical Boys Clothing, http://histclo.com/youth/youth/org/nat/hitler/prin/hj-prin.htm, accessed February 18, 2015.

21. Wulf Schwartzwaller, *The Unknown Hitler* (New York: Berkley Books, 1990), quoted in "The Unknown Hitler: Nazi Roots in the Occult," bibliotecapleyades.net, accessed February 14, 2015.

22. Ibid.

23. Alex S.Wilner and Claire-Jehanne Dubouloz, "Homegrown Terrorism and Transformative Learning: An Interdisciplinary Approach to Understanding Radicalization," *Global Change, Peace, and Security* 22:1 (2010), 33–51.

24. Eli Berman, *Radical, Religious, and Violent: The New Economics of Terrorism* (Cambridge, MA: MIT Press, 2009).

25. Lawrence Wright, *The Looming Tower: Al-Qaeda and the Road to 9/11* (New York: Knopf, 2006).

26. Ibid.

27. Bernard Lewis, "The Roots of Muslim Rage," *Atlantic*, September 1990.

28. Wright, *Looming Tower*.

29. "Analysis: Who Are the Taleban?," BBC News. December 20, 2000.

30. John Simpson, "Who are the Taliban?," BBC News Asia, November 1, 2013.

31. Ibid.

32. Tim Craig and Pamela Constable, "In Pakistan, Taliban Massacre of Schoolchildren Fuels Broad Outrage," *Washington Post*, December 16, 2014.

33. Abdulrahman al-Masri, Michele Chabin, Mona Alami, and Sarah Lynch, "Al-Qaeda Hasn't Gone Away, and Is Gaining," *USA Today*, January 8, 2014.

34. "Mapping the Global Muslim Population," Pew Research Center, October 7, 2009.

35. "Islam: Sunni Sect," Jewish Virtual Library; "Islam: Shi'a Sect," Jewish Virtual Library.

36. F. Michael Maloof, "Murder of Pilot Sparks Tough, New Question," *WND*, February 4, 2015.

37. Ellen Knickmeyer and Jonathan Finer, "Insurgent Leader Al-Zarqawi Killed in Iraq," Council on Foreign Relations, *Washington Post* Special Report, June 8, 2006.

38. John F. Burns, "Leader of Al Qaeda in Iraq Has Been Killed," *New York Times*, June 8, 2006; "Zarqawi's Pledge of Allegiance to Al-Qaeda: From Mu'asker al-Battar, Issue 21," trans. Jeffrey Pool, *Terrorism Monitor* 2, no. 24 (December 15, 2004), on the website of the Jamestown Foundation.

39. William W. Harris, *The Levant: A Fractured Mosaic* (Princeton, NJ: Markus Wiener, 2003).

40. Bobby Ghosh, "Roots of Evil: A Short Political History of the Terrorists Who Call Themselves the 'Islamic State,'" Quartz, August 13, 2014.

41. "'ISIS Wants Global Conquest, Not Tribal Conquest': Huckabee Critiques Obama's Foreign Policy," *Fox News Insider* (blog), Fox News Channel, August 22, 2014.

42. Jeremy Bender, "One Paragraph Explains How ISIS Managed to Seize Iraq's Second-Largest City," *Business Insider*, October 14, 2014.

43. Mark Tran and Matthew Weaver, "Isis Announces Islamic Caliphate in Area Straddling Iraq and Syria," *Guardian*, June 30, 2014, US edition.

44. Paul Crompton, "The Rise of the new 'Caliph,' ISIS Chief Abu Bakr al-Baghdadi," Al Arabiya News, June 30, 2014.

45. CNN Library, "ISIS Fast Facts," CNN, last updated February 11, 2015.

46. Rainer Brunner and Werner Ende, Werner, eds., *The Twelver Shia in Modern Times: Religious Culture and Political History* (Leiden, Netherlands: Brill Academic, 2001), 178.

47. Ehsan Yarshater, "Persia or Iran," *Iranian Studies* 22, no.1 (1989).

48. Michael Lipka, "The Sunni-Shia Divide: Where They Live, What They Believe and How They View Each Other," Pew Research Center, June 18, 2014.

49. An English translation of the Constitution of the Islamic Republic of Iran is available online on the website of the Foundation for Iranian Studies and elsewhere.

50. Pierre Tristam, "Twelver Shiites, or Ithna Ahariyah," in "Glossary for the Middle East, Islam and the Arab World," About.com.

51. Karim Sadjadpour, *Reading Khamenei: The World View of Iran's Most Powerful Leader* (Washington, DC: Carnegie Endowment for International Peace, 2009).

52. Karim Sadjadpour, "The Supreme Leader," in *The Iran Primer: Power, Politics, and US Policy*, ed. Robin Wright (Washington, DC: United States Institute of Peace, 2010).

53. Ibid.

54. Ibid.

55. "Iran Jets Bomb Islamic State Targets in Iraq—Pentagon," BBC News Middle East, December 3, 2014.

56. Colonel Ralph Peters, interview by Bill Hemmer, *America's Newsroom*, Fox News, January 22, 2015.

57. Drew Silver, "World's Muslim Population More Widespread Than You Might Think," Pew Research Center, June 7, 2013.

58. "The Future of the Global Muslim Population," Pew Research Center, January 27, 2011.

59. Benjamin Netanyahu, "Preparing for the War on Terror: Understanding the Nature and Dimensions of the Threat" (statement at the US House Government Reform Committee, Washington, DC, September 20, 2001), Israel Ministry of Foreign Affairs press release.

60. Indira Lakshmanan, "Islamic State Now Resembles the Taliban with Oil Fields," Bloomberg Business, August 25, 2014.

61. Tyler Durden, "The ISIS' Top Line: $2 Million in Daily Revenue from 'Oil Sales, Extortion, Taxes and Smuggling," Zero Hedge, August 25, 2014.

62. Ghosh, "Roots of Evil."

63. Ari Yashar, "'Israel the Only Place in Middle East Where Christians Are Safe," Arutz Sheva 7, israelnationalnews.com, September 23, 2014.

64. "2014 Global Terrorism Index," Institute for Economics and Peace, November 18, 2014.

65. "WARNING GRAPHIC PHOTOS (RAW)—ISIS Begins Killing Christians in Mosul, CHILDREN BEHEADED," Catholic Online, August 8, 2014.

66. Erin Cunningham and Heba Habib, "Egypt Bombs Islamic State Targets in Libya after Beheading Video," *Washington Post*, February 16, 2015.

67. "Westerners Executed by Jihadist Groups," News24Morocco, October 10, 2014.

68. Bill Sanderson, "French Prime Minister Declares 'War' on Radical Islam," *New York Post*, January 10, 2015; Michael Martinez, Dominque Debucquoy-Dodley, and Ray Sanchez, "Vignettes: More about the 17 Killed in French Terror Attacks," CNN, January 11, 2015.

Chapter 10: Deliver Us from the Evil One

1. Matthew 4:24; 7:22; 8:16, 28, 31, 33; 9:32, 33, 34; 10:8; 11:18; 12:22, 24, 27, 28; 15:22; 17:18. Mark 1:32, 34, 39; 3:15, 22; 5:12, 15, 16, 18; 6:13; 7:26, 29, 30; 9:38;

16:9, 17. Luke 4:33, 35, 41; 7:33; 8:2, 27, 29, 30, 33, 35, 36, 38; 9:1, 42, 49; 10:17, 11:14, 15, 18, 19, 20; 13:32. John 7:20; 8:48, 49, 52; 10:20, 21. 1 Corinthians 10:20, 21; 1 Timothy 4:1; James 2:19; 3:15; Revelation 9:20; 16:14; 18:2.

2. Prince, *They Shall Expel Demons*, 180.

3. Arthur Somers Roche (1883–1935; mystery writer), quoted on ThinkExist.com, accessed February 16, 2015.

4. "Guideposts Classics: Corrie ten Boom on Forgiveness," *Guideposts*, November 1972.

Chapter 11: Why I Believe in Angels

1. Pearlman, *Knowing the Doctrines*, 81.

2. Ibid., 82.

3. Prince, *War in Heaven*, 120.

4. Christine Darg, "Two Miracle Dove Stories: From Gaza 2014 and Yom Kippur War 1973," Jerusalem Channel, August 5, 2014.

5. Raphael Poch, "A Soldier's Personal Miracle," in "Rumors Abound but God's Protection of Israel Is No Fable," *Breaking Israel News*, August 11, 2014.

6. Yosef Mendelevich, "A Miracle during Operation Protective Edge," *Jerusalem Post*, September 11, 2014.

7. Pearlman, *Knowing the Doctrines*, 83.

Chapter 12: Where Angels Tread

1. Barton David, *The Founder's Bible*, (Newbury Park, CA: Shiloh Road, 2013), B1–B3; "The Indestructible George Washington," The Real American His-story.

2. James S. Hewett, ed., *Illustrations Unlimited: A Topical Collection of Hundreds of Stories, Quotations, and Humor* (Carol Stream, IL: Tyndale House, 1988), 29.

3. Ibid., 31.

4. News.com.au, "Beneath Yellowstone, a Volcano That Could Wipe Out US," *New York Post*, December 12, 2013.

5. Tariq Malik, "Active Sun Unleashes Massive Solar Flare," Space.com, December 20, 2014.

Chapter 13: The Throne Room of God

1. C. S. Lewis, *Mere Christianity*, Book III (New York: Macmillan, 1952), 120.

2. *Webster's Dictionary* definition as referenced in Pearlman, *Knowing the Doctrines*, 20.

3. C. H. Spurgeon, "The Wailing of Risca," sermon no. 349, delivered December 9, 1860, at Exeter Hall, Strand, The Spurgeon Archive, spurgeon.org.

4. John Newton, "Amazing Grace," 1779. Public domain.

5. John Hagee, "Where Will You Spend Eternity?," excerpt from sermon.

Chapter 14: Your Eternal Home

1. Victor Hugo was a nineteenth-century French poet, novelist, and dramatist whose works include: *Les Misérables*, 1862; *The Hunchback of Notre-Dame*, 1831.
2. Prince, *End of Life's Journey*, 14.
3. Adapted from Pearlman, *Knowing the Doctrines*, 369.
4. C. H. Spurgeon, "Though He Were Dead," sermon no. 1799, delivered at the Metropolitan Tabernacle, London, September 14, 1884.
5. C. H.Spurgeon, "An Awful Contrast," sermon no. 2473, delivered at the Metropolitan Tabernacle, London, July 11, 1886.
6. Clarence Larkin, *The Book of Revelation: A Study of the Last Prophetic Book of Holy Scripture* (1919); eBook. Accessed on EarnestlyContendingfortheFaith.com in "The Fifth, Sixth, and Seventh Dooms" section.
7. Adapted from Spurgeon, "Though He Were Dead."
8. F. Michael Maloof, "Iraq Invaders Threaten Nuke Attack on Israel," WND, June 23, 2014.
9. Matt Drudge, "Iran Supreme Leader: Only Solution Is Israel's Destruction," Drudge Report, *Daily Caller*, July 24, 2014.
10. Matt Drudge, "Iranian General Threatens Surprise Attack on Israel," Drudge Report, *Daily Caller*, August 26, 2014.
11. Matt Drudge, "Iran Arms Palestinians for New War with Israel," Drudge Report, *Daily Caller*, October 17, 2014.
12. Matt Drudge, "Ayatollah Publishes Plan to 'Eliminate' Israel," Drudge Report, *Daily Caller*, November 10, 2014.
13. Matt Drudge, "Iran Launches 'We Love Fighting Israel' Campaign on Social Media," Drudge Report, *Daily Caller*, December 10, 2014.
14. Yamiche Alcindor and Elena Berton, "Four Killed at Paris Grocery Store Were All Jewish," *USA Today*, January 12, 2015.
15. Martin Fackler, "Hostage's Apparent Beheading by ISIS Stirs Outrage in Japan," *New York Times*, February 1, 2015.
16. Paul Adams, "Jordan Pilot Hostage Moaz al-Kasasbeh 'burned alive,'" BBC, February 3, 2015.

ABOUT THE AUTHOR

John Hagee is the author of several *New York Times* bestsellers, in addition to *Jerusalem Countdown,* which sold over 1 million copies. His latest, *Four Blood Moons,* has sold more than 700,000 copies. He is the founder and senior pastor of Cornerstone Church in San Antonio, Texas, a nondenominational evangelical church with more than 20,000 active members, as well as the founder and president of John Hagee Ministries, which telecasts his radio and television teachings throughout America and in more than 100 nations worldwide. Hagee is also the founder and national chairman of Christians United for Israel, a national grassroots association with over 1 million members to date.